Tourism in India and India's Economic Development

Tourism in India and India's Economic Development

Kartik C. Roy and Clement A. Tisdell

Nova Science Publishers, Inc.
Commack, New York

Editorial Production: Susan Boriotti
Office Manager: Annette Hellinger
Graphics: Frank Grucci and John T'Lustachowski
Information Editor: Tatiana Shohov
Book Production: Donna Dennis, Patrick Davin, Christine Mathosian, Tammy Sauter and Diane Sharp
Circulation: Maryanne Schmidt
Marketing/Sales: Cathy DeGregory

Library of Congress Cataloging-in-Publication Data

Tourism in India and India's economic development / edited by Kartik C. Roy, Clement A. Tisdell.
p. cm.
Includes bibliographical references.
ISBN 1-56072-612-1
1. Tourist trade--India. 2. India--Economic policy. I. Roy, K. C. (Kartik Chandra), 1941- II. Tisdell, C. A. (Clement Allan)
G155.I4T638 1998 98-39202
338.4'79154045—dc21 CIP

6080 Jericho Turnpike, Suite 207
Commack, New York 11725
Tele. 516-499-3103 Fax 516-499-3146
e-mail: Novascience@earthlink.net
e-mail: Novascil@aol.com
Web Site: http://www.nexusworld.com/nova

Printed in the United States of America

CONTENTS

LIST OF FIGURES

LIST OF TABLES

PREFACE

The essays included in this volume are edited versions of those selected from the papers presented at the Fourth IIDS International Seminar held during June 4-7, 1997 on the theme: Tourism and Economic Development. Normal refereeing procedure was followed in selecting papers for inclusion in this volume.

The Seminar was organised by the International Institute for Development Studies, (IIDS) Calcutta, in India in collaboration with the Department of Analytical and Applied Economics of Utkal University, Bhubaneswar, Orissa, India and the Department of Economics, University of Queensland, Brisbane, Australia. The IIDS runs a bi-annual conference series as well as a seminar series. Usually the Seminars are held in the intervening period between the two Conferences. Therefore, for the last few years the Institute has been running either a Conference or a Seminar every year.

The central theme of this volume is Tourism in India and India's Economic Development. Although the essays dwell on such different aspects of tourism as development issues for the whole of India, policy and environmental issues for all India, income and employment generation from tourism and human relations in tourism management, regional tourism, they try to emphasise the importance of tourism in India's economic development and discuss what measures can be taken to ensure sustainable growth of tourism in India. It is hoped that the discussions contained in this volume will be helpful to policy makers in India in designing and implementing appropriate policies for the growth and development of the tourism industry in India.

The editors wish to thank Utkal University for hosting this international seminar, to the International Institute for Development Studies for allowing them to bring out this volume and to Mr Frank Columbus, the President and Editor-in-Chief of Nova Science Publishers, New York for agreeing to publish this volume. The editors wish to thank the Department of Economics, The University of Queensland for being the co-sponsor for this seminar, for providing all the facilities for ensuring the smooth running of the Conference and for preparing the manuscripts for this publication.

The editors wish to express their appreciation to all others who have been associated in one way or another with the publication of this volume. In particular, we are grateful to those who assisted us with the reviewing process for this volume. They include:

M. Alauddin
C. Arcodia
V. Gunasekara
A. Hamid
G. (Ravi) Ravinder
P. Riethmuller

P. Basu	M. Hossain	K. Roy
J. Chai	R. Jensen	L. Ryan
S. Craig-Smith	B. Prasad	C. Tisdell
G. Docwra	B. Prideaux	B. Watson
A. Duhs		

However, the usual *caveat* applies.

Finally, special thanks are due to Mrs Robyn McDonald, assisted by other secretaries in the Department of Economics at The University of Queensland, for preparing the manuscript.

Brisbane
June, 1998

K.C. Roy
C.A. Tisdell

List of Contributors

K.K. Barman
Department of Economics
Gauhati University
Guwahati
Assam
India

K.S. Behera
Professor of History
Utkal University
Bhubaneswar
India

Sridhar Behera
P.G. Department of Industrial Economics
Government College
Angul
Orissa
India

Prabir Biswas
Faculty Member
Institute of Business Management and Research
Calcutta
India

Hans C. Blomqvist
Swedish School of Economics and Business Administration
Helsinki
Finland

Saundarjya Borbora
Department of Economics
Sherubtse College
Kanglung
Bhutan

Note: Since writing his paper Dr Borbora has moved to:

Rajgarh Road
Guwahati - 781 003
Assam
India

Alak Ghosh
President
International Institute for Development Studies and Head of the Department of Economics
Calcutta University
India

Bhubaneswar Goswami
Barama College
Assam
India

Tushar R. Hathi
Department of Economics
M.T. Dhamsaniya College of Commerce
Rajkot 360001
India

Moazzem Hossain
School of International Business
Griffith University
Nathan Q 4111
Australia

G.C. Kar
Nabakrushna Choudhury Centre for Development Studies
Bhubaneswar 751013
Orissa
India

Note: At the time of writing his paper Professor G.C. Kar's address was:

Department of Analytical and Applied Economics
Utkal University
Bhubaneswar
Orissa
India

Jyotirmayee Kar
Department of Analytical and Applied Economics
Utkal University
Vani Vihar
India

Subas C. Kumar
Department of Economics
Ekamra Mahavidyalaya
Bhubaneswar
Orissa
India

Scott McCabe
Derbyshire Business School
University of Derby
Kedleston Road, Derby DE22 1GD
United Kingdom

Anita Medhekar-Smith
Central Queensland University
Bruce Highway
North Rockhampton Q 4702
Australia

Amitava Mitra
Department of Economics
Arunachal University
Itanagar
India

Pragati Mohanty
Department of Economics
S.D. Women's College
Rajgangpur, 770017
Orissa
India

Harshada S. Rathod
Department of Economics
Smt. P.N. Doshi Women's College,
Ghatkopar (W) Mumbai - 400 086
India

G. (Ravi) Ravinder
School of Leisure & Tourism Studies
University of Technology, Sydney
PO Box 222
Lindfield NSW 2070
Australia

Kartik C. Roy
Department of Economics
The University of Queensland
Brisbane Q 4072
Australia

Liam Ryan
Central Queensland University
Bruce Highway, North Rockhampton
Q 4702, Australia

Jayne Stocks
Derbyshire Business School
University of Derby
Kedleston Road
Derby DE22 1GD
United Kingdom

Clement A. Tisdell
Department of Economics
The University of Queensland
Brisbane Q 4072
Australia

BACKGROUND ON INDIA'S DEVELOPMENT AND TOURISM

Chapter 1

AN OVERVIEW OF TOURISM IN INDIA'S ECONOMIC DEVELOPMENT

KARTIK C. ROY AND CLEMENT A. TISDELL
Department of Economics,
The University of Queensland,
Brisbane Q 4072,
Australia

INTRODUCTION

No other form of economic activity transects so many sectors, levels and interests as tourism. It is often said that there are economic, social and psychological benefits of tourism as it attracts foreign currency, improves world understanding and broadens the mind (Cater and Lowman, 1994). It is true no doubt that travel opportunities can enhance the quality of human experience in spiritual as well as material ways (Krippendorf, 1987). Nevertheless there have been critical comments about tourism phenomenon. Boorstin (1961) and Fussell (1982) have commented on the transition from the qualities of travel to artificiality of tourism. Some of the main concerns relating to tourism (Murphy, 1985; Urry, 1990) stem from (i) continuing growth in numbers; (ii) increasing ability to penetrate even more remote locations; (iii) the assumption of the right to do so and (iv) the likely impact on the infrastructure, society and environment of the host country.

The destinations which rely heavily upon tourism have become fully aware of their vulnerability. They are experiencing what is happening to their society and their environment. But even those who oppose tourism, acknowledge the economic benefits it may bring. A number of developing countries in the world have been highly successful in promoting their tourism industry and deriving significant economic benefits from the growth of this industry.

India's tourism industry has remained at a dormant stage despite the fact that tourism can offer enormous benefits both directly and indirectly to the country and that India has many touristic products to offer to each category of domestic and international tourists. No genuine attempt has so far been made in Indian planning to develop its tourism industry although tourism has always produced a surplus in India's invisible trade account (Government of India, 1994). A large number of ancillary industries, both in the formal and informal sectors, in India depend on tourism. Hence, its impact on income generation and employment creation is quite considerable. However, the tourism infrastructure that exists in India is not adequate to meet the demands of modern-day tourists.

TOURISM'S IMPORTANCE IN INDIAN DEVELOPMENT: ECONOMIC ASPECTS

A severe drop in India's foreign exchange reserves and a large balance of payments deficit were the two most immediate reasons which forced India to seek the help of the IMF and the World Bank to tide over the economic crisis in 1991. In improving India's foreign exchange reserve and balance of payments position, tourism industry can play an invaluable role. Throughout the 1980s and 1990s India recorded adverse balance on its trade account and favourable balance on its invisible accounts (GOI, 1995). Within the invisible sector, the net surplus from tourism has continuously increased since the mid-1980s. Immediately after the Gulf War, the net surplus from private remittances declined considerably but this loss was more than compensated by increase in surplus from tourism receipts. Thus tourism directly has made significant contribution towards increasing the foreign exchange reserve and reducing the size of the balance of payment deficit of India.

At the micro-level tourism's economic importance is also quite considerable. Tourism generates employment opportunities for both skilled and unskilled labourers. Since tourism relies on a large number of ancillary industries for its survival and success, increase in tourist traffic increases the demand for goods produced by these industries. Increased demand for places of tourists' accommodation gives a strong boost to the construction industry. The development of basic infrastructure also gets a strong boost. A hotel requires the services of hundreds of different categories of people and the supply of hundreds of different kinds of goods. The increased demand for different varieties of services and goods benefits the local, regional and national economy.

Tourism can contribute significantly towards reducing regional imbalances in development. This is particularly important for India as there is wide disparity in the level of development achieved by different regions of the country. Under centralised planning and Nehru's leadership the central government in the early 1950s disbanded the policy of allowing the principle of comparative advantage to dictate the location of industries (Roy, Tisdell and Sen, 1992, 1995) and made conscious efforts to redirect the location of industries away from the dictates of the principle of comparative advantage by various measures, the most important of them being the passing of the Freight Equalisation Bill in the Indian Parliament in 1954.

Since that time, much of India's industrial activities have been concentrated in Southern and Western regions. As a result, the levels of income and employment of these regions have moved significantly ahead of other regions. Tourism can play an important role in redressing this problem of regional imbalances in development. Every region of India has important tourist products to offer. In Eastern and North Eastern regions which are relatively poorer than the Western and Southern regions, there are many places of tourists' interests and many types of touristic products available to satisfy the needs of different categories of tourists. For example, in Orissa alone there are historical places of interests, magnificent lakes, sea beaches, bird sanctuary, India's largest national park and temples etc. There are also a number of handicraft industries such as handloom, leather products, filigree works, cutlery, crockery etc. which produce goods which are purchased by tourists. These industries are widely dispersed throughout the state. Hence increase in tourists' demand for these products can increase income and employment throughout the state. The direct employment and income created by the tourism industry and the employment and income created by these handicraft industries can considerably reduce the level of underdevelopment of Orissa and the region.

There is also the religious tourism which is vastly popular among internal tourists. Orissa is famous for religious tourism. There are different types of handicraft and service industries which supply goods needed by religious tourists.

Since the number of religious tourists is quite considerable and since this kind of tourism continues throughout the year, proper development of such tourism can increase the level of employment in the state and region and help reduce the regional imbalance in development.

Social and Cultural Aspects of Tourism

Tourism helps travellers to come into direct contact with people of diverse cultural and social background. In India different tourist spots located in different states have different historical and cultural background. Tourists visiting these places gain knowledge about these places. The enhancement of tourists' knowledge of these places has, in the past, helped in the preservation of these places and monuments. For example, the project to reduce the level of pollution surrounding the Taj Mahal is being implemented by the central and Uttar Pradesh governments but the tourists played an important role in making the pollution level around the Taj Mahal an issue of international concern (*Statesman Weekly*, 1997). Similarly the project to establish a mobile hospital on boats to serve the minimum health needs of the population of the villages in the Sundarban Delta will be completed with the financial help from frequent foreign visitors to this delta.

One of the best ways to reduce tension between two nations is to allow the people of the two countries to travel to their neighbouring countries. A significant amount of tension would have been eliminated in South Asia if travel between India and Pakistan was less restrictive.

IMPEDIMENTS TO THE GROWTH OF TOURISM

To develop a successful tourism industry and to enhance the growth of tourism, a country needs to develop a tourism culture. Peoples' social customs and traditions may act as a hindrance to the growth of tourism in the country. Therefore, these customs and traditions need to be changed. But it is not so easy to do that in India.

Providing information to tourists about the tourist spots and about the availability of accommodation, transport and other facilities to enable tourists to make the trip more successful. Successful foreign marketing exercise requires enormous expenditure and efficient manpower. While funds available to government tourist offices to undertake such tasks are meagre, private tourist offices and tour operators have not been given the same status as the government offices. Hotel accommodation for domestic and foreign tourists to ensure their adequate comfort and safety are necessary. However, supply of such accommodation in adequate quantities still does not exist in India. The administration and maintenance of tourist places are inefficient and ineffective.

Also the unregulated entry to most tourist places has led to their overuse and gradual deterioration. The respective state governments have neither the money nor the desire to make the administration and maintenance of these places more efficient. For international tourists, the regulations governing their entry in to India are still restrictive and these do not encourage the tourists to travel to this country.

STATE VS PRIVATE SECTOR PARTICIPATION IN TOURISM DEVELOPMENT

The Indian public sector does not have enough financial resources to improve the performance of the tourism industry. Its capacity to do so has been further weakened under the current structural reform programme. Even if the state does have the financial capacity, peoples' adherence to the public sector rules and regulations governing the tourist places and tourism industry would be weak as the public perception of the state is that it is weak, inefficient and corrupt. As a result, the quality of the services offered by the tourism industry would suffer. Hence, it is worth considering whether the private sector should be allowed to manage some of those aspects of tourism industry which are wholly under state control. It is true that unregulated use of important tourist spots such as sea beaches at Puri in Orissa and at Digha in West Bengal have led to the significant deterioration in their quality.

These places could be better managed and protected by private sector agencies. Although the private sector management of tourist spots and tourism development can create greater monopoly power for the private sector, with an efficient, and honest bureaucracy, the state can exercise some control over the activities of the private sector. Eco-tourism and farm tourism have been gaining importance since the decade of the 1980s due to the world wide concern about the social and environmental effects of mass tourism. The decade of the 1990s has been predicted to become the "Decade of Eco Tourism" (Eadington and Smith, 1994). But the maintenance of ecological stability necessary for the sustainability of such tourism requires safeguarding the reproduction of natural resources (Brookfield, 1988). This requires considerable involvement of the state in the development of eco-tourism. Despite the fact that India has a total of 520 national parks and sanctuaries (Government of India, 1994; Kothari, 1996), India has made very little effort to utilise the full potential of eco-tourism. More than three million people, mostly of scheduled tribes, live inside these protected areas. Living with tribal families could be an important component in the package of eco-tourism. There are unique eco-tourist spots in Eastern and North Eastern India. These could be developed as important destinations for eco-tourists. But a successful development of eco-tourism in India would require not only the co-operation of the public and the private sector but also co-operation among the neighbouring states.

CONCLUSION

In this volume, we have included essays dealing with different aspects of tourism in India and tourism's importance in India's economic development. While several papers point out the economic benefits of development, others point out the lack of all kinds of infrastructure needed for tourism development. This is particularly true in case of Eastern and North Eastern India. Several other papers discuss the social and environmental cost of tourism development. Therefore some contributors feel that the impact of tourism on the environment, local economy and on the society should be carefully studied before it is expanded on a commercial basis.

It is also clear that the development of tourism can help reduce regional disparity which has been continuing to worsen in India. But it is beyond the capacity of any individual state of any region to solve all the problems facing its tourism industry because it does not have the financial resources and the problems relating to tourism development do not appear and end within the state borders. For example, a proper development of such infrastructure as roads and transport require the combined efforts of all neighbouring states in each region. If such an effort is made it will keep the cost down and improve the quality of the product and service. Hence neighbouring states must develop a co-ordinated and unified approach to tourism development for each region in India.

REFERENCES

Boorstin, D.J. (1961)*The Image - A Guide to Pseudo-events in America*, New York: Harper and Row.

Brookfield, H. (1988) "Sustainable Development and the Environment", *Journal of Development Studies*, 25(1).

Cater, E. and Larman, G. (eds) (1994) *Ecotourism, A Suitable Option?* Chichester: John Wiley and Sons.

Eadington, W.R. and Smith, V.L. (1994) "Introduction: The Emergence of Alternative Forms of Tourism", in W.R. Eadington and V.L. Smith (eds) (1994) *Tourism Alternatives, Potentials and Problems in the Development of Tourism*, Chichester: John Wiley and Sons.

Fussell, P. (1982) *Abroad: British Literary Travelling Between the Wars*, New York: Oxford University Press.

Government of India (1994) *India 1994*, New Delhi: Government of India.

Government of India (1995) *Economic Survey 1994-95*, New Delhi: Government of India.

Kothari, A. (1996) "Conserving Biodiversity: Doomed Without People", in *The Hindu* (1996) *Survey of the Environment*, Madras: The Hindu.

Krippendorf, J. (1987) *The Holiday Makers*, London: Heinmann.

Murphy, P. (1985) *Tourism - A Community Approach*, New York: Methuen.

Roy, K.C., Tisdell, C.A. and Sen, R.K. (eds) (1992, 1995) *Economic Development and Environment - A Case Study of India*, Calcutta: Oxford University Press.

The Statesman Weekly (1997) 18 October.

Urry, J. (1990) *The Tourist Gaze: Leisure and Travel in Contemporary Societies*, London: Sage.

DEVELOPMENT ISSUES FOR THE WHOLE OF INDIA

Chapter 2

TOURISM AND INDIAN DEVELOPMENT IN SEARCH OF A NEW PERSPECTIVE

TUSHAR R. HATHI
Department of Economics,
M.T. Dhamsaniya College of Commerce,
Rajkot 360001,
India

INTRODUCTION

Tourism as general term is very old but in consideration of its relationship with development it is a relatively novel concept. It is defined as an activity to move across different parts of the world. It is within and outside national boundaries. Touring is organised with multifold objectives covering a short or long time span, like other sectors it is also identified as an integral part of socio-economic development of the society.

Growth trends in tourism are universally recognized and have become the largest export industry. The World Bank and World Tourism Organisation also recognise tourism as a most flourishing industry. There are different indicators available to ensure this sector as a consequence and a concomitant to general development. Industrialised nations of the world like North America, Europe and the emerging economies of South East Asia underline the linkages between tourism and growth.

There are three important sectors contributing a lot to the growth of the economy - agriculture, industry and tourism are the three important sectors - out of which tourism can be regarded as the largest and fastest contributor. Tourism has assumed very high significance in the development of the economy. Exchange of knowledge, technology, marketing, commerce and industrial exhibitions are considered major factors generating the demand for tourism.

According to the information provided by World Tourism Organisation, about 56 crores 70 lakh people spent about Rs.372.6 billion and 21 crore 20 lakh people were provided employment through tourism in the year 1995. With this general trend for tourism in the world it would be worthwhile to examine the prevailing trends and prospects for tourism in India.

TOURISM IN INDIA

Tourism in India is a traditional phenomenon. Traditionally erstwhile princely states had restricted themselves to tour occasionally to attend any 'swearing in ceremony' or to attend a marriage ceremony of high officials or with religious motives. Usually tourism was not undertaken by the general mass in the historical age. It is found that in India organised tourism began in the fifties with the genesis of planned development. However after 46 years India has only a marginal share of 0.4 per cent of the world tourist trade.

In the emerging Asian markets, India has the potential to earn overseas revenue through tourism. Locationally India is well placed for tourism. Being in the central part of Asia India has the opportunity to benefit from the flow of international tourist traffic.

Culturally India is considered a country of very rich interest. India is a unique country having cultural roots so old as rarely to be seen elsewhere in the world. There are mountains, rivers, seashore, desert, forests, orchards, temples and sociological riches placing India as the best place for tourism. No less than 7.8 million persons accounting for 2.4 per cent of the Indian workforce are directly employed by hospitality services. This is exclusive of those engaged by suppliers to the services as well as related organised activities such as travel agencies, souvenir shops, village crafts persons, folk artists, carpet weavers and so on.

International tourism in India has also improved. Last year India received two million visitors from abroad. Though this figure looks impressive it is far too small a fraction of the 570 million who crossed international boarders as tourists. Even with its poor share of international traffic in 1995 foreign tourists to India spent over Rs.9,000 crores in foreign exchange making it the second largest export industry after garments if the gems and jewellery trade is left out because of the vast outgo on imported inputs.

Tables 2.1 and 2.2 provide the trends for international visitors both in numbers and also in terms of revenue generated through tourists to India.

As indicated in Table 2.1 the total number of tourists arriving in India exceeded two million in 1995. This nonetheless accounted for only 0.4 percentage of total world tourists. From the revenue point of view the exchange earned through tourism in the last three years has considerably increased.

Tourism is important to a vast and variegated country like India with considerable cross country movement that fosters a sense of unity. In other words, it contributes to national integration and promotion of an environment of social and cultural lives. It is estimated that even when ten per cent of the population travels outside one state, it involves a massive movement of 90 million people who develop the feeling that they are travelling within their own country.

Table 2.1
Number of Tourists Arriving in India from Abroad during 1993-1995

Country	1993 Nos	1994 Nos	1995 Nos
North America	206077	232938	267188
Central South America	13150	11805	16672
West Europe	624628	664820	754182
East Europe	56700	66060	53275
Africa	61975	64134	87238
West Africa	118233	114096	114748
South Asia	465655	480142	540209
South East Asia	93935	113535	129491
East Asia	77058	93844	109916
Australia	39020	43865	49941
Others	3100	1194	823
Total	1764830	1880432	2123683

Source: World Tourist Organisation.

Table 2.2
Gross Receipts of India from its Inbound Foreign Tourists, 1988-1995

Year	Revenue Rs. in Crore	Percentage Change
1988	1992.64	-
1989	2298.90	15.4
1990	2691.77	15.8
1991	4110.50	54.4
1992	5886.95	43.2
1993	6141.81	03.3
1994	7103.53	15.7
1995	8640.02	21.6

Source: World Tourist Organisation.

Initially tourism was not assigned the official status as an industry in India. Although discussions were held and some steps were taken in respect of extending infrastructural and other facilities to promote tourism, it was not given due accordance as per international standards. It was only after the second five year plan that tourism was regarded as a major tool for earning foreign exchange. Officially tourism was accorded special significance only in the Seventh Five Year Plan (1985-1990). Some regions were selected for promotion from the tourism point of view. These regions were selected on grounds of handicrafts, forestry, industrial variations. Structurally the promotion of tourism in the different regions was also thought to promote private participation. Tourism being a State matter it depends on the State government's approach to increase the opportunities. At present 22 states have declared tourism an industry entitling promoters to various tax concessions and other incentives. Sociocultural traditions, religious attachments, and business promotion have added to the significance of tourism to India. It is true that conditions had earlier changed after independence and a second major turn has come after liberalisation in respect of tourism. In spite of all these facts there are dimensional challenges against the growth of tourism which still act as major constraints.

MAJOR CONSTRAINTS - CHALLENGES

Culturally and naturally we are one of the richest in the world to provide attractions for tourists. However we have not been able to perform very well. Why is it that we are slow to make progress in matters of tourism? What is it that restricts the flow of tourists?

Tourism has grown over the years in India. It has tended to be diversified catering to a variety of visitor interests. Many destinations have been identified as places of interest. These places are destinations for leisure travellers with special interests. When the multi faceted quality of the product came to be known, it unfolded many realities indicating bottlenecks in the development of tourism.

In general it is said that of every ten persons, one is a tourist. This in turn led to an investment of $350 billion in world tourism. Spain attracts not less than 5 crore tourists a year and China has also accelerated its progress in tourism. It is quite possible and feasible for India to divert the attention of global tourists to India, subject to the development of certain amenities.

Considering future estimations, prospects are very bright for tourism and for markets ancillary to tourism. Of all the global resources tourism contributes to more than 3.5 trillion dollars. It is also acclaimed that Asia Pacific nations would be the maximum beneficiaries. In view of all these facts tourism needs to be prioritised. Yet the reality is that India has not played well in this sector.

According to Colliers Jardin, while China, Indonesia and Philippines earned $7,323, $4,785 and $2,090 million respectively in 1994, India earned only $1,020 million. This directly reveals certain inadequacies restricting the flow of tourists. A number of challenges is now considered.

INFRASTRUCTURE - A MAJOR HURDLE

The World Tourism Organisation's projections for tourists in India is 10 per cent more than our own estimations. We hope to welcome not fewer than 5 million tourists in the near future.

This estimation requires us to well equip ourselves with hotels, airways, telecommunications etc. Recent surveys have revealed the fact that in consideration of our own projected rates we will have to build every year a minimum 26,000 rooms as against our present rate of only 3,000 rooms. This will amount to not fewer than Rs.1,000 crore every year. As compared to our sources of tourism - accommodation facilities are very limited. In the year 1994 India had about 912 hotels totaling 55,455 rooms which includes all sorts of hotels. There is a significant shift from tourist class to the business traveller class categories in all hotels.

Apart from hotels, air facilities are also limited. In order to maintain or increase the flow of tourists we are required to double at least air capacities. Old defective runways and irregular domestic air services are the main limitations. It is heartening to note that private participation is allowed after liberalisation both for the establishment of airports and the introduction of air services. The airport authority of India has prepared a plan with an estimation of Rs.555.18 crores to prepare more airports of international standards. It is also found that comparatively our air services are largely uneconomic, especially on account of fuel rate.

Railways have of course recognized their role in tourism development. The launch of Shatabdi trains, Palaces on Wheels, The Royal Orient which are to be followed by privately operated luxury tourist trains are steps in the right direction. Despite these ventures Indian Railways are still far behind in terms of capacity to cater for the needs of tourists in terms of easier, quicker travelling and better hospitality.

Regarding highways we are very slow to progress ourselves. India has only a few four to six highways connecting any two points. For the last four years, there has been talk of expressway projects being handed to private operators but not one project has yet got off the ground.

Eventual privatisation of the power and telecommunication sectors has however increased hope for better dealings in tourism.

ENVIRONMENTAL MAINTENANCE

Our pattern of industrialisation has raised many issues for the preservation of natural culture. Growing demand for technological plant has worsened the situation. Historical monuments and religious centres are so intensely covered by gigantic polluting plants that natural conditions have been lost. In the name of technological development we have cared too little for the protection of cultural monuments. Tourism should be developed as a means to maintain environmental wealth, but less has been done in this regard on account of which climatic pollution and industrial pollution have affected the natural beauty of such places. It has also made life in the surrounding area so busy that a peaceful environment, as a major source of attraction, has also vanished.

GOVERNMENT POLICY

It is the political will and commitment on the part of leadership at the central, state and district levels and associations of the local people with a view to assuring them that tourism will in no way harm their interests. Government is actually not keen to strengthen tourism. It is through tourism that direct and indirect employment can be generated. Scattered attempts have been made to upgrade the status of tourism but there is no concrete and coherent implementation. Political will and commitment are required to rectify the inadequacies. Apart from the occasional declaration of national tourism policies, a major report on tourism development was prepared at the behest of the planning commission by a high powered committee. This committee recommended the establishment of a national tourist authority but that is still unimplemented. Frequent changes in policy at State level - especially regarding taxation - create the feeling of uncertainty.

CO-ORDINATION

The institutional role in respect of tourism development is very limited. It is not that there are too few institutions to strengthen tourism but there is a lack of co-ordination between the different agencies. In the world there are 15 countries where independent ministries are there to serve the interests of tourism. There are many policy issues which create hurdles in the process of tourism development. It is largely due to a lack of co-ordination between the departments that troubles arise, leading either to the proposals being left pending over the years or being rejected.

PROFESSIONALISM

Tourism development demands a skilled approach. We have failed to develop a professional approach to attract the tourists. We have some of the best places but on account of poor management we have not been able to maintain the places. Most of our religious places - inns, and hotels are so ill managed that dignified tourists would hardly like to stay. Hospitality along with courtesy brings about a lot of change. State Government Organisations have now concentrated on this aspect but we are still not dynamic enough in that regard. Modern amenities are not available even at our business centres, and education and training improvements are needed.

It is also realised that certain information provided is not always up to date due to which the tourists experience a lot of hardships and eventually some times change their programs. This requires staff training and use of media technology through which all the details can be furnished.

New Perspective

Tourism has a dominant role to play in strengthening the economy of the nation. It has great significance with regard to foreign relations. There are strong cultural roofs in tourism. India, though it provides multi dimensional grounds to attract the tourists, has yet not succeeded in this respect. It is true that even small countries like Singapore, Britain, and even Malta have proved superior to India in this regard.

A noted expert like Mr. Rehman has suggested implementing AIM formula to upgrade the standard of tourism. This AIM formula is an indicator of Awareness, Infrastructure and Marketing.

Awareness can be interpreted in terms of people's vigilance for developing tourism. Different places can be maintained by the people in the manner that tourists feel satisfied for their expenses. Different groups engaged in this profession must remain perfect and alert to ensure better services to the tourists. What is required more is a systematic positive approach for tourism. It should be recognized at all levels that tourism provides strong socio-economic linkages to foster unity and development.

On one hand there is a need for professionalisation which of course benefits in terms of payment but requires best services. Foreign visitors or local visitors should feel at home even at the hotel or business centres, which will encourage them to spend more. The hospitality approach must be conducive to the life styles of different communities. As people of different communities have their own tastes and preferences, wide scale attempts should be made to cater for their needs along with maintaining originality of the places.

Infrastructural facilities must be increased to sustain the flow of tourists. We have to understand the pattern of living of the tourists and accordingly we must provide infrastructural facilities. After making a detailed survey we are required to introduce roads, vehicles, railways and airways.

Here, what is intensely necessary is the professional approach. Tourists would like to have maximum comforts and convenience irrespective of the cost. It must be reasonable enough - along with better services.

Therefore what is required more in professionalism is training to be provided to the employees concerned with tourism corporations. Facts regarding touring places should be presented with perfection. Training is essential to have perfectness, local guides must be trained enough to evaluate the tourist's appreciation of the places. More knowledge of the history or the industry does not suffice for the purpose, since a courteous spirit and scientific presentation are also needed to enhance the need for tourism.

Secondly tourism should be regarded as a continuing activity. There must be continuity. Sometimes seasonal or ceremonial importance is given to tourism which neither brings economic benefits nor provides any local incentive. Places may have their peculiar characteristics but these must be developed and manifested as a touring place forever, continuity brings diversity at the places.

Temperament - touring and mental temperament is of equal importance for tourism. We need to induce a quicker, safer, approach to convince both domestic and foreign tourists. Some of the states have been more pragmatic in this regard. Industrial exhibitions and cultural fairs must be given due weight both administratively and academically. Such exhibitions and fairs may be given more thrust with arranging and organising intellectual cultural programs in addition to the routine scheduled programs.

Our institutional pattern in this regard needs to be reviewed further. Globally there are 15 nations having independent national autonomous departments exclusively for tourism. In India constitutionally tourism is considered as a State subject and accordingly State level corporations have been instituted. Fourteen States have done this but the remaining States have not shown much inclination.

According to R. Sahni, it is also necessary to promote private sector participation. Tourism development is virtually a process of struggle and solutions. It is in fact a balance between the two groups i.e. between individual interest and social interests, a well refined integrated approach is required to boost tourism at great length. We must successfully incorporate socio-economic and environmental plans in our annual tourism and planning policy to strengthen organised and continuous tourism.

As compared to some other Asian and European countries, public media and educational development have been a little bit slow in accelerating the growth process of tourism. However the process of liberalisation has played a positive role through extending the facilities to the companies and groups in terms of club, meeting halls along with providing secrecy required for the business purposes.

In short we need to have commitment towards tourism. Let tourism be allowed to flourish independently. Let the private participation be encouraged to co-ordinate and manifest several aspects of tourism. Human resource development must be introduced. Mere buses and roads will not attract the tourists. Thus we must think independently to have our dynamic positive pragmatic approach to make our nation a permanent paradise for tourists in the 21st Century.

REFERENCES

Anand, Nakul (1996) "Yojana", *Independent Day Issue.*

Bajpai, Alok (1996) "Yojana", *Independent Day Issue.*

Bhardwaj, Brij (1996) "Yojana", *Independent Day Issue.*

Chhiba, Somnath, "Essays on Tourism".

Dharamjivan (1996) "Yojana", *Independent Day Issue.*

Sahni, Ravindra, *Problems and Prospects of Tourism,* Ashish Publishing House.
Saloni, Ravindra (1996) "Yojana", *Independent Day Issue.*
Sheth, Mira (1996) "Yojana", *Independent Day Issue.*
Sheth, Ravindra (1996) "Hindu", *Survey of Indian Industries.*

Chapter 3

THE TOURISM INDUSTRY IN INDIA: ECONOMIC SIGNIFICANCE AND EMERGING ISSUES

SUBAS C. KUMAR
Department of Economics,
Ekamra Mahavidyalaya,
Bhubaneswar,
Orissa,
India

INTRODUCTION

Tourism is a phenomenon comprising activities of persons travelling and staying away from home in pursuit of leisure, culture, business and the quest for knowledge. It is a service industry with several allied and auxiliary activities such as tour operators, travel agents, accommodation, passenger transportation, insurance, entertainment and shopping. Thus the tourism industry by nature and structure is multidimensional; it is world wide in its operation and versatile in character.

There is a growing recognition by government and business teams of the industry's potential as a foreign exchange earner. Tourism is the world's largest export industry. It accounts for nearly 6 per cent of world trade and expenditure by some 567 million tourists in 1995 amounted to US$372.6 billion. The bulk of tourism business is concentrated in Europe and North America with one eighth of the market share going to other world regions. In the same year, it is estimated to have provided direct and indirect employment to the tune of 212 million which comes to 10.7 per cent of the total global work force. The highest growth rate in tourism, in recent years, has been registered in third world countries. Looking at the current trend, the World Travel and Tourism Council (WTTC) based at Brussels aptly stated that travel and tourism can be treated as 'economic catalysts' for emerging economies. As a consequence there has been an incessant demand for according it the status of an industry in order to provide tourism with necessary fillip in (Singh, 1988).

In the last couple of decades, tourism has emerged as the most lucrative economic venture in almost all developing countries including India as it has immense potentiality in yielding tax revenues, promoting growth of ancillary and auxiliary industries, generating income and gainful employment and in the development of industrially backward regions through its linkage effects (Sing, 1975). Apart from its economic significance, it acts as an effective means for international understanding, cultural exchanges and national integration. However, the economic significance of this industry is not readily appreciated due to wide dispersion of tourist locations in the country. At the same time it is sensitive to world economic and political conditions. It can occur on a large scale where the great majority of people enjoy some prosperity and security (Bhatia, 1983).

The economic and social effects of tourism (income, employment, regional development, infrastructure, environment, cultural values and international understandings) are interrelated and are a function of tourist expenditure i.e. the demand for tourist services such as accommodation, food, transport, shopping and entertainment etc. In India 'tourist expenditure' in the form of foreign exchange earning has registered an impressive growth in recent years. But it can acquire a meaningful perspective only if India can attract more tourists and maintain a high level of foreign exchange earnings. Instability in tourist arrivals and earnings of foreign exchange has always had an adverse impact on the development process as it creates uncertainties in planning which in turn affects investment in important ongoing projects. Although, the money spent by tourists tends to percolate through many economic activities and has a multiplier effect, significantly, the socio-ecological costs of tourism have not received the attention that is due. The benefits that a country gets from this industry, hence, should not be assessed on the basis of gross earnings of foreign exchange alone but net of these adverse effects as well.

This chapter makes an attempt to address some of these issues. The chapter is organised in four parts. Part I deals with the development of the tourist industry in India in its historical and contemporary perspectives. Part II makes an attempt to estimate the decadal compound growth rates and instability indices of tourist inflows and foreign exchange earnings for the period 1960–61 and 1994–95. It also tries to study the significance of India's tourism receipts in financing imports, its contribution to national income (GDP), the hotel industry and employment generation. Part III highlights some of the important economic, social, cultural, and ecological issues which arouse public concerns about the growth of the tourist industry in India. The concluding part of the study, while summarising the findings, tries to make some broad suggestions for the formulation of pragmatic strategies in order to realise maximum socio-economic benefits form this fast growing industry in India.

THE TOURISM INDUSTRY IN INDIA

India is a country with a history of civilisation spreading over more than 5000 years. The essence of Vedic, Islamic and Western cultures are all blended in Indian civilisation. The cultural heritage of India has a glorious past and many things to offer foreign tourists. It has immense scope for tourism which few countries of the world can equal. According to Seth (1996) "there are enough ruins, enough wild life, jostling humanity and exotica to satisfy even the jaded sightseer".

India occupies a unique geographical position. It is colourful and varied. Its climate varies between two extremes, i.e. cold in high altitudes to the hot summer of the plains. It has some of the world's loftiest mountains, best sunny sea beaches, most awesome rivers, scenic valleys, deserts and forests. Its monuments, sculptures and paintings bear testimony to the national ethos of harmony and diversities (Das and Mohanty, 1994). Above all, India can offer 'old world charms' and scenic attractions which can compete with those of established destinations like Spain (Bhardwaj, 1996).

Long before the birth of modern tourism, India being a country of varied cultures and interests attracted travelers from different parts of the world. Its travel tradition starts with pre-vedic-indus valley civilisation of Mohan-jodaro. Kautilya's Arthashastra epitomises tourism in ancient India. Among the earliest travellers, the Chinese pilgrim Fa-Hein visited India during 359–424 AD followed by Hiuen-Tsang during 625–45 AD. They have left details of accounts of their impressions on various aspects of ancient India. Similarly, the emperor Ashoka sent his emissaries to Sri Lanka, East and West Asia to preach the teachings of Lord Buddha, two and a half centuries before the birth of Christ.

TOURISM IN POST INDEPENDENCE INDIA

Being a late starter, modern tourism in India began in the early 50s. The government in British India appointed a committee in 1946 under the chairmanship of Sir John Sergent, Secretary, Department of Education to look into the prospects of tourism development in India. Although the report was incomplete it strongly recommended that steps be taken to build more tourist infrastructure and to provide more information aimed at attracting foreign tourists.

The first and most systematic step to promote tourism in India after independence was the formation of a separate Department of Tourism under the Ministry of Transport and Communications in 1958. But, tourism in India continued to languish unnoticed till 1962 – the year of Chinese aggression. To give a boost to the tourism sector an *ad hoc* committee was set up with Mr L.K. Jha as the chairman. On the basis of the Jha Committee Report, three corporations were set up to deal with the problems faced by the tourism sector. In 1966, these corporations were merged together to form India Tourism Development Corporation (ITDC) and subsequently, a separate Ministry of Tourism and Civil Aviation came into being under the Prime Minister, Mrs Indira Gandhi.

Throughout the sixties and early seventies the activities of public sector involvement in tourism in India was largely confined to the expansion of capacity of the ITDC hotels. The extent of development in tourism at least for thirty years after independence was quite insignificant. This was a consequence of India's inability to provide funds for the promotion of tourism as resources were required for more urgent needs which included supply of food and development of basic infrastructure such as irrigation, electrification, education and health care. However, in 1982 the government announced a tourism policy which assigned the development of international tourism to the central government and the promotion of domestic tourism to the states. In 1986 a National Committee under the chairmanship of Mohammed Yunus was formed to draw up plans for the development of tourism in the country. The Committee reported that state intervention was necessary in order to ensure the supply of public utility services at reasonable prices. The Committee also made suggestions for the restructuring of government institutions and the provision of incentive programmes to encourage private sector involvement in the development of tourism. As a follow-up action the central government of India instituted a Tourism Finance Corporation (TFC) in 1989, liberalised air charter policy, and simplified travel procedures and formalities.

After the introduction of the new economic policy in 1991, to achieve higher growth in tourist arrivals, foreign exchange earnings and to generate more employment in the tourism sector, the government adopted a National Action Plan in 1992. As a result, many tourist spots and some new areas have been identified for special attention in co-operation with the private sector. Attempts have also been made to convert old havelies into heritage hotels. Private entrepreneurs have also been invited to develop tourist spots in selected islands.

PLANNING ERA

Tourism development in India has passed through many stages. In the Second and Third Five Year Plans, emphasis was laid on expansion and improvement of tourist facilities. Integrated development projects in Gulmarg and Kovalam were undertaken in the Fourth Five Year Plan. During the Fifth and Sixth five Year Plans measures were taken to promote integrated area development and to convert loan assistance measures to an interest subsidy scheme. In the Seventh Plan, tourism in India was accorded the status of an industry.

In the now liberalised economy of India more emphasis is given to encouraging significant private sector participation in the development of this industry. The policy framework of the Eighth Five Year Plan has restricted the role of Government to that of regulation, facilitation and coordination. As an outcome of the liberalisation process, foreign investments with equity participation of 51 per cent and 100 per cent in case of Non-Resident Indians (NRI) have been allowed in the tourism industry.

GROWTH AND ECONOMIC SIGNIFICANCE OF TOURISM

Economists like S. Kuznets have described 'Industrial growth' to mean a sustained increase in the volume of industrial output, the absence of which means stagnation in an industry. In a similar way the growth of the tourism industry can be defined as a sustained increase in the flow of tourists and foreign exchange earnings over time. The rise must be self-sustained and exhibit stability in the trend over a period long enough to reflect more than cyclical expansion or transient factors.

The growth and economic significance of the tourism industry is not readily appreciated due to the wide dispersion of tourist locations in the country. As early as 1936, the Economic Committee of the League of Nations restricted the benefits of this industry to:

(a) its ability to generate foreign exchange earnings
(b) its role as an accelerator of development, and
(c) softening the damage of uncertain commodity price fluctuations of primary products.

But, in recent years, tourism has been widely accepted as an important element of international trade, as a segment of national economies, as a means of earning foreign exchange, as a generator of income and employment and above all as a powerful driving force for economic development through its linkage effects. Economically speaking, tourism development encompasses practically all fields of economic activity, although some other sectors too have a powerful claim on the limited resources available for economic development, regional growth and investment, especially in a developing country like India.

In this section, an attempt is made to examine the growth and fluctuations in tourist arrivals and foreign exchange earnings during the period 1960/61–1994/5. Consideration is also given to the significance of tourism receipts in financing imports, raising national income (GDP), generating employment and promoting the development of the accommodation sector – the hotel industry.

The trend in the growth of the tourism industry in India has been analysed on the basis of estimated indices and the change in the annual percentage of growth. Further, an attempt is made to estimate the compound growth rate for the entire period under consideration and for different decades. The compound growth rate has been computed from the exponential function: $Y = ab^t$

$$\text{Growth rate (Gr)} = (b-1) \times 100$$

To probe into the proximate reasons for examining another dimension i.e. stability in tourist inflow and foreign exchange earning instability indices have been estimated as suggested by Cuddy and Dellevale (Cuddy and Dellevale, 1978) as follows:

$$\text{Instability Index (I)} = CV\sqrt{1-\overline{R}^2}$$

$$\text{Where, } \overline{R}^2 = 1 - (1 - R^2)\{(N - 1)/(N - K)\}$$

The data used in the study has been collected from secondary sources like the Centre for Monitoring Indian Economy (CMIE), Data Bank – Economic Times and World Tourism Organisation (WTO).

TOURIST ARRIVALS

Table 3.1 provides details of foreign tourist arrivals in India from 1961 to 1995 together with an index of growth and percentage of annual growth. It is observed that the tourist arrival has increased 15 times more from 139.8 thousands in the year 1961 to 2123.68 thousands in 1995. The index increased to the level of 1519 in 1995. Annual growth of tourist arrival is positive except for the years 1962, 1965, 1984, 1990 and 1991.

The decadal compound growth rate (Table 3.2) of tourist arrivals is found to be the highest (i.e. 12.06 per cent) for the decade 1971–80 and the lowest (i.e. 3.97 per cent) for the decade 1981–90. Despite fluctuations, the growth of tourist arrivals in India has registered a rising trend at the rate of 9.67 per cent over the entire period of study.

It is worth mentioning that instability in tourist arrivals acts as a detrimental factor in obtaining foreign exchange which in turn adversely affects the process of economic development. Table 3.2 reveals that instability in tourist arrival is the highest for the decade 1961–70 and the lowest for the period 1991–95. However, the trend of the instability index provides evidence of a declining trend over the decades.

Tourist inflow to India is mainly from eleven countries (Table 3.3) contributing around 50 per cent of total arrivals. The share of UK is the highest, 15.86 per cent, followed by USA, 9.80 per cent in 1994. Further, it is noted that tourist arrivals from USA and UK have tended to decline over the years. The growth rate is the highest (15.89 per cent) in the case of Spain and it is the lowest (4.99 per cent) in the case of USA (Table 3.4). The countries with higher growth rates exhibit a high degree of instability. Thus, the association between growth and instability of tourist arrivals from different countries is found to be positive.

Table 3.1
Tourist Arrivals in India (1961–95)

Year	Number ('000)	Index (1961 = 100)	Annual Per Cent of Growth
1961	139.80	100.00	–
1962	134.36	96.12	–3.89
1963	140.82	100.73	4.81
1964	156.67	112.07	11.25
1965	147.90	105.79	–5.60
1966	159.60	114.16	7.91
1967	179.57	128.45	12.51
1968	188.82	135.06	5.15
1969	244.72	175.05	19.60
1970	280.82	200.87	14.75
1971	301.00	215.31	7.19
1972	342.95	245.31	13.93
1973	409.90	293.20	19.52
1974	423.16	302.69	3.23
1975	465.28	332.82	9.95
1976	533.95	381.94	14.76
1977	640.42	458.10	19.94
1978	748.00	535.05	16.80
1979	764.78	547.05	2.24
1980	800.15	572.35	4.62
1981	1279.81	915.46	59.95
1982	1288.16	921.43	0.65
1983	1304.98	933.46	1.31
1984	1210.75	866.06	–7.22
1985	1252.38	900.84	4.02
1986	1451.08	1037.97	15.22
1987	1484.29	1061.72	2.29
1988	1590.66	1137.81	7.17
1989	1736.09	1241.84	9.14
1990	1707.16	1221.14	–1.67
1991	1677.51	1199.93	–1.74
1992	1822.44	1303.60	8.64
1993	1867.58	1335.89	2.48
1994	1907.32	1364.32	2.13
1995	2123.68	1519.08	11.34

Source: Centre for Monitoring Indian Economy, India's Balance of Payments, CMIE, July 1996.

Table 3.2
Decadal Growth Rate and Instability Indices of Tourist Arrivals

Period	GR	I
1961–70	11.16	7.82
1971–80	12.06	4.85
1981–90	3.97	6.10
1991–95	5.30	2.28
1961–95	9.67	15.21

Source: Table 3.1.

Table 3.3
Main Tourist Generators
(In millions)

SL No	Country	1961	Share (%)	1971	Share (%)	1981	Share (%)	1994	Share (%)
1.	Australia	2.30	1.64	10.94	3.63	20.94	1.64	32.92	1.72
2.	Canada	1.92	1.37	7.05	2.34	25.36	1.98	59.63	3.10
3.	France	3.03	2.17	16.78	5.57	57.27	4.47	71.71	3.76
4.	Germany	4.84	3.46	17.87	5.94	54.31	4.24	48.08	4.09
5.	Italy	1.64	1.17	5.98	1.99	28.50	2.23	42.90	2.24
6.	Japan	3.94	2.82	11.62	3.86	29.03	2.27	62.59	3.28
7.	Netherlands	1.20	0.86	3.69	1.23	10.78	0.84	34.84	1.83
8.	Spain	0.19	0.14	1.08	0.36	10.50	0.82	21.83	1.44
9.	Switzerland	1.65	1.18	5.39	1.79	14.11	1.10	28.40	1.49
10.	UK	22.19	15.87	40.01	13.29	116.68	9.12	302.48	15.86
11.	USA	31.35	22.42	54.98	18.26	82.05	6.41	186.91	9.80
12.	World	139.80	100.00	301.00	100.00	1279.80	100.00	1907.3	100.00

Source: Same as Table 3.1.

Table 3.4
Growth Rate and Instability Indices of
Tourist Arrivals from Major Countries (1961–1994)

SL No	Country	GR	I
1.	Australia	7.34	22.47
2.	Canada	11.20	18.76
3.	France	10.33	24.28
4.	Germany	9.47	19.98
5.	Italy	12.22	21.20
6.	Japan	9.28	18.75
7.	Netherlands	11.35	16.66
8.	Spain	15.89	28.46
9.	Switzerland	9.86	16.63
10.	UK	8.99	10.19
11.	USA	4.99	8.92
12.	Others	11.55	20.38
13.	Total	9.54	14.26

Note: GR – Growth Rate, I – Instability Index.
Source: Same as Table 3.1.

Although India's international tourist traffic has increased significantly, its share in International tourism is very insignificant; i.e. 0.37 per cent in 1995 (Table 3.5). India's share is also small when compared with other Asian countries. In contrast to this, tourism has achieved significant growth in many countries of the world (Table 3.6). France followed by Singapore, USA and Italy continue to maintain their position at the top in terms of tourist arrivals. While France received 60.58 million tourists in 1995, it is 2.12 million in the case of India. The reasons for this are very clear. These countries enjoy prosperity and higher standards of living leading to increased leisure, improved education and further they have well developed transport and communication systems which have contributed significantly to the growth of their tourism industry.

The poor performance of India on the other hand is mainly attributable to inadequate infrastructural support, poverty, terrorism, irregular air services, rigidity in customs clearance and foreign exchange formalities etc.

Table 3.5
World Tourist Arrivals

Year	World (in millions)	India (in nos)	% Share of India
1960	69.3	123,095	0.18
1970	159.7	280,821	0.18
1980	284.8	800,150	0.28
1995	567.0	2,123,683	0.37

Source: WTO.

Table 3.6
Tourist Arrivals and Foreign Exchange
Earning by India and Some Selected Countries (1995)

SL No	Country	Arrivals (in millions)	Foreign Exchange ($ in millions)
1.	USA	44.73	58.37
2.	France	60.58	27.32
3.	Italy	29.18	27.07
4.	Spain	45.13	25.06
5.	Singapore	6.59	7.55
6.	Hong Kong	9.59	9.07
7.	Thailand	6.53	6.61
8.	Indonesia	4.60	7.94
9.	Malaysia	7.94	3.50
10.	India	2.12	2.76
11.	World	567.00	372.60

Source: WTO.

FOREIGN EXCHANGE EARNINGS

Most of the less developed countries (LDCs) are not only poor in resources but also dependent on agriculture. Recently, in the era of liberalisation and globalisation there is a race among LDCs to industrialise their economies to achieve higher rates of economic growth. This is possible either through the development of indigenous technology or obtaining it from abroad. The first option is not only costly but also time consuming. The second one though easy requires huge foreign exchange. To earn more foreign exchange there must be growth of export trade. Whether international trade fosters economic growth in LDCs has been a controversial issue. Many studies (Prebisch, 1950; Singer, 1950; Myrdal, 1956) have proved that trading between developed countries (DCs) and LDCs has led to a dual economy of the colonial type accentuating the existing economic inequalities among nations. Moreover, the terms of trade has moved in favour of DCs which in turn has led to an alarming rise in the balance of payments deficits, and decline of foreign exchange reserves in LDCs. Thus, in recent years greater emphasis has been put on invisibles for earning foreign exchange. Tourism is one of the important invisible items with the least import intensity. Imports in the tourism industry constitute just 10 per cent of foreign exchange earnings as compared to 40 per cent in engineering products, 70 per cent in gems and jewelleries and 15 per cent in garment industries. Therefore, it is widely recognised that development in the tourism industry with little foreign exchange obligations can be relied on as an export led strategy for growth.

This sub-section, while examining the growth trend of travel receipts in India, seeks to answer the following questions: how stable is the foreign exchange earning from tourism? And has instability in foreign exchange earnings been increasing or decreasing over the period?

Table 3.7 reveals that there has been perceptible growth in foreign exchange earnings in spite of wide fluctuations in the trend. An uninterrupted growth in travel receipts is marked since 1986. The earning during 1987–88 was Rs. 1856 crores thus making tourism the highest net foreign exchange earner in the country for the same year. It significantly rose to Rs 7298 crores in 1994–95.

The index of tourism receipts increased to the level of 7773 in 1980–81 and declined to 5986.6 in the year 1985. However, the index continues to rise since 1986 without any setback in the trend.

The estimates of decadal compound growth rate of foreign exchange earnings (Table 3.8) show that there is a high degree of inconsistency in the growth-rate. It varies from 8.24 per cent in the decade 1960/61–1969/70 to 50.98 per cent in the decade 1970/71–1979/80. Further, it is observed that there is a drastic fall in the growth rate from 50.98 per cent in the seventies to 5.93 per cent in the eighties. This is probably due to political instability arising out of the assassination of Smt. Indira Gandhi, the Prime Minister of India during this period. However, foreign exchange earning over the decades has been marked by a declining trend of the instability index. It declined from 78.08 in 1961/70 to 13.3 in 1990/95. When the entire period is considered the index is as high as 52.78.

Table 3.7
Foreign Exchange Earning (1960/61 to 1994/95)

Year	Receipt $ (Cores)	Index (1960/61 = 100)	Annual % of Growth
1960/61	15	100.00	–
1961/62	15	100.00	–
1962/63	16	106.70	6.67
1963/64	13	86.67	–18.75
1964/65	2	13.33	–84.61
1965/66	12	80.00	500.00
1966/67	2	13.33	–83.33
1967/68	3	20.00	50.00
1968/69	5	33.33	66.67
1969/70	32	213.33	540.00
1970/71	36	240.00	12.50
1971/72	32	213.33	–11.11
1972/73	38	253.33	18.75
1973/74	57	380.00	50.00
1974/75	94	626.67	64.91
1975/76	190	1266.67	102.13
1976/77	285	1900.00	50.00
1977/78	531	3540.00	86.32
1978/79	565	3766.67	6.40
1979/80	920	6133.33	62.83
1980/81	1166	7773.33	26.74
1981/82	1064	7093.33	–8.75
1982/83	1131	7540.00	6.30
1983/84	1075	7166.67	–4.95
1984/85	898	5986.67	–16.46
1985/86	1189	7926.67	32.40
1986/87	1607	10713.33	35.16
1987/88	1856	12373.33	15.49
1988/89	2054	13693.33	10.67
1989/90	2386	15960.67	16.16
1990/91	2613	17420.00	9.51
1991/92	4892	32613.33	87.21
1992/93	6060	40400.00	23.87
1993/94	6717	44780.00	10.84
1994/95	7298	48653.33	8.65

Source: CMIE & Data Bank – *The Economic Times*.

Table 3.8
Decadal Growth Rate and Instability Index of Foreign Exchange Earning

Period	GR	I
1960/61–1969/70	–8.24	78.08
1970/71–1979/80	50.98	21.50
1980/81–1989/90	5.93	19.5
1990/91–1994/95	26.76	13.3
1960/61–1994/95	26.40	52.78

Although foreign exchange earning from tourism increased at the rate of 26.4 per cent within the period under study it seems sluggish when compared with Hong Kong, Indonesia, Singapore, Thailand and Malaysia. For instance, while in 1995, Hong Kong, Indonesia, Singapore, Thailand and Malaysia earned foreign exchange to the tune of $9.07 billion, $6.61 billion and $3.5 billion respectively, India could earn only $2.76 billion (Table 3.6). In the same year, India's share in the World total stands at 0.74 per cent.

FINANCING IMPORTS

A developing country like India with agricultural orientation of its economy and its heavy dependence on imports of capital, technology and manufactured goods for productive as well as for domestic consumption, has encountered continuous balance of payments deficits. After all, the volume of imports cannot be restricted because the level of investment as well as the rate of economic growth of LDCs is dependent on imports (Bhattacharya, 1987). The export of merchandise and net invisible earnings constitutes the chief means of financing imports. In this section, therefore, attempt has been made to assess the significance of tourism as an invisible item of export in financing India's import during the reference period.

Table 3.9 shows that while merchandise exports financed about 56 per cent of total imports in 1960/61, it is 7.4 per cent in the case of total invisibles. It reached the highest level of 56.85 per cent in 1973–74. In the terminal year of the study the contribution of merchandise export increased to 93.40 per cent while net earning from invisibles as a percentage of total imports is almost the same as in 1960/61, i.e. 7.64 per cent.

Net earnings from total invisibles has been marked by a steady decline since 1980–81 and it even assumed a negative contribution towards financing imports in the year 1990–91. However, earnings from tourism as a single invisible item has assumed greater importance over the period. Earnings from travel though not steady have been contributing positively since 1969–70. Its contribution was only 0.27 per cent in 1960–61; it reached an all-time high of 9.10 per cent in 1979–80, and then started to decline up to 1984–85. It is interesting to observe that from 1987–88 the earnings from invisible total in financing imports mainly comes from the net travel and tourism receipts.

Table 3.9
Means of Financing India's Imports (1960/61–1994/95)
(In per cent)

Year	Export of Merchandise	Invisibles Total Net	Invisibles Travel Net	Total Earnings	Total Imports	+ OR –
(1)	(2)	(3)	(4)	(2 + 3)	(6)	(7)
1960–61	56.15	7.40	0.27	63.55	100.00	–36.45
1961–62	61.28	2.20	0.37	63.49	100.00	–36.51
1962–63	60.30	4.77	0.35	65.08	100.00	–34.92
1963–64	65.58	7.20	0.16	72.77	100.00	–27.23
1964–65	59.53	10.45	–0.59	69.98	100.00	–30.02
1965–66	55.50	5.46	0.07	60.97	100.00	–39.03
1966–67	51.92	–0.34	–0.63	51.59	100.00	–48.41
1967–68	62.50	–0.80	–0.60	61.70	100.00	–38.30
1968–69	71.61	0.42	–0.52	72.03	100.00	–27.97
1969–70	88.75	–2.40	1.07	86.35	100.00	–13.65
1970–71	85.99	–2.26	1.10	83.72	100.00	–16.28
1971–72	85.21	1.97	0.66	87.18	100.00	–12.82
1972–73	101.50	–0.05	1.02	101.45	100.00	1.45
1973–74	79.56	56.85	1.35	136.41	100.00	36.41
1974–75	70.37	7.37	1.75	77.74	100.00	–22.26
1975–76	79.35	16.33	3.19	95.69	100.00	–4.31
1976–77	101.16	23.75	4.87	124.91	100.00	24.91
1977–78	90.27	30.53	8.07	120.80	100.00	20.80
1979–80	81.56	29.20	7.36	110.76	100.00	10.76
1980–81	56.89	34.79	9.10	91.17	100.00	–8.83
1981–82	52.40	34.35	8.57	86.75	100.00	–13.25
1982–83	57.07	26.87	6.76	83.94	100.00	–16.06
1983–84	63.93	24.35	6.62	88.27	100.00	–11.73
1984–85	64.23	22.80	5.27	87.03	100.00	–12.97
1985–86	69.76	22.45	2.85	92.21	100.00	–7.79
1986–87	58.90	18.47	3.96	77.36	100.00	–22.64
1987–88	66.26	17.54	6.15	83.79	100.00	–16.21
1988–89	73.71	13.50	6.15	87.21	100.00	–12.79
1989–90	73.13	6.99	5.20	80.12	100.00	–19.88
1990–91	79.91	2.90	4.86	82.81	100.00	–17.19
1991–92	76.75	–1.01	4.42	75.74	100.00	–24.26
1992–93	93.88	8.90	7.90	102.78	100.00	2.78
1993–94	86.41	2.11	7.70	88.52	100.00	–11.48
1994–95	97.41	4.30	5.87	101.00	100.00	1.71
1995–96	93,40	7.64	3.91	101.04	100.00	1.04

Source: Balance of Payments, CMIE, July 1996.

CONTRIBUTION TO NATIONAL INCOME

Expenditure incurred towards goods and services by the tourists in other countries is reflected as national travel receipts for such country. Thus, the contribution made by the tourism industry for the growth of national income depends on the volume of foreign exchange earnings and its spread effects in the economy over a time. The amount of money spent by tourists multiplies as it passes through various sections of the economy. Therefore, tourism as a source of income is not easy to measure, at least to some degree of accuracy because of the multiplier effect (Dube, 1995). Many studies, (Clement, 1961; Richards, 1972; Vonhove, 1975 and Archer, 1977) have been undertaken to estimate the value of the tourist multiplier and its effect on macro-economic aggregates. In recent times, Fletcher, Seene *et al.* (1981), Lin and Sung (1983) and Fletcher (1993) have tried to examine the economic effects of tourism on the basis of input-output analysis. In India, NCAER (1975) conducted an elaborate study on Kashmir and Kovalam Beach Resort Project (KBRP) and measured the tourism multiplier for India. According to their findings the tourism multiplier co-efficient varies between 3.2 and 3.6.

In this study a simple measure, i.e. percentage share of travel receipts from international tourism in Gross Domestic Product (GDP) has been estimated and analysed in order to show the significance that the tourism industry has in the growth of national income of India.

Table 3.10 provides GDP figures and per cent share of tourism receipts in GDP for the period 1970–71 to 1994–95. The share of tourism receipts in GDP was merely 0.09 per cent in 1970–71. It increased to the highest level of 0.96 per cent in 1992–93 and declined to 0.85 per cent in 1994–95. Three distinct phases are clearly marked in the trend of tourism's share in GDP. The first phases, i.e. from 1970–71 to 1980–81 has been marked by a rising trend followed by a declining trend in the second phases, i.e. from 1980–81 to 1989–90. In the last phase, i.e. from 1990–91 to 1994–95, no clear trend is observed. The share of tourism after increasing for two years declined from 1992–93. The rising and falling trends in the first and second decade have been supported by the positive and negative growth rates, i.e. 35.2 per cent and –3.76 per cent respectively. On average, the contribution of tourism to the growth of national income has increased at the rate of 9.21 per cent during the period under study.

It is worth mentioning here that India's GDP has been forecast to grow at the rate of 5.6 per cent as against 3.4 per cent for the world in the coming decade. A study by the World Tourism Organisation in 1988 reveals that the average expenditure by a tourist in India is about $1000 against the average of $675 in South Asian countries. Thus the prospects of the tourism industry in generating more income for India seem to be promising.

EMPLOYMENT GENERATION

The economic significance of the tourism industry can also be assessed on the basis of the role it plays in reducing unemployment in India. The tourist industry is a highly labour-intensive service industry and hence, there is ample scope for gainful employment. It provides a vast spectrum of employment starting from highly trained managers and accountants to unskilled gardeners. It also makes much better use of certain other resources with low opportunity costs (Chattopadhaya, 1995). The demand for tourism can have direct, indirect and induced effects in the economy. Moreover, tourism has the advantage of absorbing locally available labour in backward regions of tourist importance.

Table 3.10
India's Tourism Receipts and GDP,(In Rs Crores)

Year	GDP (in factor cost)	Per cent share of Tourism
1970–71	39708	0.09
1971–72	42248	0.08
1972–73	46473	0.08
1973–74	56954	0.10
1974–75	67039	0.14
1975–76	71201	0.27
1976–77	76536	0.37
1977–78	87351	0.61
1978–79	93880	0.60
1979–80	102442	0.90
1980–81	122427	0.95
1981–82	143216	0.74
1982–83	159395	0.71
1983–84	186723	0.58
1984–85	208577	0.43
1985–86	233799	0.51
1986–87	262030	0.62
1987–88	294851	0.63
1988–89	352706	0.58
1989–90	408662	0.58
1990–91	477814	0.55
1991–92	552768	0.88
1992–93	627634	0.96
1993–94	723103	0.93
1994–95	854103	0.85

Source: CMIE, May and June 1996.

It is observed by WTO that one in every 16 workers world-wide owes his/her job to tourism (Satyasundaram, 1995). According to an estimate of WTO travel and tourism are expected to have provided direct and indirect employment to 212 million people accounting for 10.7 per cent of the global work force in 1995.

The tourism industry in India, in particular, has much relevance with regard to employment generation. Statistics and various estimates show that not less than 7.8 million people accounting for 2.4 per cent of total work force are directly employed by this industry. These include activities like travel agencies souvenir shops, village artisans, folk artists, carpet weavers and many others. It is estimated than an investment of one million rupees creates 89 jobs in the hotel and restaurant sector, a key segment of the tourism industry as against 44.7 jobs in agriculture and 12.6 in manufacturing industry (Seth, 1996). In 1994–95 the tourism industry in India has provided direct employment to the tune of 18.4 million, i.e. one million more than the estimated figure for 1993-94 (*Market Survey*, 1995). Thus, it is widely believed that the tourism industry in a populated country like India with millions of unemployed, has an important role to play in generating gainful employment in days to come.

Tourism and the Accommodation Sector: The Hotel Industry

The phenomenal increase in tourism in the 20th century has made the hotel business cross national boundaries and become global in character as accommodation services form an important segment of tourism infrastructure. The accommodation sector includes such establishments and facilities where tourists stop being travellers and become guests (Mohanty, 1992). Therefore, it is said, "no tourism without hotels". The relationship between tourism and the hotel industry can be expressed in two ways:

(a) firstly, a large component of demand for hotel services is generated by the tourism industry.
(b) secondly, the hotel industry supplies the basic requirements – food, accommodation, entertainment required by the tourists.

While analysing the impact of the tourism industry on the accommodation infrastructure, Ogilvie (Ogilvie, 1941) observes that "a nation of shop keepers has, in a large measure, become a nation of inn keepers". Thus the significance of the tourism industry in a country is also studied by examining the growth trend of the hotel industry in that country.

In India, since the economic reforms were introduced, there has been a significant growth of business travels with spin off effects on the growth of accommodation infrastructure. This phenomenon has induced entrepreneurs and existing business houses to diversify their business in the accommodation sector.

Table 3.11 reveals that there were only 363 hotels of all categories in 1981 and it has increased to 912 in 1994 registering a growth rate of 151.2 per cent between 1981 and

1994. Similarly there has been a growth of 148.6 per cent in the total room capacity during the same period. Further, the growth of five and four star hotels is fairly high, both in terms of numbers and room capacity in comparison to other classified category of hotels. This phenomenal growth is due to the expansion of the railways infrastructure, the establishment of a separate Department of Tourism, the part played by the Government of India and participation by the private sector.

Table 3.11

Growth of Hotels and Hotel Rooms

	No. of Hotels				No. of Rooms			
Category	1981	1992	1993	1994	1981	1992	1993	1994
Five Star	25	82	87	91	5498	15435	16580	17440
Four Star	18	49	59	58	1336	3543	4104	4471
Heritage	-	19	21	22	-	651	616	682
Three Star	59	115	141	163	2974	6045	7747	9104
Two Star	78	235	238	240	3248	8740	8744	9142
One Star	38	96	101	103	1262	3182	3344	3608
Classification awaited	145	202	234	235	7982	9811	10288	11008
Total	363	798	881	912	22300	47407	51453	55455

Source: Department of Tourism, Government of India.

The average occupancy rates of approved hotels for the last five years are depicted in Table 3.12. It shows that the rate of occupancy of approved hotels except two star has increased over the years. The occupancy rate has increased form 64.9 per cent in 1991 to 73.7 per cent in 1995. It is further observed that in addition to increase in foreign tourist traffic, the rate of occupancy by domestic tourists has also increased.

Table 3.12

Estimated Average Occupancy Rate of Approved Hotels

Category	1991	1992	1993	1994	1995
Five Star	69.2 (37.8)	70.1 (42.1)	69.8 (41.9)	69.9 (36.9)	72.6 (40.0)
Four Star	62.1 (22.6)	64.3 (23.9)	65.1 (23.3)	72.3 (22.4)	78.1 (25.9)
Heritage	-	-	-	53.1 (13.0)	52.1 (16.1)
Three Star	59.5 (14.7)	65.0 (14.2)	65.6 (14.3)	67.5 (12.8)	76.7 (14.1)
Two Star	69.4 (14.1)	69.8 (14.9)	70.5 (14.0)	65.4 (16.1)	65.9 (16.6)
One Star	55.0 (09.5)	57.6 (8.90)	58.4 (9.10)	74.4 0(1.1)	68.7 (3.70)
Classification awaited	62.0 (30.8)	65.4 (32.4)	64.8 (32.0)	50.1 (10.4)	39.4 (30.7)
Total	64.9 (28.8)	66.7 (30.5)	67.1 (30.3)	69.3 (28.0)	73.7 (32.6)

Source: Figures in parenthesis show the rate of occupancy by foreigners.

EMERGING ISSUES

The present section aims at raising some key issues relevant to the challenge and prospects confronting the Indian tourism industry. The single most basic proposition which appears to have set the priorities for the promotion of tourism in LDCs and India in particular, is to garner more and more of foreign exchange to meet trade deficits and leave ample surpluses to meet the import requirements for future development. But the plausibility and profitability of this proposition is by no means examined alongside the public concerns and the negative impacts that this industry has upon the economy. These are some of the important issues and challenges which require due consideration when evaluating the performance and prospects of the tourism industry, and consideration of strategies for the development of the industry and the economy at large.

ECONOMIC

The impact of tourism becomes critical when the flow of tourists in a particular place is visibly large. The numerical impact is relative to the size and spatial distribution of the host population. For instance, in the Maldives, the ratio of foreign tourists to the total population of the country is about 33 per cent. India experienced similar problems during the sixties when hippies congregated in Goa. All those economic problems and priorities that arise as a consequence are unknown to anyone. Particularly, tourism development in a locality puts severe pressure on essential but limited local resources, such as water supply, sanitation, health care, accommodation and transportation etc.

Moreover, like many other industries its actions are dictated by the market, and usually, too, by short term profit rather than long term investments. Huge investments are made for conservation and preservation diverting scarce resources from other use, and do not pay immediate dividends.

It is true that tourism brings affluence to many in the tourist localities but at the same time it increases the cost of food and housing for everyone. Such a process not only gives rise to shock wave of inflation but also to demonstration effect as locals adopt the marks of affluence exhibited by the tourist, and live beyond their means.

Tourism is labour intensive, and it helps to solve the unemployment problem in a big way. The significance of tourism in helping to solve the unemployment problem in LDCs is undermined if someone questions the nature of employment provided by the tourism industry. Tourism is always and everywhere a seasonal economic activity. It provides seasonal employment, and consequently creates seasonal unemployment. Thus, it does little for correcting structural unemployment problems – arising out of changes in technology, changes in the composition of final demand, or on a more local scale, from the changes in the location of the industry – which is one of the main causes of concern in LDCs including India.

It is said that tourism is labour intensive excluding the hotel industry – an important segment of the tourism industry. Growth of the tourism industry on the other hand is always accompanied by the growth of the hotel industry. Studies (Medlik, 1978) in Germany and Switzerland reveal that in the hotel industry the proportion of fixed assets is probably higher than in any other industry. It is therefore said with some validity that tourism as a capital intensive industry ties up scarce capital in developing countries, which could be better utilised to improve the quality of life of the people (Kaul, 1989).

In developing countries millions of artisans rely upon local craft industries. Local craft industries flourish with the growth of the tourism industry as it provides new outlets for ethnic goods. But it has been observed that growth of tourism has degenerated local crafts into cheap imitations, and caused severe damage to the local industries.

Finally, any economic activity ensuring economic development but accentuating inequality has less to recommend in a welfare state. Regarding the tourism industry, a joint UNESCO-World Bank seminar in 1976 concluded that as with so many 'improvements' tourism based development usually reinforces social divisions. It is only those who already have land or money who take full advantage of this new source of riches; and the biggest profits are often made by large firms from outside the locality.

SOCIO-CULTURAL

All over the world government bodies are being set up to encourage the development of tourism. But tourism can be more disruptive than any other industry. "Can it be made to benefit existing communities, and culture rather than destroy them?" questioned Sarah Tillostan, (Tillostan, 1988) a tourist visiting India. It is believed that tourism provides funds for conservation and grants new life to monuments. Old monuments can become profitable assets. This proposition may not hold always good. Specifically speaking what is true in DCs, e.g. in Britain, may not be true in India.

Let us take the case of Jaipur and Jaisalmer where havelis have been brought down and traditional urban habitations have been destroyed to make space for parking. Moreover conservation is not the ultimate aim of tourism. Conservation very often leads to physical destruction of buildings and streets under the pressure of tourism development. Many traditional buildings with a long cultural heritage have lost the essence in the process of 'conservation'. Tourism does not always help conservation of cultural heritage but often does the reverse.

One of the important and socially undesirable impacts of mass tourism is that it bears a positive relationship with crime. It has been observed that a spurt of thieving in Mexico, Hungary, the former Czechoslovakia and drug trafficking in Goa can be traced to foreign tourists.

Tourism development in developing countries often creates 'sex tourism' in the name of mass tourism. Prostitution increase is very much in evidence in some parts of South East

Asia, especially Thailand, the Philippines, South Korea, Taiwan, Indonesia and Sri Lanka. Consequently, sex tourism has led to the spread of many incurable diseases like AIDS.

Environmental

The relationship between the development of tourism and the natural environment is, more or less, reciprocal. With the growth of the tourism industry misuse of environment increases leading to degradation of the environment in the region. For instance, a large influx of tourists to an environmentally fragile locale holds out a threat of degradation. Once of tourist place is environmentally degraded, new locations are developed as tourist spots and there is a shift of the tourism industry from the old to the new location. The growing negative impact of the tourism industry on the environment has led the WTO Environment Committee to undertake some steps in order to preserve the natural environment. It has also been realised by many that without sustainability of the environment, the tourism industry cannot be sustained in future. Growth of the tourism industry gives rise to many environmental problems – specifically carrying capacity, ecosystem solvency, protection of cultural elements an protection of the built environment etc.

Lastly, no other international trading activity involves such critical interplay between economic political, environmental and social elements than tourism. In the extreme, developing countries perceive international tourism as a form of imperialism. The greeter the difference between the tourists and the host country in terms of race, culture and standard of living, the greater is the negative impact of tourism.

Conclusion

This article used time series data on tourist arrivals, foreign exchange earnings, import values, GDP and the number of classified hotels and rooms available primarily to study the growth and economic significance of the tourism industry in India during the period 1960/61 to 1994/95. It also throws light on some of the important economic, social and ecological issues which require due consideration in the policy framework if India is to become a major player in world tourism. The method of analysis involved is to estimate the compound growth rate from the exponential function and instability indices using the method as suggested by Cuddy and Dellavale; and the find answers to the following questions pertaining to tourist arrivals and foreign exchange earnings:

(i) What is the growth achieved over different decades?
(ii) How stable are the growth rates?
(iii) Has the degree of instability been declining or increasing over the period? and

(iv) Which countries exhibit relatively more growth and stability in the generation of tourists during the period under study?

Finally, the study has made some broad suggestions for the growth of the tourism industry in India, in particular, and the economic development, in general.

FINDINGS

The main findings of the above analysis are summed up as follows:

Despite the fact that the development of tourism in India is linked to its glorious tradition and rich cultural heritage, India was a late starter in promoting the modern concept of tourism because of historical and economic reasons. Although a separate Department of Tourism was formed in 1958 to look after the development of tourism, the extent of development was quite insignificant for at least thirty years. With the announcement of tourism policy in 1982 and National Committee Report in 1986 and followed by the National Action plan in 1992 the Indian tourism industry has experienced impressive growth in comparison to a low base during the sixties. It was only in the Seventh Five Year plan that tourism in India was accorded industry status. With the liberalisation of the Indian economy more emphasis is put on the role of the private sector for the development of the tourism industry.

Growth in tourist arrivals, though, seem impressive at 9.67 per cent per annum, but there are wide fluctuation in the trend during the period 1960/61–1994/95. It varies between 3.97 per cent in 1981–90 and 12.06 per cent in 1971–80.

The degree of instability in tourist arrivals is not only low but also is marked by a declining trend over the decades. For the entire period the instability index stands at 15.21.

Although the UK has claimed the highest share followed by the USA in the tourist inflow to India their respective shares have been declining. While Spain, out of eleven major tourist generating countries, has registered the highest growth rate i.e. 15.89 per cent, the USA represents the lowest, i.e. 4.95 per cent. Similarly, the Instability Index for Spain has been found the highest and for the USA the lowest. The association between growth and instability of tourist arrivals from major countries exhibit a positive relationship. In spite of an impressive growth in tourist arrivals over the years, India's share in the world total is very insignificant, i.e. 0.37 per cent in 1995.

A significant growth with a high degree of inconsistency in the growth rate of foreign exchange earning has been marked over the decades. The growth rate varies from –8.24 per cent during the sixties to 50.98 per cent during the seventies. However, the degree of instability has been showing a falling trend. India's share in the world tourism earnings is not only low at 0.74 per cent in 1994–95 but also insignificant in comparison to other Asian countries.

While merchandise exports have met 93.40 per cent of foreign exchange requirement of imports in 1994–95, the share of total invisible trade was only 7.64 per cent which is almost the same in comparison to 1960–61. But tourism as an invisible item of export has been contributing positively in financing imports to 1960–61. It is also observed that the share of tourism has increased significantly since 1986–87.

Similarly, in the growth of national income (GDP), the share of the tourism industry has increased at the rate of 9.21 per cent between 1970–71 and 1994–95. But a high degree of fluctuations has been evident in the growth trend of shares over the decades. In the last five years the share has increased by 9.87 per cent per annum.

The role played by the tourism industry in the generation of employment has been found to be significant. It has given employment to the tune of 18.4 million persons in 1995 which constitute 8.67 per cent of the total employment generated by the global tourism.

There has been impressive growth of the hotel industry in terms of number of hotels, room capacity and average rate of occupancy during 1991–95. The highest rate of growth is seen in the case of high spending hotels and the lowest growth is seen to be in the case of low spending hotels. The average rate of occupancy of approved hotels except two star hotels, has increased during the last five years. Average occupancy by both foreign and domestic tourists has increased during the same period.

Some of the major economic, social and environmental issues and fall outs of the indiscriminate growth of the tourism industry have also been discussed. The study, while observing the positive contributions made by the tourism industry in the process of economic development of India, critiques the efficiency of this industry because of its negative impacts aggravating the problems of over population, pressure on local resources, demonstration effects, capital intensity, regional inequality, crime, prostitution, cultural degradation and loss of essence of traditional architecture, and most importantly, the environmental degradation.

BROAD SUGGESTIONS

These are some of the broad suggestions for planning tourism development:

(i) As tourism destinations cover vast areas and larger distances, steps should be taken for the growth of tourism infrastructure such as provision for an adequate number of air-conditioned cars and coaches, aircraft, reliable flight scheduled and safety. Moreover, the Government of India should adopt a liberal policy towards foreign airlines and take steps to remove rigidities and reduce formalities for obtaining visa and custom clearance.

(ii) The hotel and transport services of the public sector has been found to be less efficient in comparison with private entrepreneurs. Thus a package of fiscal incentives may be given to the private sector for promoting more hotel construction to meet the accommodation requirement of tourists by the turn of the century.

(iii) There is an urgent need to re-orient awareness programmes abroad. Indian Embassies and High Commissions abroad should present the ambience of our cultural heritage in more detail.

(iv) A strategic marketing plan is very much needed with a focus on a select number of tourist generating countries along with exploration of new tourist generating markets.

(v) The tourism industry may be accorded the status of an exporting enterprise in order to reap the benefits and facilities that are given to other exporting enterprises.

(vi) Domestic tourism must be promoted with higher intensity for the proper utilisation of the available tourism infrastructure in order to avoid the loss caused by seasonal variations and fluctuation in tourist arrivals due to economic and political reasons.

(vii) Tourism planning should not be viewed in isolation. Tourism plans must be an integral part of the National Economic Development plans. Plans must be mutually interdependent and reinforcing each other.

(viii) Tourism planning along with general development planning should ensure protection and conservation of natural resources and heritage. Strict specifications must be made for the use of land space, water, air and local resources.

(ix) There is an urgent need to stop the concentration of development in the hands of multi national companies (MNCs) as these companies are not familiar with the local culture, problems and resources.

(x) It is urged that a conservation tax may be imposed on hotel industry – the main beneficiaries from tourism – operating in tourist places.

(xi) Lastly, there must be cooperation and coordination between different departments of the Government such as Commerce, Finance, Civil Aviation, Home and External Affairs, Urban and Land Development in order to provide a boost to the tourism industry.

Thus, the need of the hour is a comprehensive well defined national policy framework which would strike a balance between the tourism development and the socio-economic costs. A short sighted view tilting in favour of economism in its most vulgar form may lend us in a realm of ecological catastrophe.

NOTE

The author is thankful to Professor Kumar B. Das, Head of the Department of A & A Economics, Vanivihar, Utkal University (Orissa) for his useful comments on the earlier draft of the paper.

REFERENCES

Archer, B.H. (1977) *Tourism Multipliers, The State of Art Bangor*, University of Wales Press.

Bhardwaj, B. (1996) "Tourism and infrastructure", *Yojana*, 40(8), August: 23.

Bhattacharya, H. (1987) *International Trade and Finance*, Calcutta Book House, 334.

Bhatia, A.K. (1983) *Tourism Development, Principles and Practices*, New Delhi: Sterling Publishers Pvt. Ltd, 26.

Chattopadhaya, Kunal (1995) *Economic Impact of Tourism Development, An Indian Experience*, Calcutta: Kanishka Publications and Distributors, 89.

Clement, H.G. (1961) *The Future of Tourism in the Pacific and the Far East*, Washington, New York: US Govt Printing Press.

Cuddy, J.D.A. and Dellevale, P.A. (1978) "Measuring the instability of time series data", *OBEAS*, 40: 79-85.

Das, K.B. and Mohanty, P.' (1994) "Profile of global tourism in India", *Indian Journal of Marketing*, XXXI(11), January: 4.

Dube, Rajiv (1995) "Multiplier effect and the tourism sector", *Indian Economic Journal*, 42(3), January–March: 147.

"Facts for you" (1995) *Market Survey*, October: 18.

Fletcher, Snee *et al.* (1991) *An Input and Output Study of Gibraltar*, Bangor Institute of Economic Research, University College of North Wales.

Kaul, R.N. (1989) *Dynamics of Tourism – A trilogy, Vol 1, The Phenomenon*, Sterling Publishers, ND, 105.

Lin Tzong and Yun Wing Sung (1983) "Hong Kong", in T. Lin and E.A. Pye (eds) *Tourism in Asia: Economic Impact*, Singapore: Singapore University Press, 1-100.

Medlik, S. (1978) *Profile of Hotel and Catering Industry*, London: Heinemann, 85.

Mohanty, P. (1992) *Hotel Industry and Tourism in India*, Ashish Publishing House, ND, 47.

Myrdal, G. (1956) *An International Economy*, New York: Harper.

Negi, J. (1996) "Tourism and development: Some issues", *Yojana*, 40(8), August: 33.

Ogilvie, F.W. (1941) *The Tourist Movement*, London: Staple Press Ltd, 4.

Prebisch, R. (1950) "The economic development of Latin America and its principal problems", *Economic Bulletin for Latin America*, New York: United Nations.

Rabindra, Seth, *A Tourist Consultant*.

Richards, G. (1972) *Tourism and the Economy – An Examination of Methods for Evaluating the Contribution and Effects of Tourism in the Economy – Surrey*, University of Surrey.

Satyasundaram, I. (1995) "Tourism industry untapped potential", *Facts for You*, October: 17.

Seth, R. (1996) "Tourism in India, an overview", *Yojana*, 40(8), August: 19.

Sing, R.B. (1988) "Tourism development, environment monitoring and remote sensing", in R.B. Singh (ed.) *Studies in Environment and Development,* New Delhi: Common Wealth Publishers, 116.

Sing, T. (1975) *Tourism and Tourist Industry*, Delhi: New Height, 221.

Singer, H.W. (1950) "The distribution of gains between investing and borrowing countries", *American Economic Review,* Papers and Proceedings.

Tillostan, S. (1988) "Cultural tourism or cultural destruction", *Economic and Political Economy*, XXIII(38), September 17: 1940-41.

Vanohove, Norbert (1972) "Application of cost benefit analysis of tourism Berne", *AIEST*, 12.

Chapter 4

TOURISM AND INDIA'S DEVELOPMENT: ECONOMIC, SOCIAL, POLITICAL AND ENVIRONMENTAL ISSUES

HARSHADA S. RATHOD
Department of Economics,
Smt. P.N. Doshi Women's College,
Ghatkopar (W) Mumbai
400 086, India

BACKGROUND

Tourism and fashion are the two rapidly changing features of the socio-economic world. Tourism and travel need to keep constant pace with the ever changing demands and preferences of the peoples of the world. The world of tourism is as fanciful and real as it is thrilling and dangerous.

Tourism is a basic and most desirable economic, industrial and human activity which deserves the praise and encouragement of all people and government. It is an international, intra-regional as well as a domestic industry in most countries of the world.

Like many other consumer goods industries, tourism may be entering a more stabilised period of operation, following the boom years of expansionary development. Stability, however, does not mean stationarity. The industry is more diversified and flexible than ever before and should be able to respond to changing needs and preferences of visitors.

Tourism is an economic and industrial activity in which many individuals, firms, corporations, organisations and associations are engaged and is a direct concern to many others. It is economically important as it provides a source of income. It provides employment, it brings in infrastructural improvements and it may help regional development. In India, tourism has emerged as the single largest net earner of foreign exchange. It is a high employment sector, where 5.3 million people are directly employed by the tourism industry. Despite this India accounts for hardly 0.3 per cent of the world tourist traffic and 0.2 per cent of global earnings. It is estimated that tourist arrival would reach 5,000,000 by the year 2000.

The latest World Tourism Organisation data indicates that India's tourism receipts per person reached over $15 in 1996. India's economic rival, China, notched up over $20 per person in the same year, while Singapore, topped the order with $3,137 per person. Furthermore, the gap in tourism earnings has been steadily widening. While for Singapore tourism receipts per person rose by 14.6 per cent in 1996, India recorded a growth of only 10.6 per cent according to the World Tourism Organisation. India's total earnings from tourism during the period was Rs. 10,000 crore, a rise of 21.6 per cent.

It is disappointing that India has not managed to have a greater share of the tourism market notwithstanding the fact that there was an absolute increase in the number of travellers to India during the last few years. By and large, this has been due to the lack of a coherent policy and information facilities.

The above analysis shows the structural inadequacies of Indian tourism which prevent it from benefiting substantially from the global growth in tourism. This inadequacy stems from the failure of the tourism industry and the relevant ministries to understand the needs of present day tourists. Tourism brings a number of intelligible benefits. It offers educational, social, cultural and political values. It brings in international understanding. Travel widens knowledge and reduces political sources of friction and political tensions. All these benefits also accrue to India which is a vast and diverse country with rich regional, cultural heritage and languages. The movement of the people between regions is the main factor which has kept India together in the past and will help in shaping her into a fully integrated nation in the future.

Tourism has many undesirable aspects. Critics of tourism expansion point to the various social strains which are caused by tourist development. Some of the economists have serious accusations against the tourism industry. The various charges levelled against tourism are being seriously discussed in the high levels of the government, the chambers of commerce and industries, in the lecture rooms of institutes dealing with tourism, and in the editorial pages of newspapers and magazines. The industry cannot ignore these. The main charges leveled against tourism are:

- distortion of indigenous cultural expression;
- conversion of small farmers into wage earners;
- national demoralisation;
- burden of infrastructure costs;
- possibility of population explosion;
- exploiting natural landscape;
- uncertainty and risk related to dependence;
- dependence on foreign capital;
- saturation of tourist region;
- disproportional use of land etc.

When talking about cost and benefits of tourism, the economic value of tourism to an economy is measured by way of its contribution to the national income, the earnings of foreign exchange, the state revenues and to the creation of employment. The main sources of revenue to the state from the tourist industry are through taxation, customs and excise duties in goods and services bought or used by the tourists. The other benefits involved are increase in income and jobs, preservation of cultural and natural heritages, increased international understanding, building new factories such as sewage works for the whole community. But the cost at which these benefits accrue are the foreign exchange costs of capital investments in hotels, cost of land and building, cost of importing amenities, like vehicles, destruction of environment etc.

The tourist industry is no doubt a foreign exchange earner but the ill effects of tourism are causing concern to the experts in the field. It produces widespread effects on society, the economy, culture, the environment and human behaviour. It has both positive and negative effects. Some of these effects are listed below.

SOCIAL IMPACTS OF TOURISM

Tourism in developing countries has some social effects. The analysis of the social impact of tourism has been ignored by economists, in spite of the fact that most of the attack on tourism in developing countries has been levelled at its "social effects".

Tourism brings together people belonging to different countries, practising different lifestyles, speaking different languages. There is a great mingling of cultures and this naturally has some of its adverse effects. The most important is the culture shock. When people belonging to more affluent countries come face-to-face with poverty they feel very uneasy.

In addition, there is a "demonstration effect" which occurs when the presence of large numbers of tourists encourages consumption patterns which are inappropriate for the population as a whole. These can range from demands for expensive food imports to entertainment activities like gambling, whose introduction often coincides with new tourist developments. Finally, there is the pervasive influence of neo-colonialism. International tourism follows the well-established trading and political connections of former colonial empires and is seen by some as evidence that imperialism persists. These resentments are there because of ever-present reminders of foreign culture and former political and economic subjugation.

Tourism may contribute to an increase in criminal and anti-social activities. The main factors for this situation are the population density due to increase in tourist traffic, the location of tourist resorts in relation to an international border and a large difference in per capita income of tourists and hosts at destinations. Congregation at tourist destinations results in increased expenditure on law enforcement during the tourist season, heightened tension, false sense of security, burglary, vandalism, tax dodging and black marketeering.

Gambling has been largely responsible for the fame and notoriety of tourist destinations such as Las Vegas, Tijuana etc. Many cities like Atlantic City and New Jersey wanted to legalise casinos in an attempt to revive the fading tourist trade of those cities. Legalisation of casinos has a number of benefits to destination areas. Still there are some places where casinos have been banned as gambling was perceived by citizens as one of the most undesirable consequences of tourism.

Crime, particularly vandalism, drug abuse and disorderly behaviour resulting from the abuse of alcohol was perceive as the most negative of the impacts of tourism.

Tourism studies reveal that it is closely related to increases in the sale of sex (prostitution). The very recent threat of AIDS as an incurable sexually-transmitted disease will have important implications for the popularity of some tourist destinations, such as Thailand. The employment of women in this trade leads to their involvement in prostitution to maintain and upgrade their economic status.

Tourism has the dual effect of promoting health care in third world destinations but in addition, acts as a vehicle to spread some forms of disease. While promotion of tourism requires tax increases to improve the public health facilities in destination areas, at the same time it leads to a deterioration in standard of health due to the pollution of the atmosphere.

The other social impacts are resentment towards tourists in over-used areas and overcrowding and congestion due to mass tourism.

Tourism has many positive social impacts like increased communication with people, improved self-image of the community, a growing variety of employment opportunities, educational opportunities, motivation for learning, modernisation of the infrastructure and promotion of urbanisation. The increasing presence of international tourists is an important element in the process of cultural interaction , whereby people in contact with each other borrow from each other's cultural heritage.

The growth of tourism has increased the demand for tourists' handicrafts. This has stimulated local production with both positive and negative consequences. Positive effect may be found in the financial success of traditional art. On the other hand, the sheer pressure to satisfy the demand in a ready market for handicrafts has also led to a fall in the quality of workmanship and to the manufacture of cheap imitations known as airport art. Traditional designs are degraded in this way and old skills lost.

ECONOMIC IMPACTS OF TOURISM

Tourism is highly desirable to most communities because by attracting and serving visitors a community earns new or even basic income from other parts of the country and globe. Such income can be considered the equivalent of export earnings. It gives increasing national income, the government gains economic benefits from taxes and duties on things tourists use and buy. It is also labour oriented and provides employment several times more than normal manufacturing industries can provide. It is a fact that almost all developing countries use tourism for generating economic development, correcting adverse balance of payment position. It is the only export trade that earns large foreign exchange without depleting national resources and without actually exporting any material goods. It also creates new opportunities to spend.

The tourist industry no doubt has a positive impact, but there are a also some ill impacts, for example tourism could increase inflation. The more obvious instance involves increases in retail prices in shops during the tourist season and steeply rising land values, leading to a general rise in home costs and property taxes. The seasonal character of tourism leads to seasonal unemployment. It has been observed that tourism and its enticements draw scarce skilled manpower and capital resources away from manufacturing or agriculture industry with the result that the growth of industries is hampered. It also creates additional demand for land and increases competition from the potential buyers. The increase in demand for land results in the increase in its price. The high land prices which tourism contributes to and the consequent conversion of land to non-agricultural uses converts the small farmers into wage labourers. From an investor's point of view, tourism offers a low rate of return on investment compared to other industries. This leads to higher business risk and prospects of uncertain profitability.

ENVIRONMENTAL IMPACTS OF TOURISM

The environment gets disturbed as human activities encroach upon it. Changes brought about in the environment affect the ecology. Mining and mineral processing are such activities. Goa has been conscious of the impact of mining activities on the environment and the resulting disturbance to the eco-system. As a result of mining operations, the environment and eco-system has been disturbed by air and noise pollution, water pollution and deforestation. Although a smokeless industry it has environmental implications. Expanding tourism has the great capacity to pollute the environment as would any smoke-ridden industry. In recent years international tourism has been blamed for disrupting environmental balance and also disrupting cultures all over the world. Ambient conditions around an industrial township also affect tourism.

Earth is the only planet known to be endowed with an environment which supports life. Nature nurtures human beings by its valuable resources but an ungrateful human being repays by slowly destroying nature for short term material gains. Under the pretext of ambitions, development, expansion and growth, destruction of forests, senseless poisoning of the earth, air and water through chemicals, radioactive wastes and other wastes from houses, factories, hospitals and laboratories are nothing but the murder of the environment.

From the above discussion one may argue that tourism should be banned. But the solution to the adverse effects lies with the planners, developers and decision makers. Tourism is after al a peoples' industry and they alone can produce encouraging results. Holistic tourism results when tourists derive satisfaction from resources and tourist activities derive optimum benefits in terms of social, economic and ecological objectives.

Due weight to environmental aspects needs to be given in tourism development projects and restriction will have to be imposed on the number and behaviour of tourists in natural environments and other crowded historical, religious and cultural sites in the destination areas.

The planned development of tourism resources should ensure protection and restoration of degraded national resources. Excellent examples of tourism co-existing with wild life preservation are the Ranthambhor Tiger Reserve, Sawai, Madhapur, Rajasthan, the Corbett Park with a large tourist complex right in the heart of the sanctuary.

We have to accept that economic well-being is essential for achieving sustainable development and minimising the degradation of the environment is in conformity with such growth. Government and Industry must co-operate at the local, national and regional levels in using existing and, where necessary, establishing new mechanisms that promote pollution prevention, waste minimisation, cleaner production, energy efficiency and rational use of natural resources and in ensuring that these techniques and technologies are available, particularly to developing countries. This will entail the mobilisation of financial resources and enhanced technical co-operation in particular with developing countries, at the bilateral and multilateral levels. However, new and additional resources will also have to be channelled to developing countries in order to ensure their full participation in global efforts.

Economic, social and environmental elements of the decision-making process should be fully integrated and the fundamental mutual dependence between sustained economic growth and effective environmental protection must be recognised. They should not be looked upon as competitive policy objectives.

Market oriented instruments can play an increasing role, in particular by internalising environment considerations. Donors and international organisations such as UNDP will certainly consider seriously requests for assistance from countries that need to develop such instruments and to administer them.

FUTURE

The problems of the tourist industry are likely to increase with time and with the growth in the size of the industry and the next few decades may experience problems of much greater magnitude than have generally been experienced during the past. Nevertheless tourism has a bright future. Especially, youth tourism is going to be an important contributor to the tourist revenue of the developing countries.

To conclude, development of tourism will help to preserve, retain and enrich cultural expressions and heritage in all its manifestations. The socio-economic and environmental benefits that tourism brings must cause accretion and strength rather than damage social and cultural values and deplete natural resource in the developing countries.

TOURISM POLICIES, AND ENVIRONMENTAL ISSUES FOR ALL INDIA

Chapter 5

Importance of Tourism Development in India's Structural Reform

Kartik C. Roy
Department of Economics,
The University of Queensland,
Brisbane Q 4072,
Australia

Hans C. Blomqvist
Swedish School of Economics and Business Administration,
Helsinki,
Finland

Introduction

A stabilisation programme backed by the International Monetary Fund (IMF) is usually a forerunner to a structural reform programme. In any macroeconomic crisis instigated by an unsustainable growth in aggregate demand, the stabilisation policy is implemented first to bring the demand side of the economy under control with a view to reducing inflation and achieving a significant improvement in the balance of payment position. Once this is achieved, the structural adjustment programme supported by the World Bank takes effect with the primary objective of improving the supply side situation of the economy for the resumption of sustainable growth by removing market imperfections (Aghelvi, Kim and Neiss, 1987; Corbo and Fischer, 1991; Khan, 1987). Within this broad framework, the major emphasis appears to be on (1) a significant reduction in the budget deficit to contain inflation, prevent capital flight and thereby to revive business confidence and (2) improvement in the balance of payment position by removing exchange controls and import restrictions to encourage a more efficient use of resources (Erb, 1986).

However, the success of a structural adjustment programme is contingent on the ability of the economy to keep the aggregate demand in line with aggregate supply on a long term basis. This means that the stabilisation policy and structural adjustment programme form the twin components of a broader economic reform package as the distinction between the two involved no difference in practice (Mosley, Subasat and Weeks, 1995). In India's case the stabilisation policy implemented first in 1991 was accompanied subsequently by structural reform measures (Roy and Chai, 1995). However, the need for application of stabilisation policy measures on an ongoing basis has not disappeared. Since a reduction in the budget deficit also improves the current account balance of the country, the failure to achieve a significant reduction in internal deficit imposes a greater burden on the export sector to produce a surplus on the external account so as to improve the aggregate supply situation. This is what has happened in the wake of India's macroeconomic crisis which confronted the economy in 1991. In this paper, we comment on the origin of the macroeconomic crisis, illustrate the performance of the invisible trade sector and examine the importance of tourism in improving India's current account balance and thereby facilitating growth under structural reform.

MACROECONOMIC CRISIS: BUDGET DEFICIT, EXTERNAL BORROWING AND EXTERNAL DEFICIT

The macroeconomic crisis which originated in the Indian economy in 1991 was caused by two factors:

(1) On the one hand, the fiscal crisis was caused by the unsustainability of the vast system of politically determined entitlements to income streams and;
(2) on the other hand, the taxation system failed to raise sufficient revenue to match the rising government expenditure.

The tax revenue did not increase sufficiently because of repressive macroeconomic policies and tax evasion. Hence, domestic and foreign borrowing were the major source of funding such public expenditure (Lal, 1995). India did use these sources. The implications of such borrowing for India are that since more than 95 per cent of total external debt is held by the public sector, a substantial proportion of foreign loans is spent on imported goods and services thereby making the current account balance unfavourable.

The public sector borrowing in the domestic market creates a Acrowding out " effect which increases the interest rate and thereby the private sector investment. Theoretically, if the government spends the domestic and foreign funds on productive investment, then the adverse crowding out effect is neutralised. However, since a substantial part of the total borrowed fund has not gone into productive investment, growth has been stunted and increased borrowing has shifted a burden to the future generation. In such a situation, measures to reduce a deficit and achieve a surplus in the current account balance assume crucial importance for the success of India's structural reform. It is in this context that we examine the importance of an invisible trade sector in general and of the tourism industry in particular.

INDIA'S EXTERNAL DEBT, CURRENT ACCOUNT DEFICIT AND INVISIBLE TRADE SECTOR

India's external debt scenario in the 1990's is illustrated in Table 5.1.

Table 5.1
External Debt and Debt Servicing: Key Indicators for India

	1989-90	1990-91	1991-92	1992-93	1993-94
Outstanding Debt Stock					
(US $ billion)	75.9	84.0	85.3	90.0	90.7
Debt Service Payments					
(US $ billion)	7.6	8.2	8.1	8.1	8.3
Total Debt as					
% of GDP	28.5	30.5	41.1	39.9	36.1
% of Exports	447.7	454.4	467.2	476.9	399.7
Total Debt Service as					
% of Exports	44.8	44.5	44.5	42.9	36.6

Source: Government of India (1995), *Economic Survey 1994-95*, New Delhi: Government of India.

As Table 5.1 shows, India's external debt stock increased substantially during the first half of the 1990s reaching nearly U.S. $91 billion in 1993-94. Total debt as a proportion of GDP and of exports, although declining in 1993-94, remained quite high throughout the period.

But the most important indicator of debt burden is the ratio of debt service to exports. The table shows that this debt service accounted for a very substantial proportion of total exports. From a high of nearly 45 per cent in 1989-90, the ratio gradually declined, nevertheless it took away nearly 37 per cent of India's export income in 1993-94. The result is that it enlarges the current account deficit.

Table 5.2 illustrates the state of India's current account balance during the 1980s and 1990s. India's current account has consistently recorded a deficit, which rose from Rs16.5 billion in 1980-81 to Rs127.6 billion in 1992-93, representing an increase of 673.3 per cent. The reason for this development appears to be the deregulation of foreign trade combined with a largely unadjusted domestic economy. However, the size of the deficit would have been considerably higher had it not been for the surplus recorded on the invisible account. A substantial reduction in the size of this surplus was primarily due to the large outflow of funds on account of debt service payment.

Within the invisible trade sector, foreign travel and private remittances contributed the largest amount of surpluses to India's current account as Table 5.3 illustrates.

Table 5.3 shows that receipts and net surplus from foreign travel have been rising. Receipts and net surplus from private remittances increased up to 1991-92 but declined in 1992-93.

Table 5.2
India's Current Account Balance (Rs Billion)

	1980-81	1985-86	1989-90	1992-92	1992-93
Merchandise					
1. Imports (C.IF.)	125.4	211.6	406.4	514.2	688.6
2. Exports (F.O.B.)	65.8	115.8	282.3	449.2	547.6
3. Trade Balance	-59.6	-95.8	-124.1	-65.0	-141.0
Invisibles					
4. Receipts	58.9	78.8	124.8	234.5	238.6
5. Payments	15.8	42.5	114.6	191.9	225.2
6. Invisibles balance	+43.1	+36.6	+10.2	+42.6	+13.4
7. Current Account (3-6)	-16.5	-59.5	-113.9	-22.4	-127.6

Source: Same as for Table 5.1.

While the increase in remittances was quite substantial between 1989-90 and 1991-92, the decline in 1992-93, which was also quite considerable, was to a great extent due to the dislocation of work in the Middle East due to the Gulf War and the repatriation of thousands of workers back to India. In most other areas of services, there were net deficits, the largest being recorded in investment income.

An interesting point to be noted about private remittances is that payments on account of such remittances remained very small throughout the period so that the net surplus was quite large. However, the other point to be noted is that the continuous inflow of private remittance to the country depends on the social, economic and political factors in the host countries and on the growth of the international economy all of which are exogenous factors. On the other hand, the inflow of income from tourism depends considerably on the domestic social, economic and political factors over which the government and the society does have some control. Moreover, tourism may produce strong backward linkages which exert widely dispersed beneficial effects on the economy. India has a great deal to offer to the tourists of all countries and of all ages. The government has not yet made any attempt to utilise the full potential of this service industry.

Table 5.3
India's Invisible Trade Balance (Rs $Billion)

	1980-81	1985-86	1989-90	1991-92	1992-93
Foreign Travel					
Receipts	11.7	11.9	23.9	48.9	60.6
Payments	0.9	4.1	6.7	11.1	11.8
Net	10.8	7.8	17.2	37.8	48.8
Transportation					
Net	0.01	-0.2	-0.3	-0.2	-0.9
Insurance					
Net	0.01	-0.05	0.6	-0.4	0.1
Investment Income					
Net	4.8	-9.5	-48.8	-94.0	-105.0
Government not Included Elsewhere					
Net	0.4	-0.07	-1.6	-2.5	-0.9
Miscellaneous					
Net	-0.06	9.0	-0.6	5.3	-4.1
Transfer Payments					
Official, Net	4.4	3.1	9.0	11.4	10.5
Private					
Receipts	22.7	28.4	38.2	94.2	81.2
Payments	0.1	0.2	0.3	0.4	0.4
Net	22.6	28.2	37.9	93.8	80.8
Total Receipts	58.9	78.8	124.8	234.5	238.6
Total Payments	15.8	42.5	114.6	191.9	225.2
Net	43.1	36.3	10.2	42.6	13.4

Source Table: Same as for Table 5.1.

The importance of tourism in India's external trade sector is further illustrated in Table 5.4. It can be seen from Table 5.4 that despite a 730 per cent increase in earnings from merchandise exports (Col. 3), the current account deficit, except for the year 1991-92, remained very large during the period 1980-81 to 1992-93 (Col. 2). Although declining, the net invisible trade balance (Col. 7) remained in surplus during the period except for the year 1990-91. Within the invisible trade sector, income from tourism export (Col. 5) increased by about 422 per cent, to be compared with incomes from total invisible exports (Col. 4) and total private remittances (Col. 6) which grew by about 348 per cent and 281 per cent, respectively, during the same period.

Hence, tourism appears to have considerably greater potential than other sectors of the economy to improve the supply side situation of the economy and foster sustainable growth under economic adjustment.

TOURISM IN INDIA - BENEFITS, PROBLEMS AND DETERMINANTS

Tourism is one of the world's major export industries and one of the most rapidly growing ones as well. In terms of arrivals, South Asia grew by 11 per cent per year and in terms of receipts by 15 per cent a year during the period 1950C91, second only to East Asia and the Pacific where the growth rates were still higher (Forsyth and Dwyer, 1996). It should be noted that the base levels in both cases were rather low, however.

Table 5.4

Indices of Selected External Trade Indicators for India, 1980-81 = 100

Year (1)	Current Account Deficit (2)	Total Merchandise Export (3)	Total Invisible Export (4)	Total Receipt from Tourism (5)	Total Private Remittances (6)	Net Invisible Trade Balance (7)
1980-81	100.0	100.0	100.0	100.0	100.0	100.0
1981-82	127.0	118.1	99.6	91.4	97.7	88.0
1982-83	123.9	138.9	106.0	97.4	114.1	80.8
1983-84	101.8	154.6	129.3	93.1	131.0	96.3
1984-85	128.4	181.8	154.6	77.6	146.5	102.7
1985-86	267.1	175.0	147.8	102.6	133.3	96.3
1986-87	262.6	202.4	155.2	138.8	140.4	93.9
1987-88	283.3	249.2	174.1	160.3	165.7	80.0
1988-89	521.6	313.8	205.1	176.7	181.7	52.8
1989-90	513.0	429.0	234.1	205.2	179.3	27.5
1990-91	782.4	503.8	251.2	225.0	175.6	-11.7
1991-92	99.1	682.7	440.0	421.6	442.3	113.6
1992-93	574.8	832.2	447.7	522.4	381.2	35.7

Source: Government of India (1988, 1990, 1991, 1993, 1995) *Economic Survey*, New Delhi: Government of India.

The moment the foreign tourists arrive at their destination, the host country begins to enjoy the benefits. Apart from the immediate benefit of foreign exchange income, there are, as mentioned above, secondary benefits of backward linkages which increase activities in all sectors of the economy which in turn increase the consumption and investment expenditure which generate higher growth, income and employment for the economy. A particular advantage is the fact that tourism is quite labour intensive and provides employment for skilled as well as unskilled labour. This is a very important feature in a labour abundant economy like India.

Tourism is not an unproblematic industry, however. The effect on local culture is ambiguous, for instance. Although tourism is often blamed for introducing foreign habits and customs at the price of diluting local ones, it may also provide indigenous people with means to preserving their culture in changing environment (Jenner and Smith, 1992: 141). Petty criminality, prostitution and other social problems are frequent by-products of a booming tourism sector. The ultimate reason for this is the wide gap in income between the visitors and the local population, a fact that may easily incite bitterness and provide irresistible incentives for criminality. This is the case especially when attractions-such as beaches-are reserved exclusively for foreign tourists (*cf.* Lundberg, 1980: 155, 172) or when scarce resources, such as water, are diverted to the tourism industry. The effect of tourism on prices, particularly land prices, is likely to be harmful to the majority of the local population as well.

The other major problem in this context is that there is a tendency for tourism to be self-destructive, i.e. uncontrolled tourism may easily destroy the very attractions that the industry is based on. Over development and environmental degradation are the main dangers in this respect (Jenner and Smith, 1992). These problems are rampant in several leading tourist destinations in, e.g., Southern Europe. In some countries, the benefits of tourism are questionable because other industries are crowded out by a growing tourism industry. Hence, estimates of multiplier effects of tourism may be misleading. This problem is more serious when the labour market is tight, however. In an economy with an excess supply of labour this should be much less of an issue, even though competition for certain types of skilled labour may increase even there. For Sri Lanka, it has been estimated that each person employed in tourism brings about employment of 1.4 persons in other industries (Attanayake, Samaranayake and Ratnapala, 1983: 309). The figure should be similar for India.

Hence, the tourism industry is sensitive and often needs greater care than other export industries as its growth is considerably affected by unfavourable changes in domestic, economic, social, political and administrative environment as well as by deterioration of the tourist resorts themselves. The problem how to maximise the benefits is far from simple. To what extent should the government subsidise tourism through promotion campaigns, for instance? Can tourism be taxed? This may be the case if a country has some market power as to its supply of tourist services (Forsyth and Dwyer, 1996; Tisdell, 1983).

Tourism makes an enormous contribution to economic growth in, for instance, Thailand, Singapore and Hong Kong. Many Pacific island nations rely greatly on tourism for their survival. But in 1989 a temporary political disturbance in Thailand immediately contributed to a drastic reduction in export income from tourism. On the other hand, despite the rising value of the Singaporean dollar, the high cost of living and a limited number of places of tourists' attractions, Singapore's income from tourism has been increasing, mainly due to the ability of the government of Singapore to maintain a stable socio-political order, a highly efficient, administrative and law enforcement system and pro-tourism administrative regulations.

In fact both Thailand and Singapore have developed in their social environment a pro-tourism culture which has been highly conducive to the growth of this industry. Also, they have ensured adequate supply of infrastructure which includes transport, communication, hotel accommodation and package tours, proper maintenance of places of tourist attractions, and all other services which are necessary for the smooth inflow and outflow of international tourists.

India has more to offer to the international tourists of different age and interest groups than perhaps any other country in the world. Its main attraction seems to be its culture, even though the country's natural resources, encompassing all types of nature provide an excellent setting for any type of tourism (*cf.* World Tourism Organisation, 1992: 415). Hence, although tourism is already a major earner of foreign exchange for India, it is generally taken that the country's potential is far from fully utilised (World Tourism Organisation, 1992: 418). Table 5.5 shows the receipts from tourism in those East and South Asian countries for which appropriate data is available. The result shows unambiguously that India does rather poorly in comparison with other Asian countries, and, hence, that the scope for improvements should be quite considerable. According to recent data (Jenner and Smith, 1992: 8), the whole South Asia had only a 0.8 per cent market share of global tourism, as measured in number of arrivals. An increase to the present per capita level of China, which is rather modest, would more than double tourism receipts to an amount of over 3 bn. US dollars. An increase to the level of Indonesia would imply revenues from tourism of over 14 bn. dollars and an increase to the level of Thailand, to over 73 bn. dollars. The meaning of those figures becomes clear when we note that India's total deficit on the current account of the balance of payment in 1992C93 was about 4.8 bn. dollars (calculated with the aid of Table 5.2 and World Bank 1995 and converted to US dollars from Rupees).

Several prerequisites for successful tourism are not fulfilled, or are only partly fulfilled, in India. Firstly, proper infrastructure should be in place. Airports, communications, power, sewerage and hotels would have to be there. In India most facilities of this type are in short supply. Skilled management is scarce as well (Forsyth and Dwyer, 1996). Secondly, political disturbances, terrorists attacks and violence, are not uncommon in India. Many tourists are concerned about their personal safety and health as well.

Table 5.5
Receipts from Tourists Per Capita, 1992, Asian Countries

Country	Receipts per Capita, US$
Nepal	5.53
Bangladesh	0.07
India	1.60
Sri Lanka	11.44
Thailand	83.26
Malaysia	95.05
Singapore	1858.57
Indonesia	14.81
Philippines	26.03
China	3.40
Korea	74.87
Hong Kong	1040.86
Japan	28.82

Source: Compiled from World Tourism Organisation 1994 and World Bank 1994.

Another side of Indian politics in this context is that it seems to have regionalised all aspects of Indian development. Hence, all activities relating to the growth of the tourism industry have taken place in the Northern, Western and Southern parts of India. As a result, the largest concentration of international tourists has taken place in only one half of the country. Administration and maintenance of places of tourist attractions are highly inefficient and ineffective.

Since most of the tourist spots are under the jurisdictions of respective State governments, resource-strapped states, particularly in Eastern India, spend very little money on these activities. Also, since entry to most of the tourist attractions is free, it leads to their overuse and gradual deterioration, which most common property resources tend to suffer from. Even if state governments spend money to improve the administration and maintenance of tourist spots, it is unlikely that the accountability of public officials would improve. Efficient police service to quickly and effectively attend to the complaints of tourists is an essential requirement to maintain and increase the inflow of tourists to the country. Singapore has set an example in this area. In India, such a police service does not seem to exist.

Rules and regulations and the administrative apparatus governing the flow of tourist traffic into and out of India are still cumbersome and are not yet designed to reduce tourists' delays and inconveniences. Most Asian countries now allow tourists to stay in the country for between two weeks and three months without a visa. This is not the case in India. Obtaining an entry visa for India is time consuming and rather expensive, and obtaining an extension of an existing visa in India is even more difficult for a tourist who wants to stay on for a little longer. Immigration, customs clearance and checking at Indian airports are still very time consuming and often lead to harassment of tourists. Tax rates on accommodation and meals at hotels and restaurants are very high. Sales tax and entertainment tax together account for more than 40 per cent of the total cost of meals in hotels and restaurants.

The government of India did never formulate and apply an unbiased national tourism development policy which would benefit all regions of the country. In international marketing, India as a whole has never been promoted to foreign tourists. In the domestic tourist trade, the private sector has played a major role, but in the international tourist trade the private sector, so far, has played only an insignificant role. In this context it may be useful to note that intra-Asian tourism is rapidly becoming a sizeable part of total tourism. This means that promotion efforts should not be oriented only towards the traditional source regions for tourism: Western Europe, North America and Japan.

Against these negative aspects, the substantial devaluation of the Indian rupee in the wake of the implementation of the stabilisation programme has given a boost to the inflow of foreign tourists and the cost of living and the cost of all goods and services are substantially cheaper in India than in any other major tourist destination in the world.

Table 5.6 displays some forecast growth figures for the number of tourist arrivals for selected Asian countries. (Too much should not be made of long-run forecasts like this one, however, since the result may be sensitive to minor changes in the assumptions the forecast is based on.) As shown by the table, all the countries included in the table display respectable growth rates as to tourist arrivals. For the case of India, the rates are not as high as in many other countries, however. (That is the case for Singapore, too, but in that case the reason is likely to be relative stagnation at a very high level.) The corresponding world average for 1950C91 was 7.3 per cent (Forsyth and Dwyer, 1996) but it is unlikely that this rate of growth will be realised in the future, for the world as a whole. The World Tourism Organisation predicts a global growth rate of 3.6 per cent (as cited in Forsyth and Dwyer, 1996).

Table 5.6
Forecast Increase in Visitor Arrivals for Selected Asian Countries

Country	1991-96 Growth % p.a.	1996-2000 Growth % p.a.	2000-2005 Growth % p.a.	2005-2010 Growth % p.a.
Hong Kong	8.1	7.7	6.7	6.2
Singapore	7.9	6.5	5.8	5.3
Thailand	7.7	9.6	8.2	7.5
Malaysia	9.4	9.1	8.5	8.2
Australia	9.1	9.1	8.5	7.9
Indonesia	10.6	10.6	8.8	8.5
India	6.2	6.1	5.8	5.4

Source: Adapted from Forsyth and Dwyer, 1996.

It is not easy to determine, at a general level, what factors impinge on tourism to a certain country or region. This is because of the uniqueness of attractions available at each destination. Often tourists come for the very sake of these unique attractions. In addition to such highly individual features, there are some characteristics, however, that are widely believed to be related to a country's attractiveness to tourists. Such characteristics are: distance between the home country and the destination, possible cultural ties (e.g. an earlier colonial relationship), political ties, stability of government, law and order, health risks, cost competitiveness and quality of service (*cf.* Rafferty, 1993: 86; Bull, 1995: 29; Forsyth and Dwyer, 1996). Some of these factors are rather hard to operationalise, though.

Regression Analysis

In order to deepen our understanding of factors influencing receipts from tourism, we tried to construct a regression model which would elucidate the impact of different determinants on tourism receipts per capita. All East and South Asian countries, for which data were available, were included. Additionally, a random sample of other countries was included as well. Some preliminary data analyses suggested that developed countries (here defined as countries with a GNP per capita of 7,000 US dollars or more) tended to behave very differently from less developed countries proper. Hence, developed countries originally included in the sample were left out. The size of the remaining sample was then 30.

The theoretical starting point for analyses of tourism is usually standard demand theory (cf. Lin and Sung, 1983; Witt and Witt, 1992). In this case we were, in effect, interested in how tourism expenditures are distributed between countries in one particular year, 1992. Since the income level of the source countries is given in this set-up, the inflow of income from tourism can be assumed to be determined by various factors that make a certain target country more or less attractive, such as the ones listed at the end of the preceding chapter.

Disappointingly enough, although not entirely unexpectedly, it turned out to be very difficult to find significant relations in the model, even if parameter signs usually were the expected ones. One explanation for the poor results is likely to be the difficulty to operationalise relevant explanatory variables and poor data quality. In fact, the only variable with any explanatory value was the GNP per capita in the destination country. This variable was originally included to proxy availability and quality of infrastructure, such as transport, accommodation and telecommunication. It is likely, however, that the variable might partly capture, for instance, factors like personal safety and hygienic standard (it was rather stronglyCand negativelyCcorrelated with the infant mortality rate and, somewhat less strongly, with a measure of political risk). The result of a regression run with GNP per capita as the only explanatory variable is displayed in Figure 5.1.

Figure 5.1
Tourism Receipts Per Capita (Y) Explained by Host GNP Per Capita (X, GNPPC); Sample of Low Income Countries, 1992

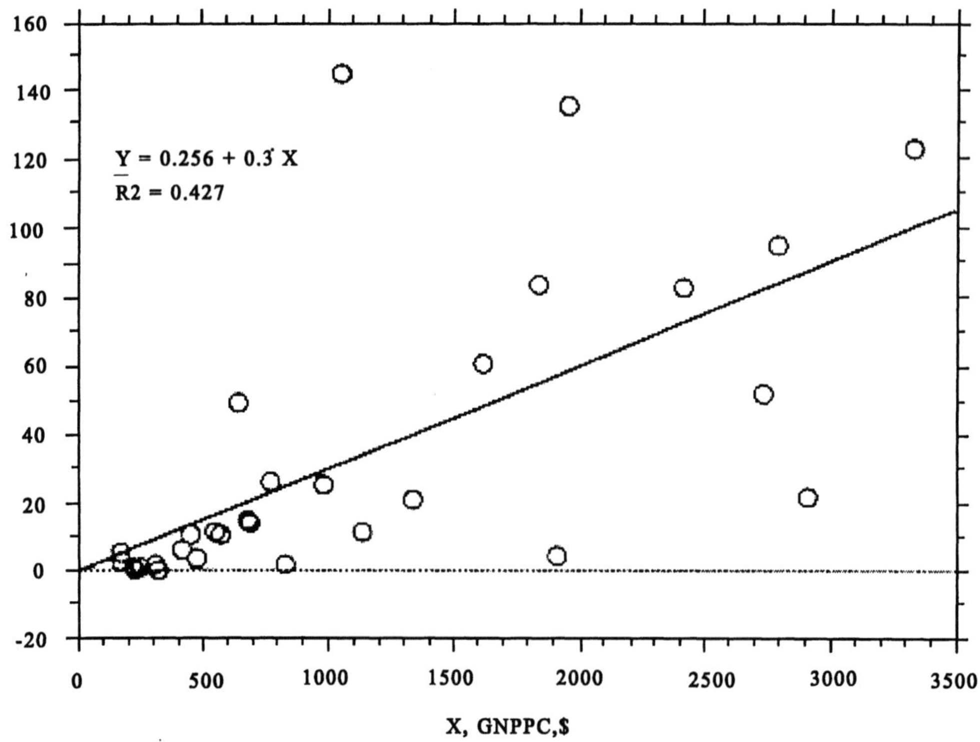

Source: The data are from World Bank, 1994 and World Tourism Organisation, 1994.

As evident from the figure (regression coefficients are presented beneath the figure itself), host GDP per capita "explains" over 40 per cent of the variation in tourism receipts, quite a good figure for a cross-sectional analysis. It is also clear, however, that many countries fit the pattern rather poorly. This is hardly surprising since, as we noted already, individual characteristics of a country are often decisive for its attractiveness as a destination for tourists.

For the case of India, an analysis of the residuals shows that a country with India's GNP per capita "should" be able to expect per capita receipts of tourism of 9.5 dollars, but the actual value of 1.6 dollars. Hence, even a six-fold increase in tourist receipts would take the country just to the "normal" level as far as tourist income is concerned. This result confirms our earlier evaluation of the Indian tourism sector as very underdeveloped.

Concluding Remarks

At the present stage of adjusting and restructuring the Indian economy to a more outward-oriented trade regime, tourism has an important role to play as a generator of foreign exchange. Even if this role is important already, it seems clear that the tourism sector in India is much smaller and weaker than it could be. The market share of the subcontinent in global tourism is low as a whole and even in that context India does not do as well as some other countries. A very modest absolute growth (although high relative growth) in tourism receipt per capita would have significant effects on the current account of India's balance of payments. According to our rough calculations a country with the income level of India can be expected to generate about six times as high tourist receipts as India does at the present time.

References

Aghelvi, B.B., Kim, I-S. and Neiss, H. (1987) "Growth and adjustment in South Asia" *Finance and Development*, 24(2).

Attanayake, A., Samaranayake, H.M.S. and Ratnapala, N. (1983) "Sri Lanka", in E.A. Pye, and T-B. Lin (eds) *Tourism in Asia: The Economic Impact*, Singapore: Singapore University Press.

Bull, A. (1995) *The Economics of Travel and Tourism*, Melbourne: Longman Australia.

Corbo, V. and Fischer, S. (eds) (1991) "Adjustment programs and bank support: Rationale and main results", *Policy Research and External Affairs Working Papers WPS 582*, Washington DC: World Bank.

Erb, R.D. (1986) "Adjustment, growth and the Fund's role", *Finance and Development*, 24(2).

Forsyth, P. and Dwyer, L. (1996) "Tourism in the Asian-Pacific Region", *Asian-Pacific Economic Literature*, 10(1).

Government of India (1988, 1990, 1991, 1993, 1995), *Economic Survey*, New Delhi: Government of India.

Jenner, P. and Smith, C. (1992) *The Tourism Industry and the Environment*, London: The Economist Intelligence Unit, Special Report No. 2453.

Khan, M.S. (1987) "Macro-economic adjustment in developing countries: A policy perspective", *World Bank Research Observer*, 2(1).

Lal, D. (1995) "India and China: Contrasts in economic liberalisation", *World Development*, 23(a).

Lin, T-B. and Sung, Y-W. (1983) "Hong Kong", in E.A. Pye and T-B. Lin (eds) *Tourism in Asia: The Economic Impact*, Singapore: Singapore University Press.

Lundberg, D. (1980) *The Tourist Business*, 4th ed., Boston: CBE Publ. Co.

Mosley, P., Subasat, T. and Weeks, J. (1995) "Assessing adjustments in Africa", *World Development*, 23(9).

Rafferty, M.D. (1993) *A Geography of World Tourism*, Englewood Cliffs, N.J.: Prentice Hall.

Roy, K.C. and Chai, J.C.H. (1994) "Economic liberalisation and the delivery of public goods to the poor", in D.T. Nguyen and K.C. Roy (eds) (1994) *Economic Reform, Liberalisation and Trade in the Asia-Pacific Region*, New Delhi: Wiley Eastern.

Tisdell, C.A. (1983) "Public finance and the appropriation of gains from international tourists: Some theory with ASEAN and Australian examples", *Singapore Economic Review*, 28(1).

Witt, S.F. and Witt, C.A. (1992) *Modeling and Forecasting Demand in Tourism*, London: Academic Press.

World Bank (1994) *World Development Report*, New York: Oxford University Press.

World Bank (1995) *World Tables*, Baltimore: Johns Hopkins University Press.

World Tourism Organisation (1992, 1994) *Yearbook of Tourism Statistics*, Madrid: World Tourism Organisation.

Chapter 6

ECONOMIC REFORMS AND THE PERFORMANCE OF INDIA'S TOURISM AND HOSPITALITY INDUSTRY

MOAZZEM HOSSAIN
School of International Business,
Griffith University,
Nathan Q 4111,
Australia

MACROECONOMIC PERFORMANCE

In the first instance, the paper presents India's growth performance along with the performance of three other nations in the region: Bangladesh, Pakistan and Sri Lanka. Overall, the countries in South Asia have achieved slow but steady economic growth since the 1960s. Table 6.1 makes this point more clear. All four countries in recent years achieved a per capita GDP growth rate of between 2 and 5 per cent. This shows that no single country has performed outstandingly which may attract attention. For Bangladesh, the decade of eighties has been a decade of almost no progress. In more recent years it has come out of the cycle of below 4 per cent rate of growth. India's overall growth performance was relatively better in the 1980s than in the 1960s and 1970s. The growth rate slipped further in recent years due to the structural adjustment programmes the economy is undergoing since the early 1990s but has recovered between 1994 and 1996. Pakistan has been consistent in achieving growth in GDP since the 1960s. The overall growth rate is hovering between 5 and 6 per cent over the last three decades. Its population growth is highest in South Asia and as a result in per capita terms the growth has been the lowest among the four countries. Sri Lanka's per capita growth rate is highest in the region. It is due mainly to its low level of population growth. The economy has suffered a great deal during the last 15 years due to ethnic violence and the continuing political crises.

Table 6.1
Overall Growth in GDP in Four South Asian Nations: 1960–1996 (%)

Country	1960–1970	1971–1980	1980–1985	1985–1988	1989–1993	1994–1996
Bangladesh	–	5.9	3.8	3.9	4.2	4.0 (2.0)
India	3.4	3.3	5.8	5.7	4.0	6.3 (5.4)
Pakistan	6.7	4.8	6.6	5.9	5.1	4.7 (1.3)
Sri Lanka	4.6	5.5	5.1	2.8	4.7	5.5 (4.3)

Note: Figures in parentheses show per capita GDP growth rate.
Source: Raghavan, S.N. (1990), ADB (1994) and ADB (1996).

India's overall rate of growth mentioned above over the last three decades was contributed by various sectors of the economy. The sectoral growth performance and dominance of any sector in economic growth tell the full story about the overall economic growth performance. These are captured in Tables 6.2 and 6.3 respectively for India. (Table 6.2 presents the information about the growth rate sector-wise, since the 1965.) The agricultural growth has been low compared to other sectors. Agriculture, however, has been the dominant sector. Industry and manufacturing growth is picking up in recent years. Manufacturing in particular, is growing very fast. This is due to India's sound historical base in manufacturing (Bhagwati and Desai, 1970). Growth rate of the service sector has been recovering from decline in previous term (1989-93). The countries in East Asia show that there is a positive correlation between overall economic growth and growth in the services sector (Chowdhury and Islam, 1993). In the case of India, it appears that this kind of correlation does not exist.

Table 6.3 presents the sectoral contribution to overall GDP formation and their dominance in India. From this table it can be seen that there is a genuine structural transformation taking place in the economy in recent years. The degree of transformation, however, varies from sector to sector. Agriculture's share to GDP is declining substantially. Industry and manufacturing sectors' contribution to GDP has been increasing continuously over the last 15 years. It is the service sector which experienced a moderate growth and its contribution to GDP has increased slightly in recent years.

From this result it can be seen that India has been experiencing similar kind of structural transformation which have been experienced by East Asian nations during their early stage of economic development in the 1960s and 1970s (Chowdhury and Islam, 1993). (There are, however, some concerns about the sustainability of this transformation.)

Table 6.2
Sectoral Growth Performance, India: 1965-96 (%)

Sector	1965-80	1980-88	1989-93	1994-96
Agriculture	2.8	0.8	2.4	2.8
Industry	4.0	7.2	3.5	9.9
Manufacturing	4.3	8.3	30.0	–
Services	4.6	6.1	5.6	6.2
GDP3.7	3.7	4.6	4.0	6.3

Source: Raghavan, S.N. (1990), ADB (1992), ADB (1994), ADB (1996).

Table 6.3
Sectoral Contribution to GDP: 1970-1995 (%)

Sector	1970	1980	1993	1995
Agriculture	44.5	38.1	30.5	27.8
Industry & Manufacturing	23.9	25.9	28.1	31.1
Services	31.6	36.0	41.4	41.2

Source: Raghavan (1990), ADB (1994), ADB (1996)

Macroeconomic Goals, Policy Instruments and Trade Offs

Soon after the independence fifty years ago, India embarked upon managing the economy through development planning at the centre. The country established an influential Planning Ministry to prepare long term development plans for the economy and to advise the government on macroeconomic management. The successive Five Year Plans introduced an 'inward-looking' import-substitution policies in both industrial and agricultural sectors. Under the import-substitution strategy the major macroeconomic goal was to make the country self-sufficient in all respects and protect the new industries from foreign competition and foreign involvement. In later years, it has been argued that the import-substitution policies have proved to be costly to the economy since the domestic production costs in many protected industries were much higher than the prices exist in the world market.

The second objective of development planning approach was to shape the economy towards mixed economy framework. The reason behind this was to transfer the command of the economy into the hands of the State, through state ownership of heavy industries and infrastructure facilities. The private sector was allowed to operate only with the small scale industries. The idea was to fulfil the goals of growth and equity. Immediately after the first oil shock of early 1970s, due to the poor economic performance, it has been realised in the planning department that the import-substitution strategy is not working. In the mean time, in late 1970s and early 1980s the World Bank and IMF have come up with a new strategy of outward-looking; export-orientation to overcome the economic problems facing by India. In other words, this strategy is commonly known as structural adjustment programme (SAP).

So far, much has been written about the SAP and its effects on the macroeconomic performance of the countries which implemented it (Mosley *et al.*, 1991, Mukhopadhayay, 1995). Over the last fifteen years the Bank and the Fund have been implementing the SAP policies in various developing countries with the financial support called adjustment policy-based lending. The major objective of the adjustment policy-based lending is to stimulate the economy through relaxation of state intervention so as to promote domestic and international competitiveness and make the economy export oriented. The Bank and the Fund have made available adjustment loans to participating countries with certain conditions. These conditionalities include a package of macroeconomic policy reform designed to correct the imbalance the economy faces.

Presently, in India the macroeconomic goals and policy instruments are oriented towards achieving the objectives of the SAP. The SAP objectives are designed under policy specific reforms. The policy reforms can be categorised into the following broad elements:

- Trade and Industry Policy Reform
- Market Reform
- Fiscal Reform
- Monetary Policy Reform
- Exchange Policy Reform
- 'Safety Nets' and Institutional Reform.

Table 6.4 provides the summary information about these policy reforms and their year of commencement in India. A brief summary of the SAP in India is provided below taking policy specific analysis.

Table 6.4
Elements of the SAP in India, 1986-94

Policy Areas	Year of Commencement of Reforms in India
I Trade Policy Reform	1986
II Market Reform	1991
III Fiscal Reform	1991
IV Monetary Policy Reform	1991
V Exchange Policy Reform	1991
VI 'Safety Nets' and Institutional Reform	–

Source: Gulati (1994) and Ahluwalia (1994).

TRADE POLICY REFORM

Trade policy reform mainly covers the reform measures in the areas of import liberalisation and export enhancement. The reform process over time involved the gradual extension of categories of imports taken out of qualitative restrictions and rationalisation and reduction on tariff barriers. Export enhancement requires the provision of currency convertibility for foreign exchange transactions (Lakshman, 1994).

A beginning was made towards liberalisation of India's trade policy regime during 1986 by emphasising two major points: on the export front there was a need to evolve an efficient system which would make exports less costly and more profitable; and on the import front, there was a need to move away from a discretionary system of quantitative import controls to a system based on tariffs (Gulati, 1994). Incentives for exports were strengthened, while cash subsidy to exports was eliminated. Custom duty reductions was begun in 1991–92 and carried forward in the subsequent budgets. In particular the import duties on capital goods have been reduced substantially. Duty on projects and general machinery has been lowered in several steps to 35 per cent and on energy it is lowered to 25 per cent (Ahluwalia, 1994).

MARKET REFORM

Market reforms covered the elimination of most price controls that operated in the domestic market and making provisions for greater autonomy to public corporations to adopt more realistic market oriented pricing policies for their products. India has introduced market reform particularly in agricultural sector. Input subsidy has been eliminated and proper relation between input and output prices has been established. Market reform in the areas such as capital and stock markets, direct foreign investment have been also introduced.

FISCAL REFORM

Fiscal reform includes the reform to achieve greater fiscal discipline. In India, restraint was exercised in expanding the real resources going to the social sectors such as education and health and certain reforms have been introduced to income and other forms of taxation. By 1993-94 the fiscal deficit has been brought down to 4.7 per cent of GDP from 8.4 per cent in 1990-91. The inflation was running below double digit (at 9.9 per cent) in the year 1992-93 (Ahluwalia, 1994).

MONETARY POLICY REFORM

The major distinctive measure of these types of reform was to increase interest rates to increase the rate of savings in recent times. This measure has also contributed to the demand management of the economy to reduce the fiscal deficit. In India, savings has increased from 21 per cent of GDP in 1981 to 24.3 per cent of GDP in 1992.

EXCHANGE RATE REFORM

This involves the creation of unified exchange rate system under a flexible exchange rate regime. At present, India has a unified exchange rate and the Rupee has been devalued to a large amount to facilitate exports and to maintain competitiveness in the world market. The reform in exchange rate has been substantial. Apart from the devaluation of rupee in 1991 by 20 per cent, the reforms in this area include scraping of the dual exchange rate system in 1994 and established a unified exchange rate regime for exports and imports (Ahluwalia, 1994).

'Safety Nets' and Institutional Reform

The main elements of these reforms cover the issue of social security to the underprivileged and disadvantaged in the society. India has not yet introduced any national programme in this regard. But numerous non-government Organisations (NGOs) are working on this problem to improve the plight of thousands and millions of disadvantaged Indians.

In summary, India has commenced implementing the SAP strategy and is committed to do so effectively in full over the next five years. The Union and State governments' commitment towards implementing such a strategy has been enhanced further by way of rewarding facilities and funds by the World Bank and IMF under the adjustment policy-based lending as discussed earlier.

The Tourism Industry

It has been argued that with the economic reform process currently in place, Indian economy will experience a sustainable growth in the future in all sectors including tourism. India's tourism industry has been making strong progress since the start of the reform process in 1991. Table 6.5 presents some basic information about the achievements of tourism industry over 1991-94. India's share of world tourist receipts has increased significantly during this period. The foreign exchange earning has crossed more than $2 billion and the sector has directly employed almost 8 million people in 1994. However, the overall contribution of tourism sector to GDP formation has still remained less than 1% of total GDP.

Table 6.5
India's Share of World Tourists

Item	1991	1994
India's share of world tourists (%)	.37	.36
Share of world tourist receipts (%)	.49	.70
Foreign exchange earnings (% of GDP)	.62	–
Amount of foreign exchange ($ million)	–	2,348.00
Direct employment (million person)	–	7.8

Source: GOI (1994).

The foreign tourist arrivals in India have been growing every year since 1991. However, Table 6.6 shows that the arrivals from Pakistan have dropped substantially. This was more for a political reason than economic. The arrivals from rest of the world have been growing by more than 8 per cent per year.

Table 6.6
Foreign Tourist Arrivals

Source	1991	1993	1994
Bangladesh	251,260	277,565(10.5)	282,271(1.7)
Pakistan	190,128	44,622(-326)	42,146(-5.5)
Other Countries	236,120	1,442,643(16.7)	1,562,016(8.3)
Total	1,677,508	1,764,830(5.2)	1,886,433(6.9)

Note: Percentage change in parentheses.
Source: GOI (1994), (1991).

Tourist arrivals from G7 countries have been growing steadily in post reform period (Table 6.7). The growth has been substantial particularly in the case of US (50%), Canada (56%), UK (42%) and Japan (36%). The tourist arrivals from G7 nations comprise more than 50 per cent of the total arrival. It is expected that with the reform process fully in place, the tourism sector will attract further interest from tourists from these countries.

Table 6.7
Tourist Arrivals from G7 Nations (1991-94)

Country	1991	1994	% Change	% of Total 1994
U.K.	212,052	300,626	42	19
USA	117,322	176,482	50	11
Germany	72,019	85,352	19	5
France	69,346	73,088	5	4.7
Japan	46,655	63,398	36	4
Italy	41,129	43,510	6	3
Canada	36,142	56,441	56	3.6

Source: GOI (1994).

PERFORMANCE OF TOURISM INDUSTRY

Tourism Industry's performance has been captured in Tables 6.8, 6.9 and 6.10. The major indicators of performance analysis include: income generation, government expenditure and investment growth.

INCOME GENERATION

Table 6.8 presents the income generated by the sector over the last ten years. In pre-reform periods, the foreign exchange earning was stabilised at $1.5 billion. However, it has increased to more than $2 billion in the post-reform period. The percentage increase of income was very high between 1990/91 and 1991/92. This was more than 87 per cent in Rupee terms and was due mainly to the devaluation of rupee in these years. However, a true picture can be found from column 3 of Table 6.8 which shows the changes in earnings in terms of US$. The figures show that, immediately after the reform process in 1990/91, the tourism sector's earnings has increased by 21 per cent. There was a decline in the following year, however, this has started to increase again (by 13 per cent) in 1993/94.

Table 6.8
Earnings from Tourism, 1985/86 to 1994/95

Year	Earnings ($ml)	% Change	Earnings (Rs.Cr.)	% Change
1985/86	1,189	-		
1986/87	1,607	35	-	
1987/88	1,418	-12	1,856	15.5
1988/89	1,503	6	2,054	10.7
1989/90	1,513	0.7	2,386	16.2
1990/91	1,757	16	2,613	9.5
1991/92	2,120	21	4,892	87.3
1992/93	2,001	-6	6,060	23.9
1993/94	2,265	13	6,509	7.4
1994/95	–	-	7,365	13.2

Source: GOI (1994), (1995).

GOVERNMENT EXPENDITURE

Table 6.9 suggests that the government allocation to tourism has been growing steadily over the last five years. The major growth areas of spending have been manpower and institutional development, marketing and publicity and the India Tourism Development Corporation (ITDC). The increase in resources for manpower and institutional development was more than doubled between 1992/93 and 1995/96. Expenditure for marketing and publicity has increased by more than 35 per cent and the expenditure on ITDC projects has almost doubled over the same period. The total budget allocation to the sector has increased by almost 40 per cent between 1992/93 and 1995/96. The projection for this sector suggests that this will grow strongly in the future.

Table 6.9

Government Allocation in Major Tourism Programmes (in Rs. Cr.)

Program	1992/93	1993/94	1994/95	1995/96
1. Manpower & Ins. Dev.	4.92	7.08	7.5	10.18
2. Marketing & Publicity	44.74	48.00	60.50	60.50
3. Dev. of Tourism in Rur.	3.14	2.10	2.5	2.44
4. Dev. of Tourism Infras.	15.21	14.80	13.56	14.90
5. ITDC	5.84	7.28	10.70	10.00
6. Total Allocation	79.49	85.52	103.51	110.70

Source: GOI (1994)

INVESTMENT GROWTH

The substantial amount of tourism investment funds has been invested in building three ranges of hotel accommodations: 5-star, 4-star and 3-star (Table 6.10). Over the last five years, investment in 5-star hotels has increased by 15 fold, in the case of 4-star hotels this was 17 fold and the 3-star hotels has increased by 9 fold. Outside hotel accommodation, the major increase has been witnessed in the area of car rentals (10 fold). This suggests that the growth has been in the area of establishing medium range hotel accommodation facilities. The regional areas of India have attracted such investment in recent years.

Table 6.10
Tourism Investment Funds for Major Development Projects (in Rs. Cr.)

Industry	1989/90	1994/95	Change
5–Star Hotels	3.30(30)	49.55(36)	15 fold
4–Star Hotels	.70(4)	12.29 (9)	17 fold
3–Star Hotels	5.80(45)	50.59 (37)	9 fold
Car Rentals	.90(7)	9.00 (6)	10 fold
Amusement Parks	1.80(14)	1.98 (1)	no change

Note: Figures in parentheses are per cent of total investment.
Source: GOI (1994).

Overall, due to the economic reform process the Indian economy has been opened up to the outside world particularly in terms of foreign investment in aviation and telecommunications industries. The liberalisation and privatisation of aviation industry have contributed directly to the growth of tourist arrivals from G7 nations, particularly, from North America, Europe and Japan. The growth in tourist arrivals and growth in earnings from tourism made the Indian governments to invest further for the expansion of the industry. It becomes an added burden to the governments when the resources are becoming limited to the hands of the government. To address this problem the government must make further initiatives to attract investment from overseas. The final section makes a few recommendations in this regard.

POLICY RECOMMENDATIONS

India's tourism industry has a long tradition and history. Most of the tourist attractions are historical places and mountain resorts. The country has major potentials to improve the current status in tourism provided new initiatives and innovative projects are created. The economic reform process mentioned in the beginning of the paper is mainly industry and agriculture oriented. Foreign interest in tourism in India for investment purposes has not been overwhelming as against the public utilities and aviation industry. It is necessary to generate foreign investment in tourism sector rather than leaving the recently growing investment burden to the hands of the governments. To generate foreign interests in India's tourism the following measures need to be taken immediately:

1. To make the industry competitive, more and more private operations should be allowed with a regulator overseeing the operation to ensure quality.
2. Promotion of India's tourism industry in more developed regions of East Asia (Japan, South Korea, and ASEAN) should be targeted.
3. Development of tourism infrastructure should be a priority agenda by the government.
4. Tourism services should be upgraded through training and development of the field level staff.
5. An investment plan, particularly, for attracting foreign investment with further incentives should be initiated.
6. Regional cooperation between tourism authorities must be enhanced by conducting seminars, meetings and workshops on new products.
7. Research and development activities on tourism should also be strengthened.

REFERENCES

Asian Development Bank (ADB) (1996) *Asian Development Outlook 1996*, Oxford: Oxford University Press.

ADB (1995) *Key Indicators of Developing Asian and Pacific Countries,* Vol. XXVI, Manila: Economic and Development Resource Centre, Asian Development Bank.

ADB (1994) *Asian Development Outlook 1994*, Oxford: Oxford University Press.

ADB (1992) *Asian Development Outlook 1992*, Oxford: Oxford University Press.

Ahluwalia I.J. (1994) "New economic policies: Reform of public sector enterprises and privatisation in India", presented to the ASARC conference on Liberalisation and Privatisation, Australian National University, Canberra, November.

Bhagwati, J.N. and Desai, P. (1970) *Indian Planning for Industrialisation: Industrialisation and Trade Policies Since 1951*, London: Oxford University Press.

Chowdhury, A. and Islam, I. (1993) *The Newly Industrialising Economies of East Asia*, London: Routledge.

Government of India (GOI) (1996) *Annual Report*, New Delhi: Department of Tourism.

GOI (1994) *Tourist Statistics*, New Delhi: Department of Tourism.

Gulati, A. (1994) "India poised for take-off: Reforms in trade, industry and agriculture: stock-taking and future challenges", presented to the ASARC conference on Liberalisation and Privatisation, Australian National University, Canberra, November.

Lakshman, W.D. (1994) "Structural adjustment policies in Sri Lanka: Imbalances, structural disarticulation and sustainability", presented to the ASARC conference on Liberalisation and Privatisation, Australian National University, Canberra, November.

Mosely, P., Harrigan, J. and Toye, J. (1991) *Aid and Power: The World Bank and Policy Based Lending*, London: Routledge.

Mukhopadhyay H. (1995) "Structural adjustment programs: Some new findings", Discussion Paper, Boston: Institute for Economic Development, Boston University.

Raghavan, S.N (1990) *Macroeconomic Performance and Policy Framework in the SAARC Countries: A Review*, New Delhi: Interest Publications.

Chapter 7

TOURISM PROMOTION AND DEVELOPMENT IN QUEENSLAND 1980–1996: RELEVANCE FOR INDIAN STATES

LIAM RYAN AND ANITA MEDHEKAR-SMITH
Central Queensland University,
Bruce Highway,
North Rockhampton Q 4702,
Australia

INTRODUCTION

By the commencement of the 1990s, international tourism had become the world's largest industry generating US$ 2.7 trillion in 1990 (Waters, 1991). The industrialised countries dominated the top rankings in the tourism earner list in 1991, but the High Performing Asian Economics (HPAEs) were resolutely making their presence felt with Hong Kong in tenth position, Singapore, eleventh, Thailand, fifteenth, South Korea, eighteenth, and Japan, nineteenth. Australia occupied thirteenth position with tourism earnings of US $4.2 billion in 1991. (See Table 7.1.) Needless to say, India, having a relatively underdeveloped tourism industry, did not make this top-twenty list.

The average annual growth rate of 1.7 % in tourism in India between 1983 and 1993 was the lowest of any of the five South Asian countries covered in Table 7.2 and ten percentage points below the world's average annual growth rate.

Between 1970 and 1973, India obtained a disproportionately high share of the small South Asian trade – 53% of total tourist arrivals and 68% of receipts. The average expenditure per international tourist in India in 1993 was $US 757, somewhat above the region's average of $US 591 and the world average of $US 648, (Vellas and Becherel, 1995: 13–16, 49–54).

Table 7.1
World's Top Tourism Earners in 1991 (millions U.S. dollars)

Rank	Country	Income
1.	USA	45,551
2.	France	21,300
3.	Italy	19,668
4.	Spain	13,956
5.	Austria	13,956
6.	UK	12,588
7.	Germany	10,947
8.	Switzerland	7,064
9.	Canada	5,537
10.	Hong Kong	5,078
11.	Singapore	5,020
12.	Mexico	4,355
13.	Australia	4,183
14.	Netherlands	4,047
15.	Thailand	3,923
16.	Portugal	3,700
17.	Belgium	3,468
18.	South Korea	3,446
19.	Japan	3,435
20.	China	2,845

Source: *World Travel and Tourism Review*, 3: 6, 1993, CAB International.

Table 7.2
Average Annual Tourism Growth Rates, 1983–93

Country/Region	Arrivals (%)	Receipts (%)
World	5.5	11.7
South Asia	3.3	2.0
India	3.1	1.7
Sri Lanka	2.9	5.2
Pakistan	–0.03	–5.1
The Maldives	12.5	14.1
Nepal	4.7	12.6

Source: Vellas and Becherel (1995), p. 49, Table 2.9.

Table 7.3
International Tourist Arrivals and Receipts in South Asia, 1970-93

Year	Arrival s (000)	Change %	Share of Total World Arrivals	Receipts US$ million	Change %	Share of Total World Receipts %
1970	912	–	0.55	100	–	0.56
1975	1557	70.72	0.70	329	229.00	0.81
1980	2280	48.44	0.79	1549	370.62	1.50
1985	2540	11.40	0.77	1400	-9.62	1.21
1986	2731	7.52	0.80	1677	19.07	1.19
1987	2707	–0.88	0.74	1875	12.48	1.09
1987	2707	–0.88	0.74	1875	12.48	1.09
1988	2881	6.43	0.72	1929	2.88	0.97
1989	3054	6.00	0.71	2022	4.82	0.95
1990	3179	4.09	0.69	1990	–1.58	0.77
1991	3279	3.15	0.72	1968	–1.11	0.76
1992	3509	7.01	0.73	2076	5.49	0.70
1993	3459	–1.42	0.69	2015	–2.94	0.62

Source: Vellas and Becherel, p. 50, Table 2.10.

Table 7.3 shows that South Asia did not share in the spectacular growth of international tourism between 1970 and 1993.

TOURISM GROWTH IN AUSTRALIA

In 1996, Australia's tourism industry generated approximately US $12 billion, employed half a million people and had acquired the status of top export earner. The spectacular growth performance of an industry that had been comparatively neglected until the early 1980s was largely due to a concerted approach to tourism industry planning, promotion and development in which federal, state and local governments participated. It did not happen automatically.

In Australia, from 1983 onwards, the tourism industry was earmarked as the growth industry of the remainder of the second millennium and beyond the year 2000.

Hall (1989: 3) notes that by 1985, the contribution of the tourism industry to Australia's economy was equivalent to that of the textile, footwear, clothing and motor vehicle industries combined. This was indeed fortuitous for Australia as these manufacturing industries had been nurtured behind a high protective barrier and would find it difficult if not impossible to survive in a competitive free trade environment.

In the single year from 1992 to 1993, overseas tourist arrivals grew by 15 per cent with the majority originating in Asian countries – principally Japan (*Cornell Hotel and Restaurant Quarterly* – August 1994: 10). With 3 million overseas visitor arrivals in 1993, Australia accounted for only one per cent of the world-wide tourism market and had tremendous expansion potential being located on the fringe of the fastest growing economic region in the world. This remarkable growth of Australia's tourism industry was accompanied by increased tourism research activity, and many regions across Australia experiencing a sustained decline in the demand for traditional primary commodity exports, viewed the expanding tourism industry as their saviour and adopted tourism-led growth strategies.

The State of Queensland, located in Northeast Australia, adopted a proactive approach towards increasing its market share of inbound (international) tourists as well as attracting a larger share of Australia's domestic (interstate) tourism market. This paper provides an overview of the strategy adopted and the results achieved. The Australian experience, and the Queensland experience in particular, provide useful policy pointers that can assist in enhancing Indian tourism industry performance. The State of Orissa, in particular, which has a lot in common with Queensland, could benefit from the successful Queensland tourism experience.

Queensland – The Sunshine State

Queensland became a state of the Commonwealth of Australia in 1901 and Brisbane, the State's capital, was proclaimed a city in 1902. Queensland is the second largest of the six Australian States with an area of 1,727,000 sq.km, and importantly from a tourism perspective, 7,400km of mainland coastline plus an additional 1,400km offshore island coastline. The Great Barrier Reef, a massive tourism attraction, flanks the coast for 1,200km.

In June 1995, Queensland had a population of 3.27 million of which approximately 80% lived in urban areas and 75% in the south-east portion of the state. This contrasts sharply with Orissa State with an area of 155,707 sq.km, that is one eleventh the size of Queensland, and a population of 31.98 million – nearly 10 times that of Queensland.

Queensland's climate is typical sub-tropical to tropical with wide variations from the temperate south to the tropical north and from the dry hot interior to the moist coastal plains. Climate is a dominant factor in attracting both overseas tourists and domestic tourists from the colder southern states. In the hot, humid Summer months, (December, January and February) sea breezes temper the hot conditions on the coast. Winters in Queensland (June, July and August) tend to be dry and sunny and temperatures mild. Overseas visitors find the climate pleasant and healthy and conducive to pursuing a wide range of outdoor activities. In October, a typical low rainfall month, the south-west of the state experiences 11 hours sunshine and the remainder of the state between 8 and 10 hours (Queensland Yearbook – 1997: 18). It is not surprising, therefore, that Queensland is promoted as 'The Sunshine State'. Queensland's tourism industry success can be attributed to the adoption of a strategic approach in developing and promoting the industry with the private sector encouraged to take a pro-active role and the state and federal governments taking on supportive and facilitation roles.

The strategy was developed through broad-based consultation with key tourism industry stakeholders after considerable research on international tourism trends and segmented market research on the needs and expectations of tourists. Only the key elements of the strategy are documented here.

Key Elements of Queensland's Tourism Development Strategy

- It was agreed from the outset that it should be private sector driven.
- In identifying the tourism product/products, accessibility was considered to be a major consideration.
- On the basis of existing tourism destination popularity, two or three destinations were singled out for international promotion. Brisbane – Gold Coast – Sunshine Coast on the South-East coast, the Whitsundays on the central coast and the Cairns region on the north coast were chosen as the three key tourism regions.
- The Gold Coast, Australia's premier tourist venue, is approximately, an hour's drive by freeway from Brisbane, has a domestic airport and is serviced by Brisbane International Airport. It is an all-year-round tourism venue with top class hotel and restaurant facilities, a wide variety of attractions, is internationally famous for its numerous surfing beaches and caters for a large convention trade.
- Cairns/Tablelands, in the far north, combines coral reef and rainforest attractions and experiences some seasonality with lowest patronage during the wet (cyclone) season. It has an international airport with gateway status. The Mackay/Whitsundays region is serviced by a domestic airport on the mainland at Proserpine and Mackay and a domestic airport on the prestigious Hamilton Island. The region is a popular yachting area and abounds in easily accessible coral islands and cays. All three regions are serviced by rail and all-weather highways.
- The unique features of these destinations were highlighted in promotion material. Promotions targeted international travel agent conferences.
- It was agreed that the accommodation mix should range from the exclusive five star hotel/resort facility (beyond the affordability of the 'budget packaged holiday traveller') through the two and three star family style resort/hotel facility to on-site caravan, cabin and backpacker hostel facilities and serviced camping facilities in National Parks and on Barrier Reef Islands.
- The natural and unique attractions at the short-listed prime destinations had to be complemented by developing a depth and variety in terms of leisure/entertainment facilities.

- The prime target market, because of its high and rising living standards, its comparative proximity, and its long-established strong trading links with Australia, should be Japan.
- Research of the potential Japanese tourist market aimed to isolate the main market segments towards which promotions should be aimed, such as,
  - Corporate golfing enthusiasts
  - The honeymoon segment
  - The retired segment
  - Corporate single females
  - Diving and snorkelling enthusiasts.
- Queensland's affable climate should be stressed in attracting Northern Hemisphere winter visitors.
- Travel times between destinations and between attractions at particular destinations should be minimised by using modern air-conditioned coaches and catamarans.
- Tourism facility operators were urged to achieve high all-year-round capacity utilisation which would require off-season discounting to the domestic and package tour markets.
- The Federal Government's primary role was to act as a facilitator in accessing overseas markets and attracting venture capital for tourism facility development; in addition it promised to provide tourism monitoring and strategic information services.
- The State Government agreed to co-operate with federal and local governments in promoting hallmark events (also known as major or special events). Two such events were the Commonwealth Games (1982) and an International Trade Exhibition in 1988 (Expo'88) both held in Brisbane.
- All tourism developments had to satisfy federal and state government environmental protection regulations.
- In collaboration with the Federal Government, the State Government agreed to share key infrastructure development funding on a 50/50 basis.
- Tourism industry training was formalised and allocated additional funding. The objective was to ensure that tourism services would be world class.
- Up to the late 1980s the Australian Government owned one international and one domestic airline carrier, Qantas and Trans-Australian Airlines. These two airlines along with the privately owned second domestic carrier under the two-airline agreement, Ansett, would be expected to cooperate in schedule synchronisation and package discounting. Both airlines owned and operated several luxury island resorts.
- The State Government agreed to complement the Australian Bureau of Statistics (ABS) data in monitoring tourism industry performance and set up the Queensland Tourist and Travel Corporation (QTTC) in 1979 to ensure that strategic market

information was regularly distributed to industry operators. Performance monitoring was the key function of this body.

- By promoting a few prime destinations, there would be 'trickle down' and 'spread' effects that would benefit other regions.
- The dominant slogan was to be 'Queensland–Sunshine State'. Operators across the state were encouraged to develop their own strategies to increase their market shares of inbound and domestic tourists.

TOURISM INDUSTRY PERFORMANCE IN QUEENSLAND

Queensland is Australia's prime holiday State and tourism is the State's number one growth industry. In recognition of the tremendous potential of tourism growth and development in Queensland, in 1979 the State Government established the Queensland Tourist and Travel Corporation and charged it with the responsibility of fostering the State's tourism industry. Since that time there has been a substantial growth in tourism activity and substantial expansion and upgrading of tourism infrastructure. In fact, Queensland's tourism industry has been growing at more than double the rate recorded by the rest of Australia which is clear evidence of the ever-increasing popularity of Queensland as a holiday destination for both domestic and international visitors.

Table 7.4 shows the remarkably successful performance of the Queensland tourism industry. In just fourteen years, tourist spending quadrupled having grown at an annual average rate of 11%. In 1988 – Expo year – tourism spending contributed 11.7% of Gross State product (GSP) and in 995 it contributed 10%.

The five-year period from 1984 to 1989 was one of solid performance with Queensland's share of the Australian tourism market rising from 19.7% to 23.3% in terms of visits and from 22.9% to 28.8% in terms of visitor nights. (See Table 7.5.)

The five-year period from 1984 to 1989 was one of sanguine growth performance. Table 7.5 documents Queensland's growing market share of domestic tourism in terms of number of visitors, trips and visitor nights in commercial accommodation.

The domestic market, however, is the backbone of Queensland's tourism industry. Table 7.6 shows that there was an increase of 34 per cent from 46 million visitor nights in 1984/85 to almost 62 million visitor nights in 1988/89 – an average growth rate of 7.6 per cent per annum. Over the same period, nights spent by visitors throughout the rest of Australia decreased by almost 2 per cent (from 155 million to 152 million). Queensland's share of international tourists increased by 156 per cent from 6.2 million nights in 1985 to 15.8 million in 1988, or 36.8 per cent per annum, while nights spent in the rest of Australia increased by over 78 per cent (from 23.3 million to 41.6 million) or 21.3 per cent per annum.

Table 7.4
Expenditure by Overnight Travellers in Queensland

Year	Traveller expenditure	Gross State Product	Ratio of GSP
	$m	$m	%
1982	1,960	24,460	8.0
1983	2,123	26,483	8.0
1984	2,194	30,323	7.2
1985	2,372	33,114	7.2
1986	3,177	36,021	8.8
1987	3,719	39,897	9.3
1988	5,381	45,860	11.7
1989	4,591	53,101	8.6
1990	5,045	56,421	8.9
1991	5,656	57,758	9.8
1992	5,623	62,275	9.0
1993	6,236	66,697	9.3
1994	7,005	72,977	9.6
1995	7,671	76,890	10.0
	%	%	
Average Annual Growth	11.1	9.2	

Source: Australian Bureau of Statistics, *Queensland Year Book* 1997, p. 150.

Table 7.5
Queensland's Marketshare of Domestic Tourism, 1984/1985 – 1988/1989

Year	Visits (000)	% of Aust	Trips(000)	% of Aust	Nights (000)	% of Aust
1984/1985	10,643	19.7	8,859	19.5	46,104	22.9
1985/1986	10,596	19.6	8,711	19.3	48,321	23.1
1986/1987	11,420	21.4	9,528	21.2	53,369	25.3
1987/1988	11,504	20.7	9,485	20.3	55,671	25.7
1988/1989	12,749	23.3	10,669	23.2	61,722	28.8

Source: Queensland Tourist and Travel Corporation, *Domestic Tourism Monitor,* August 1990.

Table 7.6
Domestic Visits, Trips and Nights in Queensland, 1984/1985 – 1988/1989

Year	Visits	Trips	Nights	Av. nights per visit	Av. nights per trip
1984/1985	10,643,000	8,859,000	46,104,000	4.3	5.2
1985/1986	10,596,000	8,711,000	48,321,000	4.6	5.5
1986/1987	11,420,000	9,528,000	53,369,000	4.7	5.6
1987/1988	11,504,000	9,485,000	55,671,000	4.8	5.9
1988/1989	12,749,000	10,669,000	61,722,000	4.8	5.8
Av. Annual % growth 85–89	4.6%	4.8%	7.6%		

Source: Queensland Tourism and Travel Corporation, *Domestic Tourism Monitor*, August 1990.

Table 7.7 shows that in 1995–96 in terms of total overseas visitors, Queensland was second only to New South Wales with Japanese making up 33% of all overseas visitors. The dominant trip purpose was holidaying accounting for 76% of the total – the highest for any state; neighbouring New Zealand provided 11% of all overseas visitors and Korea, a market that has recently been cultivated, 7%.

Table 7.7

Distribution of Overseas Visitors between Australian States, 1995-96

Country of Residence	New South Wales		Victoria		Queensland		South Australia	
	('000)	%	('000)	%	('000)	%	('000)	%
New Zealand	286.7	13.0	111.1	12.0	199.0	11.0	31.3	11.0
Japan	538.2	24.0	111.9	12.0	596.2	33.0	27.5	10.0
Hong Kong	89.8	4.0	44.5	5.0	60.2	3.0	8.9	3.0
Singapore	57.2	3.0	36.2	4.0	77.7	4.0	4.9	2.0
Malaysia	43.8	2.0	34.7	4.0	31.1	2.0	5.3	2.0
Indonesia	51.5	2.0	30.5	3.0	25.2	1.0	5.5	2.0
Taiwan	106.7	5.0	59.7	7.0	100.6	6.0	0.6	*
Thailand	40.1	2.0	24.0	3.0	17.2	1.0	1.6	1.0
Korea	137.8	6.0	14.1	2.0	124.0	7.0	4.0	1.0
China	29.6	1.0	15.4	2.0	17.1	1.0	0.2	*
Other Asia	39.1	2.0	27.8	3.0	15.7	1.0	2.7	1.0
USA	208.2	9.0	102.2	11.0	131.4	7.0	34.1	12.0
Canada	41.6	2.0	18.6	2.0	25.6	1.0	9.7	3.0
United Kingdom	208.8	9.0	92.3	10.0	130.8	7.0	47.1	17.0
Germany	89.5	4.0	48.8	5.0	65.8	4.0	28.6	10.0
Other Europe	194.0	9.0	99.7	11.0	135.7	7.0	61.7	22.0
Other Countries	109.1	5.0	40.8	4.0	68.5	4.0	11.4	4.0
Main Purpose of Journey								
Holiday	1444.8	64.0	495.7	54.0	1385.9	76.0	167.9	59.0
Visiting friends & relatives	326.2	14.0	181.8	20.0	216.5	12.0	53.7	19.0
Business	259.1	11.0	127.1	14.0	77.4	4.0	27.6	10.0
Other	241.3	11.0	107.6	12.0	142.1	8.0	35.9	13.0
Total	2271.4	100	912.2	100	1821.9	100	285.1	101

Source: Bureau of Tourism Research, personal communication, 1997.

Domestic travel has always been the bread and butter of the tourism industry in Australia and Queensland. Domestic visitors currently generate 79 per cent of all nights spent in Queensland. In 1978 a survey of Domestic Travel in Australia was commenced to monitor the trends in domestic travel patterns.

Figure 7.1
Visitor Expenditure on Commercial Accommodation:
Market Shares 1984

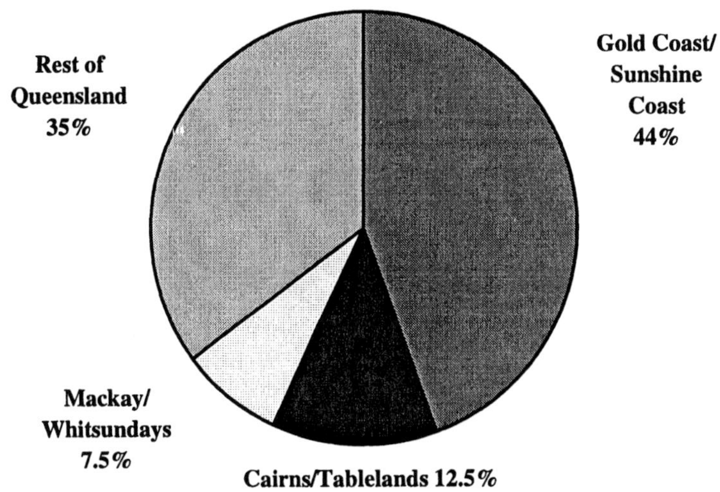

Figure 7.2
Visitor Expenditure on Commercial Accommodation:
Market Shares 1988

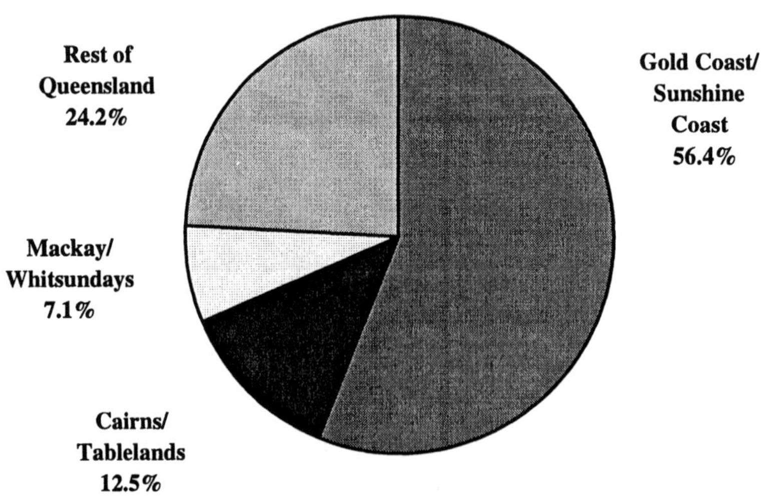

Figures 7.1 and 7.2 show the significance of the Brisbane/Gold Coast/Sunshine Coast region in the Queensland tourism market with 44% of visitor expenditure on commercial accommodation in 1984 and 56.4% in 1988, an atypical year when, due to their close

proximity to Brisbane, the host city for Expo 88, both coastal attractions would have benefited from spillover.

Cairns/Tablelands, held its 12.5% market share in 1988, despite some patronage loss due to Expo 88 but Mackay/Whitsunday region suffered a slight market share loss of 0.4%.

The 1995-96 Queensland State Budget allocated $ 12.5 million to the Queensland Tourist and Travel Corporation in addition to its base grant of $ 23.6 million with the special purpose of promoting Convention Tourism to coincide with the opening of world class Convention Centres in Brisbane and Cairns.

The 'Tourism drive into Asia' was to continue and this was supported by the opening of a new Government Tourism Office in Seoul, South Korea. (State Budget 1995-96, Budget Paper, Queensland Government: 19)

The emphasis in 1995-96 was on winning a larger share of the Asian & International Convention markets.

The Queensland Government is planning to win a major share of the 2000 Olympic Games swimming/training patronage and enticing visitors to Sydney to enjoy an adventure or leisure holiday in Queensland.

Foreign Investment in the Queensland Tourism Industry

In 1990, the Queensland Government carried out an investigation to ascertain the extent and nature of foreign investment in the Queensland tourism industry.

Foreign ownership in the 5 star accommodation category was 50.2%, in the 4 star and 5 star categories combined 43.3% and in the combined 3–5 star group 28.6%. The 1 and 2 star categories were 100% domestically owned.

The growth in tourist numbers had been accompanied by a parallel increase in foreign investment in tourist accommodation.

Along with being the major source of tourists, Japan was the dominant source of foreign investment in tourist accommodation in Queensland with 92.5% of all foreign investment in that sector.

Given the three tourism region promotional/development adopted, it is interesting to note that the Gold Coast topped the list for foreign investment in tourist accommodation with 28.6%. Cairns was second with 26.9% and the Sunshine Coast had 12.5% (Queensland Treasury Department, 1991).

India's Tourism Industry Performance

The impact of the tourist trade on the Indian economy has been quite modest: in 1988, while tourism accounted for 10.3% of India's exports, it comprised just 0.6% of GDP, earning India $US 2 per capita. This is despite extensive government sector involvement (including investment e.g. hotels) in tourism. By contrast, tourist receipts generated 9.7% of Singapore's GDP at $905 per capita (Harrison, 1992: 14).

While India has recently exceeded the threshold of 2 million international tourists per year, it has been well outperformed – as indicated above – by most of its Northeast and Southeast Asian neighbours, even Australia. In 1992, Singapore and Malaysia attracted 5.5 and 6 million international tourists respectively, Hong Kong almost 7 million, and Australia about 2.6 million.

By any measure, the physical impact of tourists on the local population and land area of India, is comparatively low. For example, the comparative Tourist Intensity Rates (TIR – tourists/local population) and Tourist Density Ratios (TDS – tourist nights over the land area in square kilometres x 365) for India and Singapore for 1988 were 0.2 (161.0) and 0.04 (34.4) respectively (Harrison, 1992: 12). This suggests – particularly in light of the growth of India's population over the 1951-95 period from 361 million to 916 million – that at least on a nationwide basis, India has the gross physical capacity to absorb a greatly expanded annual flow of tourists, even though much of India's environmental resource base is under considerable stress (India Development Report, 1997).

As to the origin of the region's overseas tourists, Vellas and Becherel (1995: 51) observe that, in 1992, 41.5% of tourists to the South Asian region came from Europe; intra-regional trade provided a low 28.1% of total visitors; tourists from the East Asian and Pacific region comprised 13.7% , and American tourists, 9.2% of the total.

THE NEED FOR A FRESH APPROACH

This history of policy failure suggests that for the Indian tourist trade to grow at anywhere near its potential, it has to break free, permanently, of the stultifying impact of government macro- and micro-economic policy-making and the dead hand of the public sector with its extensive but lacklustre involvement in tourism promotion and investment. So, to succeed, the future of Indian tourism must somehow be radically different from its recent past – somewhat like love, which according to Dr Samuel Johnson may be described as the 'triumph of hope over experience'. The future of India's tourism, as was perceived to be the case in Queensland, lies in the hands of a rejuvenated private sector, with extensive foreign direct investment both in tourism industry-specific infrastructure and economic infrastructure generally. Perhaps the most that can be expected of government in terms of sustained policy reform is:

- opening up the tourist industry and infrastructure generally to foreign direct investment;
- some reduction of the regulatory burden (bureaucratic red tape etc.) on the tourist trade and development;

- ensuring that only environmentally sustainable new tourism development is undertaken, and that that adverse environmental impact of existing development is substantially reduced;

- a partial or privatisation of public sector tourism assets, and use of the proceeds to preserve heritage property and its immediate environment;

- development of a better integrated nationwide tourism policy in consultation with the states and the private sector, and a clearer demarcation and assignment of the private/public roles.

- the selection of three or four tourism regions to become market leaders and to spearhead a concerted promotion campaign.

It is also not necessary, and counterproductive, to try to attract foreign direct investment by over-reliance on tax incentives, unsupported by an attractive business climate as a whole (as the Indian government is now doing). As Anwar Shah (1995: 25) of the World Bank noted in his overview of *Fiscal Incentives for Investment and Innovation*:

> Developing countries would be well advised to limit the use of such tax preferences and instead concentrate on eliminating disincentives to investment that arise from infrastructural deficiencies, the regulatory regime, and lack of a legal framework, institutions and enforcement.

The regulatory burden on new investment in India is still severe. Only 22.6% of the $US 14,995 million of approved direct foreign investment project funds over the period 1991-95, were actually invested, Datt and Sundharam (1997: 214). While the Far Eastern Economic Review (March 7, 1996: 40) reported that:

> In New Delhi, for instance not one new 250-room five-star hotel has been opened since 1982. *A new 250-room, five-star hotel which has been ready for the last 15 months is still unoccupied, mired in red tape.* (emphasis added)

India is well endowed with diverse natural landscapes and possesses an exceptionally rich and diverse cultural heritage and enjoys a wide range of climatic conditions all of which are attractive to the international tourist:

> More than 5,000 years of history, immense diversity, centuries-old culture preserved, and a distinct heritage. A land of magnificent monuments, with more palaces and forts than all of Europe, (*Far Eastern Economic Review*, March 7 1996: 40)

Although developing countries have tended to regard international tourism principally in terms of economic expectations, the international tourist hopes to obtain unique sociocultural and psychic 'need satisfaction' in an exchange governed by the justice principle. That exchange as Ap (1992: 677) explains, 'must be viewed as fair in the context of each actor's social environment'. Failure to comply with the justice principle, will foster either a negative attitude to tourism by host residents (as to costs and benefits), or dissatisfaction by tourists about the destination, and possibly feelings of being 'ripped-off' owing to their inadequate local knowledge etc, leading to a loss of repeat business.

THE NEED FOR CAREFUL PLANNING

Poorly managed or uncontrolled tourism development, in some locations, has caused an imbalance of social, cultural and environmental needs at best, and environmental degradation at worst. Successive Indian state governments have typically failed to develop comprehensive planning schemes in conjunction with state tourism development programs, especially in relation to land usage and the use of scarce natural resources as well as not ensuring that regulations are complied with. Tourism developers, usually enjoying political patronage, have a track record of breaking local environmental legislation with relative impunity. Although concerted action by some disenchanted communities such as in Goa (the former Portuguese colony where an active campaign was led by a militant anti-tourism group, the JGF) including successful court challenges to illegal hotel construction, has obtained better compliance with environmental safeguards, and even a moratorium on tourism development, Lea (1993: 708-10). Though victories are often not permanent. In Goa's case, by late 1995, as Wilson (1997: 73) notes:

> The most noticeable feature was the accelerating pace of development and proliferation of new buildings .... There was also evidence of growing conflict between the different types of tourism in Goa and the vested interests that support them ... If anything, the local authorities appeared even more powerless to implement and enforce appropriate development plans and policies, and the outlook for the future thus seemed bleaker than during the 1994-95 season ...

The carrying capacity of some rural tourism locations may be quite low. For example, the high growth in trekking tourism in Nepal has had adverse environmental impacts on specific locations with a small carrying capacities. Shackley (1994) noted that although just 500 trekkers, in highly organised parties, had visited the remote Himalayan kingdom of Lo (Nepal) since it was opened up in 1992, there was already signs of environmental difficulties and that its cultural carrying capacity had already been exceeded. Economic benefits to local people were also minimal. There is a danger of inadvertently causing the emergence of local hostility towards tourists.

ORISSA – THE LAND OF TEMPLES

In the State's promotion material Orissa is described as "…an un still largely undiscovered by tourists" ("State of Orissa – Welcome to Orissa – a largely undiscovered beauty", p. 1).

Orissa Tourism Development Corporation, in cooperation with Swotsi Travels, Hotel Toshali Sands of Orissa and Pugmarks of Calcutta, has been active in packaging and promoting the rich culture, unique architecture, wildlife sanctuaries and ocean beaches of Orissa with Puri, Gopalpur-on-Sea and Bhubaneswar – the Lord of the Universe – featuring prominently. This is a good start. A public and private sector partnership has been formed. An attempt to catalogue and package the State's attractions has been made.

Orissa, despite its much higher population density, has a lot in common with Queensland. Its climate is described as tropical wet-dry with January the coldest month and from June to October the Southwest monsoon heavy rainfall months. It has a wide range of fauna, tigers, elephants, monkeys, wild buffalo, blackbuck, four-horned antelopes, crocodiles and a massive variety of wild fowl. Orissa is well endowed with ocean beaches with excellent surf. It has a rich artistic heritage and has hosted many famous festivals like the Boita-Bandana (boat worshipping) festival in October or November (date set by Hindu calendar). It has many wildlife reserves like Simlipal Tiger Reserve and Bhutarakamka Mangrove Swamp Sanctuary and Chilika Lake near Chandabali in Balasore District. Then there is Chandeka elephant Reserve which also contains sambar, bears, wild dogs, pythons and pea fowl, all living in their natural surroundings and in harmony (most of the time).

These wildlife sanctuaries can compete internationally with many similar attractions that have become famous in Africa – but they need to be further developed and promoted.

The jewel in the Crown of Orissa has to be its temple heritage. The architectural richness of the Buddhist heritage at Dhauli, Lalitagiri, Ratnagiri and Udayagiri (all within 100 kms of Bhubaneswar) is a great tourism asset. Konark is magnificent and both Puri and Bhubaneswar are crowded with temples and monuments.

The reservoir of tourism potential has been tapped but not drawn on to any extent.

Orissa can benefit from the experience of Queensland in growing a tourism industry that is not threatening or intrusive on the lifestyles of its people but can provide revenue and employment in an industry that caters for enjoyment and leisure. Good policies that are implemented and policed to ensure compliance are needed if tourism development is to be environmentally friendly.

CONCLUDING COMMENTS

Orissa, and India for that matter, can benefit from the highly successful Queensland tourism experience. A feasible strategy has to be devised and key infrastructure gaps identified. The domestic market may not have the glamour of international tourism, nor will it provide the foreign exchange earnings but it has to be the prime focus of a tourism development strategy.

In targeting international tourists, Australia concentrated on its main trading partners – Japan, Korea, the United Sates and New Zealand. India could do likewise.

This industry, more so than most, requires an unwavering customer focus. Repeat business is good business. A happy homeward-bound tourists becomes a voluntary ambassador. High hygiene standards, comfort and safety of person and property rank high among overseas tourists' expectations.

The tourism industry in India is in its infancy. The drive to maturity will provide tough challenges but the rewards are high also.

The State of Orissa possesses a rich mix of tourist attractions but needs to develop the support facilities in order to be able to provide international class tourist services.

Whilst hotels like Bhubaneswar's Oberoi are 5 star plus standard, the accommodation mix in Orissa will need to be broadened to cater for a range of budgets. Investment in upgrading existing accommodation facilities and building new facilities will need to be encouraged.

REFERENCES

Ap, John (1992) "Residents perceptions on tourism impacts", *Annals of Tourism Research*, 19: 665-90.

Australian Bureau of Statistics (1997) *Queensland Year Book*, 1997.

Bureau of Tourism Research, Canberra, personal communication.

Cornell Hotel and Restaurant Administration Quarterly, "Australia: Tourism strengths", 35, August 1994.

Datt, R. and Sundharam, K.P.M. (1997) *Indian Economy*, 36th revised edition, S. Chand & Co Ltd: New Delhi.

Far Eastern Economic Review, March 1997: 40

Forsyth, P. and Dwyer, L. (1996) "Tourism in the Asian-Pacific region", *Asian-Pacific Economic Literature*, 10(1): 13-22.

Hall, C.M. (1989) "Hallmark tourist events: Analysis, definition, methodology and review", in G.J. Syme, B.J. Shaw, D.M. Fenton and W.S. Mueller (eds) *The Planning and Evaluation of Hallmark Events*, Sydney: Avebury, 20-39.

Harrison, David (ed.) (1992) *Tourism and the Less Developed Countries*, London: Belhaven Press.

Lea, John P. (1993) "Tourism development ethics in the Third World", *Annals of Tourism Research*, 20: 701-15.

India Development Report (1997) New Delhi: Government of India.

Queensland Tourist and Travel Corporation (1990) *Domestic Tourism Monitor*, August.

Queensland Tourist and Travel Corporation, *Queensland Visitor Survey 1995-96*.

Queensland State Budget (1995-96) Budget Paper Queensland Government, p.19.

Shackley, Myra (1994) "The land of Lo, Nepal, Tibet: The first eigh
Tourism Management, 15(1): 17-26.

Shah, Anwar (ed.) (1995) *Fiscal Incentives for Investment and Inn*
Oxford University Press.

Vellas, F. and Becherel, L. (1995) *International Tourism: An Economic Perspective*, London: Macmillan Business.

Waters, S.R. (1991) "Travel industry world yearbook: The big picture", New York.

Wilson, David (1977) "Paradoxes of tourism in Goa", *Annals of Tourism Research*, 24(1): 52-75.

Chapter 8

TOURISM AND ENVIRONMENTAL CHALLENGES: THE CASE OF INDIA

PRAGATI MOHANTY
Department of Economics,
S.D. Women's College,
Rajgangpur,
770017, Orissa, India

INTRODUCTION

The history of tourism indicates that its development prospects depend on the interaction with the natural environment. It is the most important factor that helps broaden the base of international and national tourism. In fact there is a reciprocal relationship between tourism and development. A sound and suitable environment is one of the most important resources that causes the advancement of tourism. The increased activity of tourism involves a misuse of the environment resulting in a decline in the quality of the environment in the region; it leads to the destruction of one of the important elements upon which tourism is dependent.

Rapid growth of the Indian tourism industry, particularly the inbound sector, has resulted in the development of new infrastructures, programmes and facilities. These developments have in many cases led to competition and conflict with other uses of resources and in turn have generated a wide range of environmental impacts.

There is a general acceptance at the policy level on the need for tourism to make land use sustainable, but there are obvious deficiencies in the implementation of such policies. The conundrum which this raises is how can the concept of sustainable development best be incorporated in tourism development? Implicit in addressing this question is consideration of whether tourism development is sustainable economically, socially, politically and environmentally. Resolution of this question is critical to the industry and the society at large from both economic and political perspective.

This contribution addresses these questions in three principal ways: *Firstly* it assesses whether tourism indeed can make land use sustainable and notes that the concept of sustainable use is ambiguous and potentially contradictory unless viewed holistically. *Secondly* the paper reviews some of the emerging issues which need to be addressed in tourism planning and management if sustainable development is to be achieved. *Finally* it identifies some of the critical pre-conditions for sustainable development, particularly at planning and developmental levels. In all these areas, this paper argues that a fundamental reappraisal of roles of agencies and individuals in the development process is needed.

GLOBAL TOURISM

Tourism has become the focus of interest for many countries because it is regarded as a productive sector. The interest in upgrading tourism and developing it as a production sector has increased considerably. Tourism has created in the community a desire to raise the standard of living and health of the population, besides putting an end to environmental pollution. Tourism has now sanitary, environmental, aesthetic and cultural dimensions that have to be considered. If we want tourism industry to grow and expand, the protection of the natural environment and maintaining the ecological balance become matters of great importance for tourism. The comprehensive plan for tourism development in the country must set up a balance between interests of tourism and other public interest of the state including political, economic, social and psychological interests and between the different geographical regions of the state.

Rapid growth of tourism has been highlighted in numerous reports and enquiries over the past decade. Much of that growth has occurred with the active endorsement and support of both public and private sector management agencies. In fact a cursory perusal of such reports suggests that they have actively prompted the benefits of tourism, while downplaying the costs. Advocates of tourism make no mention of the negative impacts of tourism, while claiming more pointedly that tourism:

- helps to diversify the economy
- assists the decentralisation process
- sells the same product over and over again, and
- assists in conservation of natural resources.

Such claims are understandable in both policy and practical context. In the former, the emergence of the tourism industry and a belated recognition of its economic significance prompted a range of policy initiatives. From the policy context measures are slowly being taken to ensure the sustainable growth of the industry in the long run. From the practical perspective, by the early 1980s despite evidence of undesirable environmental consequences, the general perception of tourism was that of a smokeless industry, one that is commonly nominated as a desirable form of land use to achieve conservation objectives. However the perception of tourism is changing as more evidence of the undesirable effects of tourism growth becomes available and recognition of the cumulative effects of development grows.

GROWTH AND SUSTAINABILITY

The concept of sustainable development is both complex and multi-dimensional. As a consequence several recent studies (Goodland and Ledec, 1986; Chambers, 1987) have proposed a range of different interpretations which, while having common elements, vary in degree and emphasis. These studies suggest that sustainable development has a primary objective of providing lasting and secure livelihoods which minimise resource depletion, environmental degradation, cultural disruption and social instability. The WCED (Bruntland Commission) report further extends this basic objective to include inter-generational and intra-generational equity concerns and includes two key aspects:

(a) an emphasis on needs, particularly of economically marginal populations, and
(b) the idea of limitations – imposed by the state of technology and social organisation on the environment's ability to meet present and future needs.

While tourism ostensibly seeks to meet the key elements of the primary objectives of sustainable development, there are many considerations both within the concept of sustainable development and within the nature of tourism which inevitably must mean that all aspects of the concept of sustainable development may not be realised. For example, as Pearce *et al.* (1988) note, sustainability implies an infinite time horizon, whereas practical decision making requires the adoption of finite horizons. In an industry as dynamic as tourism, long term planning is complicated by factors such as market change, segmentation, investment, confidence and industry coordination. While these factors complicate the attainment of sustainable development objectives, they are not hard barriers. Rather they serve to emphasise the precondition for tourism to become sustainable. Paramount amongst these is an effective coordination and control mechanism of a system which is able to give practical and ongoing effect to the policy interest of sustainable development.

POLICY PRACTICE CONUNDRUM

The multi-dimensional nature of the industry and the often poorly defined linkages between its many elements are the major barriers to the integrative strategic planning which is required for sustainable development. There are currently many hotels and tourist facilities under construction. While the provision of these units reflects a perceived market need there is increasing concern about the social (equity) and environmental effects of such concentrated investments to say nothing of their appropriateness to the tourist experience.

The current control system for such development is fragmented and poorly coordinated, both spatially and temporally – ideal pre-conditions for the tyranny of small decision (Odum, 1982). The net effect of such small decision is contrary to the objectives of sustainable development and yet is occurring within a formal policy context where sustainable development objectives are being formalised. The poor record of synchronisation of policy and practice therefore appears to be one of the major impediments to the attainment of sustainable development objectives.

Tourists' experience has a central role in the tourism market system. It is the psychological outcome of the forces of supply and demand. However the nature of tourists' experience is extremely dynamic. Like any product, tourism and tourist destinations have a limited lifespan. Throughout the world there are numerous examples where previously buoyant tourism regions have experienced rapid and dramatic declines in visitor popularity, because of either changing fashions or because of alternations in the tourist product (Clary, 1984). Therefore the existence of tourist infrastructure and ready-made attractions may not ensure the long-term future of tourist destination (Murphy, 1985).

The Indian tourism is slowly coming out of its status as a cottage industry in the postwar era. There was little evidence to suggest that the nature and scale of tourism activities were not sustainable. It is only since the rapid growth of tourism began in the late 1970s and the early 1980s that the question about factors affecting sustainability has risen to prominence. Given the growing community awareness of the prospect of the industry and the current rate of growth it is not surprising therefore that the need for sustainable development has only now emerged as one of the key management issues in Indian tourism. The efficacy and implementation of such guidelines is heavily dependent upon voluntary acceptance by selected agencies. As was noted above, the fragmented nature of tourism management in India tends to emphasise the gap between policy and practice. To compound this problem, most public sector agencies are charged with a responsibility for resource protection, while private sector agencies generally make use of these resources.

LOOKING AHEAD

The key to resolution of this problem lies in making the industry aware of the importance of incorporating sustainable development principles into both planning and operations. This can be achieved by:

(a) *Cooperative control system*: the present ad hoc approach to tourism planning introduces distortions, which may disadvantage both operators and regions/communities. An integrative planning approach to tourism planning and management at all levels would distribute benefits more equitably.

(b) Development of industry coordination mechanisms.

(c) Raising consumer awareness

(d) Raising producer awareness.

(e) Strategic planning to supersede conventional approaches.

The dependence on tourism, in turn, brings costs as well as benefits to the local population. Economic benefits come from direct and secondary employment and income. Net effects, however, are reduced by the seasonality of tourism, limited facilities and leakage of earnings outside the region. Tourism also has social and cultural impacts on the resident population. Local lifestyles and customs are disrupted and changed, often in ways that are considered undesirable for the locality. All of these issues are interrelated and they must be acknowledged and addressed in a systematic manner. The anatomy of tourism cannot be understood apart from the environment and society within which it functions. It is a symbolic industry. It means that tourism development cannot be planned on a narrow sectoral basis if we are to capitalise on new opportunities and solve existing problems.

The creation of a viable long-term sustainable tourism industry requires supply side analysis and planning. Within this perspective, tourism development is linked to socio-environmental management. It recognises that tourism is environment-dependent. Figure 8.1 depicts the environmental and social aspects of tourism management.

Figure 8.1
Environmental and Social Dimensions of Tourism Management

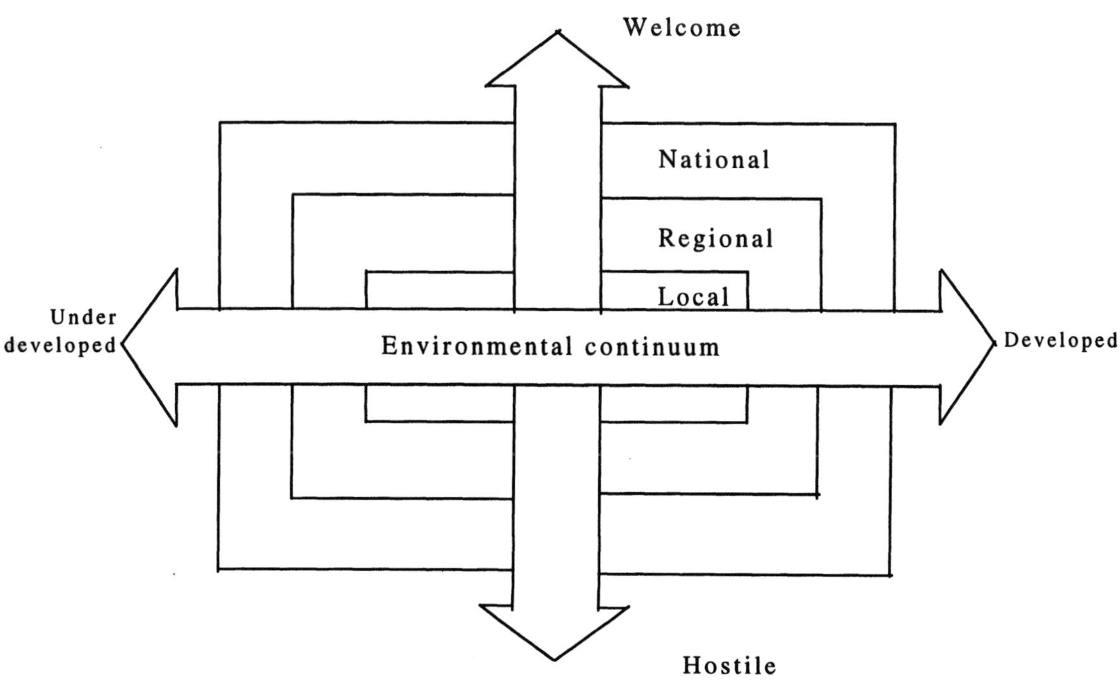

The emphasis should be given to environmental and socio-economic components which have been neglected to date. The environmental dimension in the figure correlates the degree of impact with the level of development – the socio-economic dimension focuses on the nature of community responses to tourism. In reality, the integration of tourism development with environmental and socio-economic conditions and constraints is a complex process. So the importance of coordinated planning and impact management at national, regional and local levels, should be given due emphasis.

Key suggestions are:

(i) Tourism planning should be multi-sectoral, and part of comprehensive development and land-use planning;

(ii) Policy directives, based on national needs and resources, should give overall direction to the planning process; and

(iii) Environmental Impact Assessment (EIA) should be applied to large-scale projects.

References

ATRI (1989) *Environmental Guidelines for Tourist Developments,* Second discussion draft, Sydney: Australian Tourism Research Institute.

Bandyopadhyay, J. and Vandana, S. (1989) "Political economy of ecology movements", *IFDA Dossier,* 71, May–June: 37–60.

Barbier, E.B. (1984) "The concept of sustainable development and the environment", *Journal of Development Studies,* 25(1): 126–35.

Chambers, R. (1987) *Sustainable Livelihoods, Environment and Development: Putting Poor Rural People First,* Brighton: Institute of Developmental Studies, University of Sussex.

Clary, D. (1984) "The impact of social change on a leisure region (1960–1982)", a study of Nord Pays D'Auge in J. Long and R. Hecock (eds) (1984) *Leisure, Tourism and Social Change,* Dunformline College: Centre for Leisure Research, 51–56.

Cohen, E (1988) "Authority and commoditisation in tourism", *Annal of Tourism Research,* 15(3): 351–86.

Goodland, R. and Ledec, G. (1986) *Neo-Classical Economics and Principles of Sustainable Development,* Washington DC: Office of Environmental Sustainable Development.

Gunn, C. (1988) *Tourism Planning*: New York: Taylor and Friends.

Meadows, D. *et al.* (1972) *The Limits to Growth,* New York: Universe Books.

Murphy, P. (1985) *Tourism: A Community Approach,* London: Methuen.

Odum, W.E. (1982) "Environmental degradation and the tyranny of the small decisions", *Bioscience,* 32: 728–50.

Richter, Linda K. (1989) *The Politics of Tourism in Asia,* Honolulu: University of Hawaii Press.

WCED (1987) *Our Common Future*, World Commission on Environment and Development, London: Oxford University Press.

TOURISM AND UNEMPLOYMENT, AND HUMAN RELATIONS IN TOURISM MANAGEMENT IN INDIA

Chapter 9

TOURISM: ITS GROWTH AND IMPACT ON EMPLOYMENT GENERATION

SAUNDARJYA BORBORA
Department of Economics,
Sherubtse College,
Kanglung, Bhutan
(Under University of Delhi)

INTRODUCTION

Tourism denotes the temporary, short-term movement of people to destinations outside the place where they normally live in and work and their activities during their stay at these destinations. Thus tourism is a summation of movements of people outside their normal work areas. The destinations may be within or outside the national boundary of the country. Accordingly, their movements result in domestic tourism and foreign tourism. The prime motive of tourists is pleasure and leisure, but may be supplemented by business, educational, religious, cultural etc. motives. These motives vary from person to person in varying degrees.

Tourism has now grown to such dimensions and importance that it is now rightly added to the list of established industries with tremendous economic and social potentiality.

Today, tourism has acquired the structure of a major industry, playing an important role in the world economy. In fact, travel and tourism taken together constitute the largest industry in terms of turn-over and employment. According to the World Tourism Organisation (WTO), about 500 million tourists travelled internationally in 1993, spending about US$304 billion. It employs more people than any other single industrial sector and has an infrastructural (lodging, transportation and restaurants) investment estimated to exceed US$3 trillion.

Tourism is one of India's most successful industries. Firstly its contribution towards foreign exchange earnings helps improve the country's balance of payments situation, secondly, its impact on employment generation is also quite considerable. As per a study on Tourism by the National Council of Applied Economics & Research (NCAER), New Delhi, tourism generated employment for 934 thousand persons in 1972-73 which has risen to 6,400,000 persons in 1978. The notable feature of this is that a good percentage of those employed belong to the unskilled and semi-skilled categories.

Tourism has enormous potential for utilising the natural attractions like landscapes, mountains, beaches, rivers etc. It also applies equally to a multitude of man-made attractions like monuments, places, forts and temples which were constructed over the years. This is particularly true in the case of India, where 80 per cent of the international tourist arrival is singularly attributed to Taj Mahal, one of the wonders in the world.

It is estimated that India received over 1.87 million international tourists during 1993-94 and earned foreign exchange worth Rs 65,090 million. There has been an impressive growth in domestic tourist traffic also over the years. While the total domestic tourist visits during 1987 were about 34.8 million, the same increased to 81 million by 1992 registering an average annual growth rate of about 18.4 per cent. Table 9.1 shows the achievements of India in the tourism sector during 1991-94, while India's share of world tourists receipts has increased significantly, the foreign exchange earning has crossed $2 billion and tourism directly employed about 8 million people in 1994.

Table 9.1
Statistics on India's Tourism Industry

Item	1991	1994
India's share of world tourist (per cent)	0.37	0.36
Share of world tourist receipts (per cent)	0.49	0.70
Amount of foreign exchange ($ million)	NA	2,348
Direct employment (million persons)	NA	7.8

Sources: GOI: Government of India tourist statistics 1994, New Delhi, Government of India.

EMPLOYMENT POTENTIAL

Although a considerable amount of research has been undertaken on effects on national income of tourists' expenditure, less is known about the impact of tourism on the creation of employment opportunities, specially indirect employment. In this connection, a number of questions crops up on relationship between tourism and employment such as - number of employment created, type of job opportunities, skill-required and cost-benefit from employment, geographical distribution of employment etc.

Newer and newer methods are being adopted for compilation of more accurate and comprehensive tourist-employment statistics. But there is a general agreement that tourism creates employment and it is a beneficial effect. There are employment opportunities in hotels etc. and tourists spending money outside their hotels create additional income earning opportunities for Taxi-drivers, Restaurants, Travel Agencies and Entertainment Facilities. The building of hotels and the up-gradation of transportation, sanitation and water supply facilities provide employment in construction. Increased demands for food could also increase the number of employment opportunities in the agricultural sector.

So we see three types of employment are generated by tourism:-

1. Direct employment resulting from visitors' expenditure in tourist places - such as hotels;
2. Indirect employment created in the tourist supply service sector although not resulting directly from tourist expenditures;
3. Induced employment resulting from the effects of the tourism multiplier as local residents re-spend the additional money income they have earned.

From studies, it is found out in general that the visit of each foreign tourist provides employment to one person and 6.5 domestic tourists generate one job. The value added during 1992-93 was Rs 744.76 million registering an annual rate of growth of 14.7 per cent per annum in India. The direct employment figures rose to 6.96 million by 1992-93, registering a growth rate of about 5.9 per cent per year.

Over and above, the huge pilgrim movement, both seasonal and regular, contributes to large scale employment generation at many parts of India. (For example, the villager in the Pahalgam tehsil in J & K is a classic case wherein about 8000 inhabitants are supported by the pilgrims visiting Amarnath. E.g. of Sabirmala in Kerela, Badri-Kedar belt in UP and Tirupati in AP, Puri in Orissa etc.) Thus total employment generation due to tourism will be more than 16.41 million, accounting for about 5 per cent of the total workforce.

Apart from its direct contribution to the economy, tourism has significant linkages with other sectors of the economy - agriculture, horticulture, poultry, handicraft, construction and service sector etc. Several items of tourist expenditure induce a chain of transaction in these sectors and each such transaction calls for the supply of some kind of goods and services. Further, those directly or indirectly employed following the development of tourism may also demand more goods and services as a result of such employment than what they would have demanded otherwise. The additional consumption demand thus emanating from tourist expenditure will not only induce more employment but also generate a multiplier effect through a successive chain of transactions.

Most assessments of jobs created by tourism make reference to direct employment only. Some detailed investigations have been undertaken by different researchers. But as the studies employ different terminologies, categories and methodologies, it makes comparison difficult. There is a paucity of detailed empirical studies on tourism and employment. But from the studies available, we can make some general observations which are noted below.

(a) Employment and income effects are closely connected though not perfectly related. They are analogous in that direct employment and income can be distinguished from indirect employment and income. There is a casual relationship between tourism generated income and employment but they are not necessarily of equal size nor need they be created at the same time. Income and employment multiplier are not identical and the maximisation of income may not lead to the simultaneous maximisation of employment.

(b) The effects of tourism on employment are influenced by the type of tourist activity. Some are more labour-intensive than others (e.g. accommodation-hotels etc.). They also require large capital and this requirement varies with hotel size.

(c) The effects on employment are influenced by the types of skills which are available locally. Tourism creates few jobs at the managerial and professional level and these are often filled from other sectors of the economy or by people brought in from outside the region. As many jobs are seasonal, women employees outnumber males. The employment structure and the cyclical pattern of employment are often cited as disadvantages of the tourist industry.

(d) The character of most employment in tourism is highly seasonal and this contributes to fluctuation in the level of local and regional employment. Seasonal employment has inherent disadvantages as it tends to attract those on the periphery of the labour force. This discourages outward mobility of labour to more productive employment.

In a nutshell, it is true that tourism creates employment and is generally beneficial to the economy.

In India, there is a great potentiality for growth of tourism and Government of India adopted a **National Action Plan** for tourism. The plan among other things, envisages an increase in the employment opportunities from the present level to 30 million. This will be done through a series of measures, which include improving the infrastructures like hotel and other accommodation facilities and developing special tourism such as Pilgrim Tourism, Cultural Tourism, Island Tourism, Adventure Tourism and Eco-tourism etc. Since a substantial amount of expenditure is required to establish necessary infrastructure several measures have been initiated to attract foreign and domestic private investment. These include a package of fiscal and financial incentives to investors and placing tourism within priority sector for foreign investment.

Besides the Government's measures, private sector and peoples' co-operation and participation are a necessity. Different promotional strategies need to be adopted to realise the target of attracting 5 million international tourists by 2000 A.D.

Under the current program of economic liberalisation attempts are being made to privatise many of the public sector activities. Privatisation of several of the public sector activities in the tourism industry can and should also be considered.

REFERENCES

Bhatia, A.K. (1991) *Tourism Development, Principles and Practices*, 6th edition, New Delhi: Sterling Publishers Pvt. Ltd.

Burkart, A.J. and Medtik, S. (1974) London: Heineman.

Chopra, S. (1991) *Tourism and Development in India*, New Delhi: Ashish Publishing House.

Economic Impact, 29 (1980/1) Washington, D.C., USA: International Communication Agency.

"Government of India" (1994) *Tourist Statistics*, New Delhi: Department of Tourism.

Kumar, R.B. (1995) *Coastal Tourism and Environment*, New Delhi: APH Publishing Corporation.

Mathieson, A. and Wall, G. (1982) *Economic Physical and Social Impact*, London: Longman.

Selvam, M. (1987) *Tourism Industry in India*, Bombay: Himalaya Publishing House.

Singh, R. (1994) *Tourism Today*, 2, New Delhi: Kasishka Publishers Distributors.

Sudheer, S.V. (1993) *Tourism, Problem and Prospects*, Trivandrum: CBH Publications.

Tewari, S.P. (1994) *Tourism Dimensions*, New Delhi: Atma Ram & Sons.

Yojana, December 1995.

Chapter 10

INCOME MULTIPLIER EFFECT OF TOURISM: A SAM APPROACH

JYOTIRMAYEE KAR
Department of Analytical and Applied Economics,
Utkal University,
Vani Vihar,
India

INTRODUCTION

Undoubtedly, development of the tourist sector increases the aggregate income of an economy. Many a study has highlighted the income generating impact of the tourism industry and have assessed the multiplier effect (Menges, 1975; Clement, 1961). Menges (1972), in an attempt to examine sectoral multiplier effect developed a theoretical input-output model with tourism as a separate sector. Fletcher *et al.* (1981), Li and Sung (1983) and Fletcher (1983) extended the model to test its empirical validity in the context of different economies.

The concept of multiplier, as developed by Keynes, examines the impact of an exogenous change in expenditure on the level of income. The multiplier is quantified as the ratio of the rise in total income to rise in the initial expenditure. However, the Keynesian concept of multiplier examines the income changes in a macro perspective. But the real problem is at the sectoral level, for which an assessment of investment-induced changes in demand and hence in income, in different sectors of the economy is required. Some studies have examined the sectoral multiplier effect by using input-output model developed by W.W. Leontief. Yet others have studied the multiplier effect with Social Accounting Matrix (SAM).

Development of tourism leads to an increase in income in related sectors including transport, hotels, the information network and, importantly, the government exchequer.

Milne *et al.* (1995) have examined one key strategy for downstream percolation of the benefits of visitor expenditure, i.e. the linkage between tourism and the region's art sector. The paper examines vital issues and problems encountered in the process of implementation of such a strategy. It concludes that while the residents of the area are supportive of tourist inflow, different interest groups express mixed concern as they differ on the type of interaction that should occur between tourism and the local art sector. The present study is an attempt to examine the income generating impact of tourism via its impact on the cottage industries sector. The study compares the income generating effect of the tourist sector with that of the other sectors like agriculture, trading, services etc. by comparing how an exogenous increase in expenditure of a certain amount in different sectors brings about an increase in income. This is done by examining the sectoral multiplier effects which are estimated by using a Social Accounting Matrix (SAM).

The present work is a case study undertaken in a village of Orissa. The village is famous for its appliqué work, a cottage industry. This industry thrives mainly on the sales proceeds from the tourists. The inflow and expenditure of the tourists determine the income level of the households engaged in this sector. Other groups of people are engaged in agriculture, trading, services and different types of miscellaneous activities. These sectors are completely unrelated to tourism and income and expenditure in these sectors are not directly affected by inflow of tourists and their expenditure.

Considering the labour market of the village the artisan sector is dominated by family-based household industries. The appliqué skill is learnt mainly from the senior family members practising the same. Therefore, age or caste is no bar for market work participation. Students and persons below and above the working age group contribute to family income by working during leisure hours. Work participation in other sectors of the village is mainly determined by caste, education and the size of land holding. Educated people generally receive higher earnings in the town while owners of large land holdings hardly participate in non-farm work. The farm sector is dominated by agricultural labourers who are hired mainly for seasonal work. As such, they are not provided with full time employment and a majority of them live below the poverty line. The non-farm sector is dominated by caste-based occupations or family-owned businesses.

This paper is intended as a demonstration of the use of a Social Accounting Matrix in the calculation of economic impact multipliers at the local level. This technique has commonly been used for this purpose in a number of countries, and has become the standard approach to economic impact estimation at the small-area level. This demonstration exercise has been presented in the form of a simple example with a highly-aggregated table, as an illustration of the use of the technique for readers with less familiarity with economic analysis. In practice, applications of this approach would be carried out with more detailed or disaggregated inter-industry tables.

SOCIAL ACCOUNTING MATRIX FOR THE VILLAGE

Based on the occupational pattern the village economy is categorised into five sectors: agriculture, cottage industries, i.e. appliqué work, trading services and miscellaneous activities comprising construction, transport and communication and other small industrial activities. On the basis of the information on income and expenditure in different sectors a 5 x 5 social accounting matrix is constructed. The matrix provides a detailed picture of all transactions taking place within the village economy. Inter sectoral deliveries are presented along the rows which reflect the receipts or income side. The columns show the expenditure incurred by the sectors. As entries into the matrix are made on the principle of double entry book keeping, each row total will be equal to the corresponding column total. For example in a social accounting matrix at the national level the total income of the household sector is represented by the income received from the domestic production sector (Y) and the net factor income from abroad (F). The row along the household sector will, therefore, represent Y + F, the total income of the household. This income, in turn, is spent either for consumption (C) or is saved (S). These two reflecting the total expenditure are presented along the columns of the household sector. Thus the total income along the row equals total expenditure along the column.

Table 10.1
Social Accounting Matrix (in Rs x 100)

	Agriculture	Cottage Industry (Appliqué)	Tradin g	Services	Miscellaneous	Total
Agriculture	--	171	118	70	22	38
Cottage Industry (Appliqué)	--	--	270	--	--	27
Trading	105	11	--	147	125	38
Services	232	88	--	--	--	32
Miscellaneous	44	--	--	103	--	14
Total	381	270	388	320	147	.

As revealed by the social accounting matrix the agricultural sector receives its income from cottage industries, trading, services and miscellaneous activities. This sector spends a major part of its income on services, mainly on that of the hired labourers. Next in order comes expenditure on trading as agricultural operations require purchase of fertiliser, seeds and other agricultural implements Some expenditure is also incurred on the miscellaneous sector for transportation and other services. In the cottage industries sector, income comes from the sales proceeds of the finished products, that is, mainly from the trading sector. The expenditure of the cottage industry sector is mostly on agricultural products which they do not produce. This sector also spends on hiring labour for the industry and purchase of raw materials and implements from the trading sector. The major source of income of the trading sector is from services while it spends mainly for cottage industry products, thus acting as a mediator between the cottage industries and the tourists. The service sector in the village dominated by wage-earners obtains its income from the agriculturists and the cottage industries sector. The miscellaneous sector earns its income from the agricultural and service sectors and spends on agricultural products and traded commodities.

Multiplier Analysis

Values of sectoral multiplier from the social accounting matrix could be obtained in two different methods. The first one is based on the assumption of unitary elasticity of demand for each product for which the average and marginal expenditure propensities are assumed to be equal. Average expenditure propensity for each account is obtained by dividing each element in the matrix by the respective column sum. This gives another matrix for average or marginal expenditure propensities from which the value of multiplier could be obtained in the standard way.

In an attempt to make the analysis more realistic, the marginal expenditure propensities for each product are calculated directly by considering the national sample survey records on consumer expenditure. The difference in income between two income classes is taken as the change in income and the respective pattern of expenditure gives the marginal expenditure propensities (Parikh and Thorbecke, 1996). The difference in the level of income and expenditure between the higher and lower income groups thus provides data for the marginal propensity to consume of the lower income groups. With the marginal expenditure matrix thus calculated, the multiplier could be obtained in the usual fashion as:

$$\Delta Yn = (1 - Cn)^{-1} \Delta x = Ac\, dx$$

Where Δ Yn is the change in income, Δx is the exogenous change in demand for village goods and services, Cn is the coefficient matrix of marginal expenditure propensities. The multiplier matrix presented below reveals how changes in exogenous demand will bring about incremental change in income of different sectors.

Table 10.2
The Multiplier Matrix

	Agriculture	Cottage Industry	Trade	Services	Miscellaneous
Agriculture	1.02	0.90	1.10	1.70	0.60
Cottage Industry	0.70	1.90	1.60	0.60	0.30
Tradc	1.30	1.50	0.70	0.50	0.40
Services	0.70	0.60	0.80	0.64	0.20
Miscellaneous	0.20	0.40	0.70	0.50	0.30
Total Multiplier Effect	3.92	5.40	4.90	3.94	1.80

The multiplier value of any column presents the effect of Rs. 1.00 increase in the demand of that account on the total income incorporating both direct and indirect changes.

As revealed by the matrix, the cottage industry sector yields the highest value of multiplier followed by trade and services sectors. The cottage industry sector mainly thrives on the sales proceeds of the appliqué products, the market for which is dominated by tourist buyers. Therefore when the objective is maximisation of regional income, promotion of tourism will yield the highest benefit. Simultaneously, this study also throws some light on other developmental projects to be undertaken in the neighbouring areas. The multiplier matrix also reveals that any developmental activity leading to promotion of trade and commerce in the area has a larger cumulative effect than those promoting agriculture and other services. A boost to the trading sector simultaneously facilitates the marketing of the cottage industries products which has a high incremental income effect. Moreover, it could be noted that agriculture has a low value of multiplier thus suggesting that activities leading to agricultural promotion is of relatively less importance. The multiplier assessment in the present study however does not capture the total cost-benefit of exogenous increase in income in any sector and this calls for further study.

REFERENCES

Clement, H.G. (1961) *The Future of Tourism in the Pacific and the Far East*, Washington: US Government Printing Press.

Fletcher *et al.* (1981) *An Input-Output Study of Gibraltar*, University College of North Wales: Bangor Institute of Economic Research.

Fletcher (1989) "Input-output of analysis and tourism impact studies", New York, *Annals of Tourism Research*, 16: 514–29.

Li, T.B. and Sung, Y. (1983) "Hong Kong in tourism in Asia. The economic impact", T. Lin and E.A. Pye (eds), Singapore: Singapore University Press, 1–100.

Menges, G. (1972) "Methoden der Touristischen Statistik und Markt Froschung", Berne: Editions Gurter.

Menges, G. (1975) "Macro-economic approaches to the problem of investment in the tourist industry", *The Tourist Review*, 4.

Milne, S. *et al.* (1995) "Linking tourism and art in Canada's Eastern Arctic: A case of Cape Dorset", *Poland Record*, 31(176): 25–36.

Parikh, A. and Thorbecke, E. (1996) "Impact of rural industrialisation on village life and economy: A Social Accounting Matrix Approach", *Economic Development and Cultural Change*, 44(2): 351–77.

Chapter 11

HUMAN RESOURCE ISSUES IN INDIAN HOTELS: AN EXPLORATORY STUDY

G. (RAVI) RAVINDER
School of Leisure & Tourism Studies,
University of Technology,
Sydney, PO Box 222,
Lindfield NSW 2070,
Australia

INTRODUCTION

Tourism is a growing industry; indeed it is seen by many countries as a panacea for economic development in the context of increasingly competitive international markets for the traditional products, a burgeoning population and as a quick-fix solution to increasing employment and a standard of living.

The Indian government sees the future of tourism in much the same way; they have seen a growth in international tourist visitation from 2.12 million international visitors in 1995 earning US$ 3 billion in 1995/96. As well, the domestic tourist visitation has increased at a rate of nearly 13% from 1991 to 1995 to reach 108 million visits in 1995 (Department of Tourism, Govt. of India, 1996). The Department also estimates direct employment of 7.8 million people in 1994/95.

One of the key drivers in this push towards tourism development lies in the realisation that the provision of tourism products and services is human-resource intensive. It is already an employer of significant sections of the populace. The workforce is comprised primarily of those who are in the *delivery* of tourism services, often in a real-time face-to-face encounter with tourists.

To ensure quality, this service delivery can be standardised to the extent that it approaches the consistency of output of mass-production in factories. Levitt (1976) cites the approach of fast-food chains in this regard. But this leaves no room for flexibility in approach and delivery to a wide, diverse range of tourism customers. However, some degree of industrialisation is possible in tourism industries – with respect to cookery and housekeeping in hotels, pilots and coach drivers in the transport sector and in automated reservation systems, to cite a few examples.

But, consider the variety in the nature of the interactions between the service provider and the customer in the following environments:

a. In a non-automated reservations office, or the front office, or guest relations departments of a hotel, even often in the F&B service areas of a restaurant.

b. In the retail offices of airlines or in their in-flight service

c. In the role of tour guides in a coach tour

d. In retail travel agencies.

One can see the need for a more flexible, empathic interaction being required, if the desired outcome is to achieve customer satisfaction. Indeed, the trend in most countries around the world is to provide a more customised tourism product. This has arisen from customer demand, on the one hand (more discerning customers and the wide variety of their social and cultural backgrounds), and a keenly competitive market, wherein each product supplier is keen to secure some form of competitive advantage. Quite often, this advantage is sought in the area of the quality of the service provided.

The question that this research poses is CAN INDIA PROVIDE THIS CUSTOMISED, FLEXIBLE DELIVERY OF TOURISM PRODUCTS? Indeed India has an immense variety of natural, historical and cultural attractions – and these could be packaged in a multitude of ways to suit every taste and budget. But, as mentioned before, a critical issue here is also the delivery of these services by the tourism industry.

This paper will therefore first look at some of the key writings and paradigms on service delivery and service quality. The paper will then review a limited range of Human Resources research and case studies in India. Whilst they do not always represent current practice in the tourism industry, the author has selected critical points from them which may be of relevance to the issue of tourism service delivery. As well, four interviews were also conducted with HR and Training Managers in some of the 5-star chains in India as these are reported upon.

Based on these sources, the author will pose some questions to the audience. Keeping in mind that this research is very exploratory, some of these questions might appear to be presumptuous, culturally insensitive, irrelevant or even just superficial. But this is just the feedback that the author hopes to get from an expert audience such as yourselves in the hope that it would refine the authors' conclusions and point the way to more in-depth and focused research – if indeed such research is warranted.

THE MANAGEMENT OF SERVICES

Most, if not all, tourism products are in fact services. A *service* has been defined in a number of ways, but primarily they are seen as providing an intangible benefit to the recipient (be it financial services from a bank, technical assistance from a software supplier or accommodation in a hotel); this benefit is intangible in spite of the very tangible resources (bank premises, mainframes or PCs, hotel buildings) that are *used in* the provision of the service. The service is provided in a time-bound service environment and the benefit derived is experiential (Lovelock, 1992), even though such services could have tangible elements to them – e.g. food and beverage and the furnishings and appointments of the hotel room.

The management and marketing of these intangible services are recognised to be quite different from those of tangible (usually factory-produced) goods. The differences arise from four factors (Lovelock, 1992), three of which are relevant to this research. They are

A. *The Intangibility of Services*: Because they are intangible, customers evaluate the services post-consumption and largely on the experiential aspects of the service.
B. *The Inseparability of Services*: Production and consumption of services occur in real-time with the service provider and the customer usually present together (causing, as Jan Carlsson put it, "moments of truth"). This leaves little room for error. This is dependent therefore on the availability of appropriately skilled personnel. The author is presuming that numbers of providers (i.e. labour in India) is not a problem, and that perhaps their 'technical' skills can be taught, but their 'functional' skills could still be an issue (Gronroos, 1982).
C. *The Heterogeneity (or variability) of services:* Inconsistency in service delivery and the (resulting) perceived experience by the customers can arise from the variations in the service environment, and/or variations in the knowledge (of the service) and attitudes of the customers, and/or variations in the skills and attitudes of the service providers. Tourism industry firms cannot always control the service environment (for example, delayed flights, poor weather, the number and type of other customers present); and, as for the customers, their differences are presumed to be largely out of management's control. So, the onus falls on the service provider and their management to provide consistent service quality, in spite of the above two factors. Tourism industry firms rely on a clear understanding of their target markets and their needs.

Such firms are therefore looking at providing services in the form of an experiential product to a diverse range of customers in real-time and changing environments. Do their front-line service personnel have the skills to do this? After all, these skills could be inherited or acquired in the course of day-to-day living or learnt in a more formal educative or training process.

THE COMPONENTS OF SERVICE QUALITY

Most theorists and researchers (Lovelock, 1992; Gronroos, 1982; Berry and Parasuraman, 1991) agree that the quality of services has to be judged from a customer's perspective. Indeed, given that it is primarily an experiential benefit that they are receiving, customers have few tangible clues or parameters to enable them to judge its quality. Therefore, they rely on their *prior expectations* to serve as their benchmark. Service quality is therefore seen by these researchers as the ability to meet or exceed customer expectations.

But then again, overall service quality cannot be easily evaluated as an overall measure. One would judge the quality of a car by several *discrete and tangible* features – its comfort, its power, its running costs, its manoeuvrability. Customers judge the quality of services on the strength of their tangible features too. But, as Berry and Parasuraman (1991) point out (on the basis of ongoing research), customers also evaluate services on the basis of

- its reliability
- its empathy
- its responsiveness
- its assurance.

The tangibles of a service (the rooms, the frequency of flights, the itinerary of a tour) and its reliability (cleanliness, punctuality, et cetera) constitute what Gronroos (1982) calls the *technical quality* of a service. The other three factors, could be said to contribute to the *functional quality* of the product but are also more difficult to measure and control for consistency.

The importance of each of these determinants to a customer, and their evaluation of a firm's service can be researched by its management. But this step by itself is not enough to ensure service quality. To illustrate how a shortfall in service quality appears even after such research, Zeithaml *et al.* (1985) postulated a *Conceptual Model of Service Quality* which identified where 'gaps' might occur, which lead to a fall in service standards and delivery. This is illustrated in the following Figure 11.1.

GAP 1 relates to management's perceptions of customer expectations. As mentioned previously, this can be obtained through various forms of consumer research.

GAP 2 relates to the translation of these expectations into *service quality specifications*. If managements profess a strategic commitment to provide superior quality, then they would and do break down key quality determinants and prescribe specifications for them, in order that quality can be monitored.

Figure 11.1
Conceptual Model of Service Quality

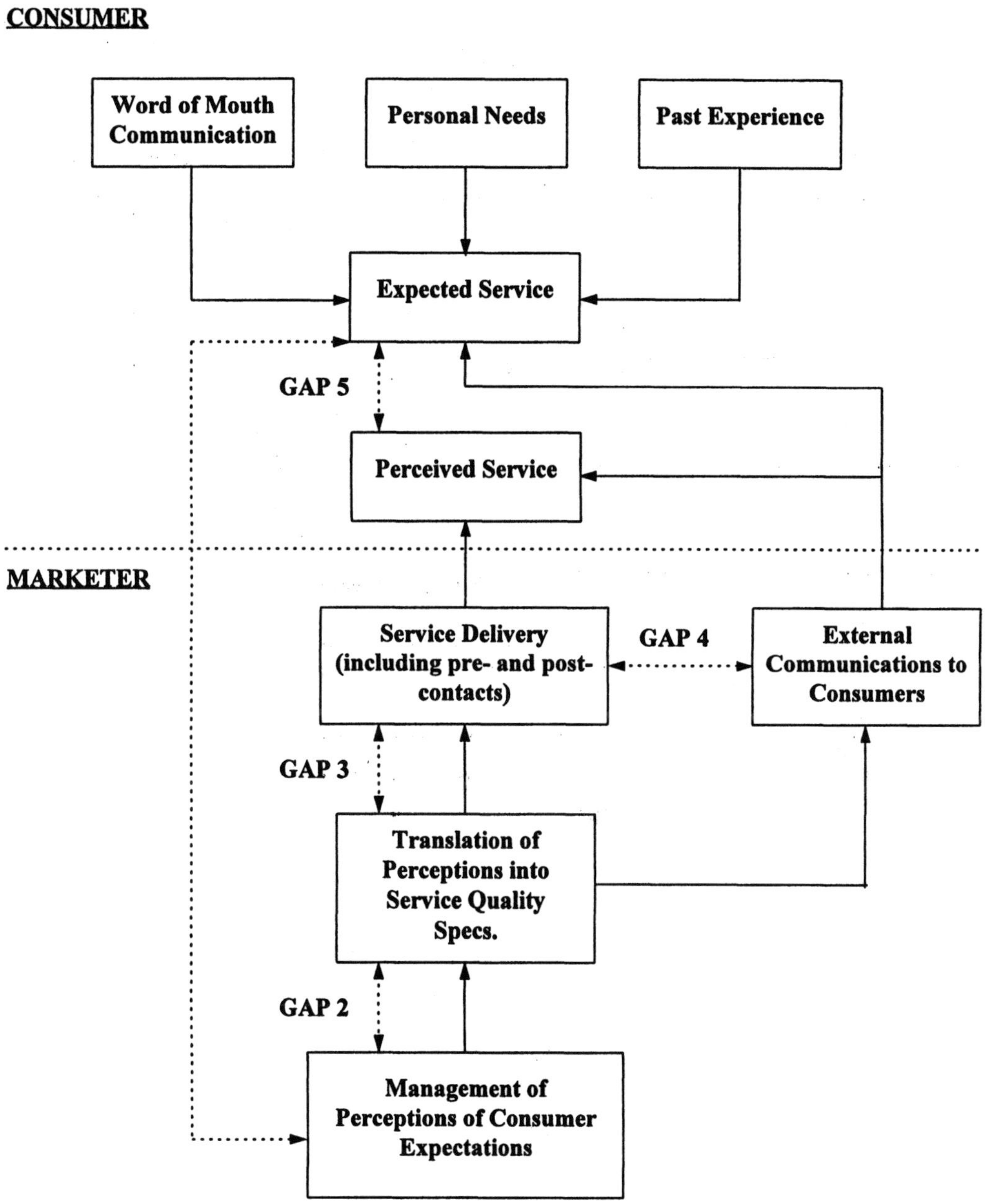

Source: Based on Zeithaml, Barry, Parasuraman (1988).

GAP 3 occurs when delivery is not in accordance with the above specifications. It could occur when ample resources are not provided (staff numbers, support systems, adequate numbers of planes or hotel rooms, adequate maintenance facilities for the same); it could also occur when the human resource employed is not trained and/or motivated to provide this level of service.

The cumulative effects of these gaps results in GAP 4 which leads to service delivery not matching what management promises the customer (through promotional messages), and, as a consequence, matching what customers expect or are led to expect (GAP 5).

This paper, however, looks particularly at what might contribute to GAP 3 occurring in the Indian context. It is therefore assuming that Indian tourism service providers know what their customers expect, are truthful and realistic in what they are saying they can deliver, and that they have a commitment and resources to providing customer-focused quality. But as D'Costa (1994) points out, 90% of the 'moments of truth' that occur in the service environment "take place beyond the immediate control of the senior management and are handled directly by employees who are in the frontline" (p.176).

THE INDIAN EMPLOYEE – THE SOCIO-CULTURAL & INDUSTRIAL MILIEU

Arora (1996) says that the prospects for worker participation in industry is dependent on the balance of power between managements and workers, and that this is contingent upon

- the value system in the country
- its stage in economic development
- the social characteristics of the labour force, and
- the institutional arrangements that exist.

These factors form the basis of this review of literature on the Indian employee. They necessarily interact with each other and feed off each other in producing impacts on the Indian labour force.

It is worth, at the outset, citing the words of arguably India's most respected industrialist of the twentieth century:

> "The worker is a mere cog in a soulless machine. His attitude towards the management becomes one of indifference, mistrust and coldness often tinged with hostility. He is easily led to feeling himself the victim of callous and unfair treatment and little is needed to make him look upon his employers as his enemies and break out into open conflict with them at the first opportunity"
>
> J R D Tata quoted in Silvera (1988: 227)

The interesting point is that he made these remarks in 1943, five years after he took over the giant Tata Iron and Steel Company. Many gathered here might comment that nothing has changed much in the last 55 years.

What was the milieu in those days? According to Silvera (1988), British rule did not inculcate an "industrial culture" in India. Most Indian managements still thought and operated like traders, rather than industrialists. Immediately following independence in 1947, Pandit Nehru's socialist vision of a self-reliant economy, driven primarily by public-sector participation in infrastructure and many core industries, fostered a bureaucratic mentality amongst large sections of the fledgling industrial work force.

Socio-culturally, the Indian worker, has had to move from an agricultural or low-skilled environment to a more modern industrial one, but some writers say he has found it difficult to achieve the level of status and relative equality in society because of the prevailing and dominant Hindu culture (and its casteism) and a perceived superiority of urban culture over traditional rural values (Saur, 1993). Sheth (1979), however, argues, that principal Hindu institutions may be rigid, but they had a "propensity to make adjustments with changing environments" (p.279). As an example, he points to how Indian employers and workers "easily compartmentalise their social behaviour at home and in the office" (p.299). It would appear, therefore, that Hindu religious tradition is not at fault.

But, according to Saur (1993), the Indian education system does not encourage

Coming back to the present, management attitudes to their workers do not seem to help either. They are seen to be paternalistic (Silvera, 1988; Saur, 1993). Silvera (1988) also observes amongst management a

> "surfeit of crawling and cringing before bosses and government authorities and compensating aggressiveness in front of the subordinates; what has been called the lick-above-and-kick-below syndrome" (p.16).

There are exceptions to this, of course; the author quotes Russi Mody (till recently the CEO of the aforementioned Tata Iron and Steel Company) as being quite impatient with "this ji-huzzori (yes sir) business" (p.229). The latter might arise from the employees' view of their manager as a "nurturant and assertive father-figure" (Kakar, 1974). Further, Saur (1993) opines that there is a lack of empathy. When there is a 'father-son' type of relationship between management and worker, it breeds a sense of brittle trust in the latter, which is liable to be broken by "punishment, threats or manipulation" by the former. The implication is that not many employers or managers possessed the egalitarian perspective of the likes of Russi Mody.

Bhattacharya (1993) finds managements not action-oriented; perhaps, he says, they are too concerned with their relationships with the government of the day (Silvera, 1988), than with their trade unions or their workers. Ray (1996) points out that managements today however are more demanding – they want greater freedom to hire and fire employees, for example. But, they still do not emphasise employee development and career progression (echoed by Rao, 1991). The unions themselves appear to face a crisis of confidence once the liberalising reforms of the 1980s started gathering pace with active government backing.

Venkatraman and Srivatsava (1991) point out mandatory employee welfare measures are often ignored. EIS (Employee Insurance Scheme) coverage is low even in the organised sector. The fact that some state governments (under whose jurisdiction this falls) are tardy in enforcing coverage does not help matters.

Some writers do not exempt academia or educated management either from bearing some responsibility for this divide. Chatterjee (1984) decried the buzzword – "the barefoot manager" – as "political claptrap" coming as it does from urban, middle-class, bourgeois protagonists.

What about the workers themselves? Sharma and Singh (1991) conducted an organisational climate study at Hindusthan Computers Ltd (HCL) and found that employees rated their overall organisational commitment at 8 on a 0 – 15 point scale. This was not found to be correlated with the employees' individual education or income, but rather with staff policies (advancement, benefits provided and recognition), job characteristics (work technology and status of position), their own personality (especially conscientiousness) and their previous work experience. HCL employees are, of course, highly skilled. But, Singh (1974) found much the same at the Premier Automobiles plant in Mumbai – in that workers are more committed to the organisation when s/he feels 'a sense of meaning and control over the work process' (p.167) and when they have had prior industrial experience. Interestingly, though, he also found that there seem to be no significant differences between employees with a rural or urban background and that the "socio-cultural background ... is not the most critical factor (p.167)" in developing or inhibiting commitment.

As implied above, status and prestige seem to be an important variable in an employees' satisfaction levels, even amongst middle-level and younger managers (Ganguli, 1974). At the lower levels, though, it does appear that the workers derive pride, recognition and self-worth from their work environment, especially if it involves technical skills.

Is the worker therefore alienated in the western sense of the term? Sheth (1979) argues that this may not be so, but the workers are indeed apprehensive of a widening gap between the haves and the have-nots, and are frustrated at their powerlessness in this regard.

Is there participative management in Indian industry? Virmani (1995) finds that it 'exists on paper', but their working and employee participation in them is undermined by trade unions, who still believe in the power of collective bargaining. But the author argues that the old adversarial role directed against an entrepreneur or his family is no longer valid, since the majority ownership now usually rests with financial institutions, who are often investing the employees' own savings in company stock. Ray (1996) disagrees. He feels trade unions still have a role to play in *empowering* the employee to demand his/her own organisational well-being.

But Sachdeva, Arora and Chaudhury (in Rao *et al.*, 1994) point out that misunderstood empowerment could be "akin to handing over a loaded gun to a person not familiar with it and without explaining the responsibility that becomes his simply by virtue of its being in his possession" (p.46).

In summary, therefore, the Indian workforce is one that still has some way to go in accepting responsibility for their own motivation and innovation beyond what is required of them. In many ways, they are constricted by union power and management attitudes which are not changing fast enough to facilitate or nurture such development.

But there are positive signs. Verma (1992) cites figures from the Annual Survey of Industries which show a 75% increase in real productivity between 1961 and 1985-86, with a concurrent 83% increase in real wages. There are also reported examples of organisations overcoming some of these problems. Silvera (1988) cites Steel Tubes of India's contributory fund schemes and Maruti Udyog's productivity improvements based on the Japanese work ethic of their foreign collaborators, Suzuki Motor Company.

Rao *et al's* (1994) collection of papers from the National HRD Network Conference (on the 'Changing Role of HRD in the New Economic Environment', Jan 20-22 1994, Bombay) include a number of instances of changing attitudes of employees after their companies undertook HR reforms..

Increases in satisfaction were reported on a range of dimensions (communication, job security, performance conditions) at the Modi-Xerox plant after a deliberate strategy to raise employee motivation. Further, once the Indian Telephone Industries plant at Bangalore achieved ISO-9000 accreditation, there was a large increase in voluntary employee participation in decision-making. D'Costa (1994) cites many examples of practices within the Taj Group of Hotels which engender employee participation, motivation and innovation.

This report up to this point has presented a review of HR-related studies undertaken in India. They do emanate from specific geographical and industrial contexts, and in most cases are studies in manufacturing organisations divorced from the need to interact in real-time with actual customers. To this extent, the above review is limited (from the point of view of this report); as yet, though, there is no published evidence of whether, in fact, the average tourism/hospitality industry employee comes from a different socio-economic or cultural milieu, or whether they may have different motivations and career expectations from factory workers. Evidence cited in the next section reveals that this might well be the case to some extent.

As yet, though, there does not appear to be any research on the tourists' (domestic or international) level of satisfaction with hospitality employees. Selvam's (1989) Ph.D thesis surveyed tourists' satisfaction with hotels in TamilNadu. The major problems were with the tangibility and reliability features (Berry and Parasuraman, 1991) of the hotel – e.g. their sanitation, maintenance, adequate facilities etc. Service delivery by employees did not rate either positively or negatively; although the 'people' (the general Indian population) were rated as one of the most satisfying features of foreigners' satisfaction. This might indicate that there is not an unbridgeable cultural divide between Indians and foreign visitors. Incidentally, tour guides were given a very low satisfaction rating by both domestic and international tourists in his study. The reasons for this low rating were not explored.

PRIMARY DATA

Interviews were conducted with HR management personnel from five executives from Welcomgroup-Sheraton, Taj, and Oberoi group of hotels. All these hotel chains are clearly in the 5-star category and have their own management training institutes from which they select their management trainees (they do recruit from other institutions as well). Interestingly, none of them offer operations-level courses. The findings of these interviews are summarised in the sections below.

THE BUSINESS MIX & THE MARKET

The Oberoi group say that 60% of their clients are foreign business persons. But most of the hotels interviewed indicated an approximate 60-40 split in favour of domestic tourists, primarily domestic business tourists and some leisure visitors amongst their international clientele. The foreign businessperson accounts for a higher percentage in Mumbai and Delhi. Their needs, according to the Taj Residency, are for prompt and efficient service and for guidance with respect to weekend leisure activities. Approximately 60% of the hotels' total revenue comes from room rentals, and a further 30% from food and beverage.

None of the hotels saw any difference in the needs and expectations between foreign and Indian business people, because as the Oberoi points out, the latter are quite well-travelled nowadays. At least at the 5-star level though, the employee would need to perform to the same level and excel along the same dimensions regardless of the customer mix.

PERCEPTIONS OF THE HOTEL INDUSTRY AS A CAREER

School-leavers do have a positive image of the hotel industry as a career option. Its desirability is not as high as for careers in Business Management, Medicine or Engineering, but Welcomgroup has no difficulty recruiting mid-level students from Delhi's convents and public schools (in the British sense of the term). This is a view echoed by the Oberoi, Bangalore, but they identify some incorrect preconceptions amongst such students (e.g. the expectations of a rapid rise to managerial positions). Female applicants are also concerned about shift and night work and the 7-day operation of a hotel. Social biases against hotel women workers also still linger even in the larger cities. The same can be said for positions in the kitchen.

RECRUITMENT SOURCES

Most operational level staff are recruited from good high schools and vocational schools. The latter are more relied upon for skilled staff at the Taj Residency, Bangalore. Students should have completed their '+2' level. Greater care seems to be taken in the recruiting for the Front Office (Welcomgroup generally insists on the completion of an undergraduate degree). But at the Oberoi, Bangalore, 90% are graduates having no hotel management skills. The Taj Residency also prefers 'freshers'. Obviously, each hotel prefers to train their staff in their own style and systems. Reservations (affirmative action for members of Scheduled Castes and Tribes) apply; in this sense, not all employees are from an urban, middle-class background.

The oldest Hotel Management Training programme is run by the Oberoi group. Recruits are given a choice of 1 out of 4 streams – Human Resources, Hotel Management, Kitchens and Mercury Travel (their own tour company). Usually selected from the Catering Institutes, based on personality (the 'spirit of hospitality and body language', rather than physical characteristics), they are placed under a mentor and are continually assessed on the basis of key result areas.

By and large, therefore, there does not seem to be a problem in the availability of good trainable personnel; and the vocational schools are (although hotels do see the need to be selective here – there are 12 in Madras alone), quite effective. The Welcomgroup in the South liaises closely with some of these Schools in terms of curriculum. However, the hotels studied in this research are all in the major metros (including Bangalore). Whether there is a problem in smaller cities and resort areas remains to be seen, although Mahesh (1993) points how HR development could be achieved in such areas (using the example of the Taj Gateway resort at Chiplun).

TRAINING

All hotels pay what they perceive is a competitive wage (or stipend during an apprenticeship). The training undertaken is broadly the same and given below are only a few special training inputs provided by these hotels.

The Taj Group undertakes a Training Needs Analysis which is approved by Head Office. The Taj Residency in Bangalore is obliged to recruit from rural areas. They take them initially to fill unskilled positions as apprentices (18 months in Housekeeping and 3 years in Kitchens). They spend up to 1 year in the Training Centre before coming on on-job, during which they also undertake a 3-month exposure to all departments of the hotel. The Oberoi recruits spend 4-5 days in various departments as well during their 3-year apprenticeship.

Ongoing training workshops are conducted by the Taj Group, often conducted by external faculty. They could include role plays, play-acting and are centred around interactive sessions. No managers are present at these workshops.

Executives at the Oberoi also undertake courses in Leadership and Team Effectiveness, as well as advanced courses in Sales and Food and Beverage.

MINIMUM CONDITIONS OF EMPLOYMENT

Labour laws do not recognise the hiring of part-time and casual staff, unlike many other countries. Probationary employees are obliged by law to be made permanent after 240 days uninterrupted service. Some states have laws restricting the employment of women in hotels. Their safety and security even outside the hotel becomes an issue with Welcomgroup sending female employees home by taxi.

INDUSTRIAL RELATIONS

There is no national trade union for the hotel employees. Hotels mainly have internal unions, except in Mumbai (at the Oberoi). The government-run India Tourism Development Corporation hotel have an external union. The Oberoi, Bangalore, does not have a union; they say that their General Manager has a an open-door policy for his employees.

Union power, therefore, is not as strong as in other industries, or even companies – except in Mumbai. There is scope therefore for managements to work from the ground up with unions in improving working conditions and employee motivation.

THE SOCIAL MILIEU OF THE HOTEL

The Oberoi, Bangalore offers various avenues for social interaction and hopefully building a greater team-spirit amongst its employees. They organise picnics, a sports day and two staff parties a year. They also have a Staff Welfare Committee, a Round Table with the General Manager and 10 staff members twice on Saturdays. Their cafeteria is patronised by operational and managerial personnel and its affairs are managed by a staff-run Cafeteria Committee.

Doubtless, this should contribute to an involved, aware team contributing to a sense of commitment and loyalty to their workmates, and to the hotel.

CAREER PROGRESSION

All the hotels surveyed expose the new recruits to all the functional departments of a hotel during their training or apprenticeship period. Multi-skilling across these departments is also practised at the Welcomgroup; where appropriate, a Taj group employee may be moved to another hotel in the chain to provide this opportunity. Having provided employees these opportunities, the Taj and Welcomgroup undertake performance appraisal using quantitatively based instruments. Further progression is dependent on the results of such appraisals.

Career Planning is still in its infancy in all the chains. The Taj group admits that this is not a structured process at the moment and promotion is usually to a more senior role in a smaller property. The Oberoi also now allows supervisors to be promoted into managerial positions (this was not encouraged before), but this is controlled by their Head Office.

TURNOVER

Turnover is highest in the Front Office area; where staff are poached by the hotel's own guests (who may be senior executives in large business houses). Housekeeping also suffers high attrition rates; women do not seem to take the physical demands of the job, according to the hotel executives.

IMPLICATIONS AND CONCLUSION

As mentioned earlier, this survey of hotels' HR practices is very exploratory. The original intention in this study involved a more representative, systematic data collection exercise, but this was to be contingent upon a updated review of HR practices in Indian hotels or service industries from academic sources. This turned out to take a lot longer time than anticipated, which left very little time for a larger, representative study. Indeed even this literature review is by no means comprehensive. The author has the feeling that he has just scratched the surface.

That said, it is not the author's intention to end the study here. Rather this paper clarifies a few issues (summarised below), but highlights further areas for research as well.

Riley (1993) highlighted several dynamics of the hospitality industry labour force, which he said have universal applicability. Those that seem to be applicable to India include

a. The relatively small unit structures of hotels

b. The transferability of skills within the industry, although the hotels surveyed preferred to recruit employees with no hospitality experience.

c. Occupational rigidity within organisations, although hotels seem to be tending towards multi-skilling their employees.

d. High-skilled jobs requiring mastery of complexity, rather than depth of knowledge.

e. Unsocial and often long hours. (p.48)

At the macro-level, there are already long-established government-run Institutes for Catering and Hotel Management in major urban centres, all of whom follow a common core curriculum. In addition, these are well-regarded by HR professionals in the industry. A plethora of private institutions abound, but of variable quality; there seems no central accreditation program for their courses. All together, the Dept. of Tourism (1996) estimates that they are turning out 5000 students per year. 5 food-craft institutes are also planned. The government recognises the need for accreditation. Some work has already been done on this with occupational skills standards for 8 occupations being specified through the South Asia Integrated Tourism Human Resource Development Project.

Management training for this industry is undertaken by the large hotel chains turning out 500 students per year. The Indian Institute of Tourism and Travel Management is attempting to fulfil a need for managers in the broader tourism industry, but their first graduates are yet to complete their course. Two more such institutes are planned. It is proposed to give them the status of a Deemed University.

The broader question posed by this paper is regarding the effect of the socio-cultural and economic environment in India, and its effect on the applicability of Western models of service quality and service delivery. This is the issue that needs to be researched in some depth; and the answers that may emanate may need to be incorporated into the curriculum at vocational schools as well as Management Institutes. One suspects that the Indian hotel employee needs to be resourced, trained and encouraged to accept responsibility and initiate customer service, and even provide uniquely Indian forms of hotel service innovation. But, by the same token, they cannot be expected to perform off their own bat. Hotel managements would need to share much of the responsibility, and perhaps even initiate strategies and foster an organisational climate to encourage such development.

References

Arora, B. (1996) "Private enterprise and authentic worker participation", *Management and Labour Studies*, October, (21)4: 213-19.

Berry, L.L. and Parasuraman, A. (1991) *Marketing Services: Competing Through Quality, Free Press*, New York: Macmillan.

Bhattacharya, S.K. (1989) *Achieving Managerial Excellence: Insights from India's Organisations*, New Delhi: McMillan.

Chatterjee, N.N. (1984) *Industrial Relations in India's Developing Economy*, Calcutta, India: Allied Books.

D'Costa, L. (1994) "The role of the human resources factor in the service sector", in T.V. Rao, D.M. Silveira, C.M. Srivatsava and R. Vidyasagar (eds) (1994) *HRD in the New Economic Environment*, New Delhi: Tata McGraw-Hill.

Department of Tourism, Government of India (1996) *Report of the Working Group on Tourism for the Ninth Five-Year Plan 1997 – 2002*, New Delhi: Ministry of Civil Aviation and Tourism.

Ganguli, H.C. (1974) "Role of status and money as motivators among middle management personnel", *Indian Journal of Industrial Relations*, 10(2): 189-96.

Kakar, S. (1974) *Personality and Authority in Work*, Somaiya, Bombay.

Levitt, T. (1972) "Production-line approach to service", *Harvard Business Review*, 50(5) Sep-Oct 1972: 41-52.

Lovelock, C.H. (1992) *Managing Services*, 2nd ed., Englewood Cliffs, NJ.: Prentice-Hall.

Mahesh, V.S. (1993) "Human resource planning and development", in T. Baum (ed.) *Human Resource Issues in International Tourism*, Oxford: Butterworth-Heinemann.

Rao, T.V. (1991) *Readings in Human Resource Development*, New Delhi: Oxford and IBH.

Rao, T.V., Silveira, D.M., Srivatsava, C.M. and Vidyasagar, R. (eds) (1994) *HRD in the New Economic Environment*, New Delhi: Tata McGraw-Hill.

Ray, P. (1996) "In search of participation", *Management and Labour Studies*, 21(4): 246-41.

Riley, M. (1993) "Labour markets and vocational education", in T. Baum (ed.) *Human Resource Issues in International Tourism*, Oxford: Butterworth-Heinemann.

Saur, D. (1993) "Work value formation amongst young managers", *Management and Labour Studies*, 18(2): 73-80.

Sharma, B.R. (1974) *The Indian Industrial Worker: Issues in Perspective*, New Delhi: Vikas.

Sharma, B.R. and Singh, S. (1991) "Determinants of organisational commitment", *Management and Labour Studies*, 16(2): 63-75.

Silvera, D.M. (1988) *H R D: The Indian Experience*, New Delhi: Newsindia.

Venkatraman, C.S. and Srivatsava, B.K. (1991) *Personnel Management and Human Resources*, New Delhi: Tata McGraw-Hill.

Verma, P. (ed.) (1992) *Emerging Issues in HRM*, New Delhi: Oxford and IBH.

Virmani, B.R. (1995) "Redefining industrial relations", *Indian Journal of Industrial Relations*, 31(2): 153-77.

Zeithaml, V.A., Berry, L.L. and Parasuraman, A. (1988) "Communication and control processes in the delivery of service quality", in C.H. Lovelock (ed.) *Services Marketing*, 2nd ed., Englewood Cliffs, NJ: Prentice-Hall, 406-23.

REGIONAL TOURISM IN INDIA

Chapter 12

BUDDHISM AND THE TRI-RATNA (TOURISM) TRIANGLE OF ORISSA: LALITGIRI, UDAYAGIRI AND RATNAGIRI

K.S. BEHERA
Professor of History,
Utkal University,
Bhubaneswar, India

Orissa possesses an extremely rich Buddhist heritage which includes among others, Buddhist images, *stupas, viharas and temples*. The beautiful Buddhist images of Orissa can vie with the best works created anywhere in India.

It was in this land of Kalinga that the mighty Maurya Emperor Ashoka (269-232 B.C.) was converted to Buddhism after the famous Kalinga War. In the words of his Rock Edict XIII.

"When Piyadasi, the beloved of the Gods, had been consecrated eight years Kalinga was conquered. 150,000 people were taken away from the place, 100,000 were killed there and many more than that died. After that, now that the Kalingas are taken, there commenced in the mind of the Beloved of the Gods, ardent desire for the practice of *Dhamma*, love or Dhamma, and teaching of Dhamma. On conquering Kalinga, there is regret on the part of the Beloved of the Gods".

Thus it is evident that the people of Kalinga, through their suffering, changed Chandashoka into *Dharmashoka*. Ashoka gave up the policy of military conquest and adopted the new policy of *Dhamma* Vijaya which was flavoured with love. It was from this land that the message of peace and non-violence began to spread throughout India.

The conquest of Kalinga by Ashoka led to a phenomenal growth of Buddhism in the province. Ashoka is said to have built a monastery called *Bhojakagiri Vihara* for his brother. It is quite possible that an Ashokan column once existed in Bhubaneswar. In the

1st century B.C., there was a Buddhist *stupa* in Bhubaneswar of which a few railing-posts are left behind and preserved in the Orissa State Museum. In the 6th century A.D., copper plate inscription of Gopachandra, discovered from Jayarampur in Balasore district, refers to the construction of a *Vihara* at Bodhipadraka with Avalokitesvara as its presiding deity. The Chinese pilgrim Hieun Tsang, who visited Orissa in the seventh century, saw more than 100 Buddhist monasteries including the famous *Puspagiri* monastery in a mountain. Many of the Bhaumakara Kings, who ruled in the 8th-9th centuries, were devout Buddhists. In 795 the Chinese Emperor Te-tsong received an autographed manuscript of the *Gandavyuha* from a Buddhist King of Orissa.

Buddhism prevailed in Orissa till about the 16th century, long after it had disappeared in most other areas. Even now Buddhism is a living religion in a few villages of Cuttack district.

This holy land has, over the centuries, seen the growth of several Buddhist establishments. The Buddhist vestiges are now scattered all over the state.

The three jewels among the ancient centres of Buddhism in Orissa are Lalitagiri, Udayagiri and Ratnagiri in Cuttack district, and for all lovers of art these have strong claim to their attention like other Buddhist monuments of India such as Bodhagaya, Nalanda and Sarnanth.

Lalitagiri (charming hill) is a place of natural beauty, which provided an ideal environment for the Buddhists. Even now the hill-top offers fascinating views of the villages and green rice fields all around. The Buddhist establishment, which existed here, has now been reduced to extensive mounds which are spread over the Parabhadi and the Landa hills. A multitude of Buddhist sculptures from the site have found their way into the local museum. The Boddhisattva images of Orissa are some of the most beautiful figures produced anywhere in India and particularly those from Lalitagiri are the loveliest of all Orissan creations. R.P. Chanda, was of opinion that "no connoisseur will hesitate to include the Boddhisattvas found on the Lalitagiri among the most lovely things shaped by the hand of man". They are extremely graceful and are more lithe in body proportions having long and pliable limbs. Among the important images of the place mention may be made of figures of Padmapani, Manjusri, Maitreya, Jambhala, Tara and Aparajita. A colossal image of Buddha, in earth touching attitude, is an outstanding specimen of the Lalitagiri art. Another colossal Buddha head provides an idea as to its original size and its missing lower portions.

Limited excavations conducted by me in 1977 brought to light Buddhist images, imitation Kushan coins, a gold coin of Chandragupta II (now in State Museum), architectural fragments and other antiquities indicating the great importance of the site. Further excavations conducted by the Archaeological Survey of India in a portion of the Landa hill have revealed remains of a few small stupa, an apsidal *Chaityagriha,* and a series of Buddhist Viharas. The stone *stupa,* situated near the site Museum, is unique for having yielded reliquary caskets, which indicate its remarkable sanctity. A large scale excavation of the mounds, is sure to shed new light on the past glory of this great centre. The site, on grounds of epigraphic evidence, dates back to the early centuries of the

Christian Era. The construction of one *Vihara* is attributed to Chandraditya who is identified with the Gupta ruler Vishnu Gupta (C. 6th century A.D.).

The Buddhist establishment at Udayagiri, beyond the Birupa river, sprang up in a semi-circular plain set against picturesque hills. Amidst the ruins can be seen a large rock-cut stepped well and a brick *stupa* with fine images of Buddha attached to it. The existence of monasteries, suspected from an ornate doorframe (now in Patna Museum) and a large image of Buddha in a mound have been confirmed by excavations conducted by the Archaeological Survey of India. One of the hills contain rock-cut reliefs of a series of Buddhist figures. With recent archaeological excavations, the monuments and images are slowly emerging from the darkness of the past to enable us to visualise the glory that was Udayagiri. The seals, discovered from the site indicate that it was known as *Madhavapura Mahavihara* in the past.

Ratnagiri, the brightest jewel of the triad, is located in Cuttack district, close to Udayogiri and about 100 km. away from Bhubaneswar. The nucleus of the monastery-complex dates back to the Gupta period. It assumed great importance during the early medieval period. The *Ratanagiri Magavihara,* like *Puspagiri Vihara* was known throughout the Buddhist world as a great centre of learning, and a rival to Nalanda. The importance of Ratnagiri in the 10th century is documented in the *Pag Sam Jon Zang* where it is stated that Acharya Bitoba went through magic to Sambhala where he obtained the *Kalachakratantra,* brought it to Ratnagiri and explained the doctrine to Abadhutipa Bodhisri and Naropa. The importance of Ratnagiri as a centre of Buddhism was considerable enough to attract the attention of Lama Taranath in the sixteenth century.

The Buddhist monuments, brought to light by excavations, are located on the summit of a low hill. The main *Stupa* at Ratnagiri, is now survived by its lofty base and a few courses of the circular drum, the core of which was in the form of a wheel. The *Stupa* was constructed before the 9th century, over the ruins of an earlier edifice of the Gupta period. The excavation has revealed that the *stupa* was renovated after the 11th century with construction of two circular walls which altered its original plan. The restored *stupa* was subsequently enclosed by a quadrilateral compound wall. Surrounding the great *stupa* are several small *stupas.* Apart from these, Ratnagiri is exceptionally rich in monolithic votives *stupas.*

The Viharas are located, quite close to the *Mahastupa* in the northern area. The monastery No. 1, is the most beautiful Buddhist Vihara of Orissa. The magnificent monastery is quadrilateral in plan with rows of cells along the sides of the inner stone paved courtyard. The entrance-complex of the monastery is quite elaborate with a front porch and a rear porch. The richly ornamented doorway of the Ratnagiri *Mahavihara* is perhaps the only of its type of India. The shrine chamber at the back has a huge seated image of Buddha in the *Bhumisparsa Mudra* flanked by standing figures of Padmapani and Vajrapani. The monastery was built about the 7th century and sometime after the 11th century, a planned overhauling was made to prolong its use.

The plan of monastery No. 2 with open courtyard, cells and a shrine-chamber, is similar to Monastery No. 1 but it is on a smaller scale. The monastery was built on the ruins of an earlier monastery, sometime between the 7th and 11th century. The brick works of the monasteries are exceptionally fine. There is evidence of the ceilings of the cells being spanned by semi-circular arches.

The remains of eight brick temples have been discovered but none of these preserve their superstructures. The only extant structural temple, made in the usual Orissan style, is the temple of Mahakala.

Ratnagiri is rich in Mahayana and Vajrayana sculptures, which are notable for their artistic qualities and iconographic details. Images of Tara, Jambhala, Manjusri, Vasudhara, Heruka, Vajrapani, Dhyani-Buddha. Colossal Buddha heads are among the reach treasures of Ratnagiri. Indeed, with its superb stone statues, stupas and impressive *viharas*, Ratnagiri offers brilliant gems of Buddhist art.

Chapter 13

ROLE OF STATE IN THE DEVELOPMENT OF THE TOURISM INDUSTRY IN ORISSA: PROBLEMS AND PROSPECTS

G.C. KAR
Department of A&A Economics,
Utkal University,
Bhubaneswar,
Orissa,
India

SRIDHAR BEHERA
P.G. Department of Industrial Economics,
Government College,
Angul,
Orissa,
India

INTRODUCTION

Tourism has been accorded the status of industry in India since the VII Plan. The role of the state has become crucial in the promotion of tourism industry especially in terms of the contribution of the tourism industry to foreign exchange earnings and its creation of employment opportunities. In spite of huge tourist resources, India has a very insignificant share of 0.5 per cent of the world tourist arrivals.

Infrastructure is the basic requirement for industry in general and tourism is no exception to it. Basic infrastructure like roads, accommodation, communication and so on are necessary for sustainable tourism development. Therefore, the state has to play a constructive role in the promotion of the tourism industry.

A package of policy initiatives were taken by the Government to develop the tourism sector. The strategy of tourism development aims at achieving the twin objectives of balanced infrastructural development and preservation of Orissa's rich cultural heritage. The Government of Orissa has also formulated policies from time to time in line with the national policy for the development of tourism industry in the state. The present study involves an incisive analysis of the role of state in the development of tourism industry in Orissa.

OBJECTIVES OF STUDY

The present study is based on the following objectives:

- To provide a profile of the tourism potential in Orissa.
- To provide a comparative assessment of the tourism policy of the Governments of India and of Orissa.
- To identify the problems of tourism development in Orissa.
- To explore Orissa's tourism potential and suggest alternatives in state policy for the development of tourism industry in Orissa.

TOURISM INDUSTRY

It is debatable whether tourism is an industry or a service. In this context, three groups of opinion are worth mentioning. One view recognises tourism as an industry because it is related to almost all the areas of the economy and includes all suppliers of goods and services which the tourists require. Tourism according to this approach is a large and highly fragmented industry and the level of Atourist " expenditures reflects the existence and scale of tourism industry. An opposite view is that Athere is no such thing as tourism industry ". Tourism is a collection of several industries with purposeful, direct and indirect links with the tourists. According to this approach, tourism only provides a link between different industries. Third there is an intermediate position. According to this view, tourism industry comprises the organisations in the business of providing goods and services to the tourist and cooperate with one another.

However, because of the economic impacts, profits, employment generation, foreign exchange earnings, most countries have accorded tourism the status of industry. Developing countries are now formulating tourism policy for the growth of this industry through the development of infrastructure. By contrast to this, many developed countries consider tourism as a service rather than an industry since they have achieved perfection in terms of infrastructural development and emphasis is laid on the consumption of services. Thus, in the absence of adequate infrastructural facilities in the developing countries like that of India, tourism is an industry rather than a service.

NATIONAL TOURISM POLICY

In the global perspective, tourism contributes about 6% of world output, one in 15 jobs and 7 per cent of capital investment, and it can double its contribution. The World Tourism Organisation (WTO) forecasts a bright future for the industry since tourism is at the leading edge of the service sector. The WTO also forecasts that the world tourism will shift from Europe to the Pacific region which will account for more than 35% of travel by the year 2000. In this decade and beyond, tourism will continue to globalise, privatise and consolidate i.e. tourism will be focussed on the Liberalisation-Privatisation-Globalisation triangle.

The liberal economic policy in India since 1991 and the move towards privatisation have renewed interest in India as a tourism destination. Nowadays golf tourism is most attractive to the world's highest spending travellers. China is having the major share in attracting golf travellers and the Chinese are planning 400 new golf courses in the next 15 years. Similarly, Thailand now has 50 golf courses of international standard. But in India, although many golf clubs are old, they are below international standard. Therefore, in order to get a larger share of the world tourism market we have to develop new golf courses.

In India, in the early 1960s, the Indian Tourism Development Corporation (ITDC) was established. The main purpose of ITDC was to attract international tourists by providing them with Western comforts. The ITDC was to play the role of a catalyst in developing modern superstructure for foreign tourists. The Government of India also set up infrastructures like Air India International and tourism promotion offices in London and Frankfurt. The private sector was in addition invited to participate in the development of infrastructure i.e. to establish luxury hotels and other facilities for high spending tourists.

Tourism was not a department but a cell in the Ministry of Civil Aviation till the late 1960s. It was later upgraded into a department and Mr S.M. Chib was appointed as the first Director-General of Tourism. He is regarded as the father of India's tourism policies. He gave importance to mass tourism without any bias towards foreign or domestic tourists. He invited UN experts to identify a modern Indian tourist product that would attract tourists. However, the golden triangle of Delhi-Agra-Jaipur still remains the main Indian attraction for tourists. Nevertheless, most tourists did not see India as a holiday destination.

The Tourism Department was separated from the Ministry of Civil Aviation in the 1970s to become independent. In order to strengthen the tourism infrastructure, the State Tourism Development Corporation was established which provided accommodation and transport facilities at the tourist centres. By now almost all the states have a separate tourism department to formulate their tourism policies and strategies for tourism development.

India's tourism policy during the early 1980s emphasised the expansion of international tourism and had the target of attracting 1 million foreign tourists, but this target was not achieved. Similarly, a target of 40 million domestic tourists was set. Yet domestic tourism was never visualised as the main form of tourism development by India's authorities.

Development of foreign tourism was given importance on the grounds of the balance of payments crisis in the country up to the end of VI Plan. However, domestic tourism was given more importance in Orissa's state policy.

The 1 million target of foreign tourist of the early 1980s was only achieved in 1990 and it remains a milestone in the development of tourism in India. In 1992, the National Action Plan (NAP) was formulated by the Government of India (Department of Tourism). It aimed at doubling India's share of the international tourism market from 0.5 to 1 per cent by increasing the hotel capacity to 80,000 rooms in the classified accommodation sector. The NAP also stressed the diversification of products and discovery of new markets like those for adventure tourism, fairs and festivals, golf and other traditional and cultural attractions in the country. This Plan will develop circuits which will cover the main tourist destinations and in this context, the Government of India has identified 11 circuits and 6 destinations for intensive tourism development.

The NAP further encourages private investment in tourism. Along with the NAP-92, the policy of economic liberalisation adopted by the Government of India since 1991 promotes private sector development of the tourism industry. Thus, the decade of the 1990s may aptly be termed as one involving the coincidence of liberalisation, privatisation and globalisation in the tourism and other industrial spheres in India. The Government of India is initiating a campaign to attract investors to the tourism sector. The state governments have been urged to identify their tourist potential and suitable sites for the construction of hotels.

Tourism was accorded the status of an industry in the VII Plan. So the development of tourism industry was listed in the planning process for the first time. The Tourism Finance Corporation was set up by the Government of India in 1989 to provide financial assistance for the development of tourism and tourist-related activities. Several new policy measures were adopted to develop the tourism sector both from the social and economic viewpoints.

In the VIII Plan, tourism policy and strategy was given even more attention. The VIII Plan strategy was mainly intended to develop the tourism sector on the principle of low-costs, high productivity, efficient use of infrastructure, and the promotion of clean and economical tourist facilities. A "Tourism Areas" concept was developed which implies that areas with high tourism potential were to be identified and promoted and given priority for development of infrastructure. All the infrastructural development in the VIII Plan was based on two objectives, namely, balanced infrastructure development and preservation of India's cultural heritage. This policy provided the formulation of masterplans for the states on the basis of the tourism potential present in each state. This policy also focussed on the dynamics of tourism, marketing and publicity, strategies using new technology, co-ordination, innovation and imagination in an attempt to attract the high spending foreign tourists. The VIII Plan gave strategic importance to the role of private sector in tourism with government playing a promotional role.

Apart from infrastructural facilities, various fiscal concessions were given to the tour and travel operators. Concessions were given under section 80 HHD of the Income Tax Act by which 50 per cent of the income earned in foreign exchange by a hotel is exempted from income tax and the remaining 50 per cent is also exempted if reinvested in the tourism industry. Hotels set up in specially identified areas or in the rural areas, hill stations, pilgrim centres were exempted from expenditure tax. The Government of India also provided infrastructure subsidy of 5 per cent on loans advanced for construction of new heritage hotels. The Government plans to liberalise and streamline procedures for recognising travel agents and tour operators dealing with adventure tourism as well as those promoting conventional tourism.

TOURISM POTENTIAL IN ORISSA - A PROFILE

Orissa is an Indian state with tremendous religious and cultural heritage and contains a large number of historic and architectural monuments and vast reserve of natural flora and fauna. The geographical location and climate of the state is unique in India. The golden triangle of Puri, Konark and Bhubaneswar, the Peace Pagoda of Dhauli, relics of the Kalinga war of Emperor Ashok, numerous temples and inscriptions, convergence of various ancient cults, and Hinduism, Buddhist and Jain monuments/caves are special attractions. Its rare sea beaches fringed by extensive mangrove and casuarina forests, Chilika Lake with its beautiful bird sanctuary and rich fishing grounds, the zoological and botanical gardens of Nandan Kanan provides ample prospects for the comprehensive development of tourism in Orissa.

These spots are within the easy reach of large urban centres of Cuttack, Bhubaneswar, and Puri. There are so many beautiful tourist centres scattered in remote parts of the state which are not developed. The tourist centres of the Khurda and Puri districts are most promoted and upgraded and the tourist centres within these two districts are the main attraction for both domestic and foreign tourists. In Orissa, there are 192 tourist centres scattered over 30 districts of the state. Of these 15 are in Puri district (highest) and 12 are in Khurda district. Out of 192 tourist spots of Orissa, only 27 spots located in these two districts are amply developed in terms of accommodation, communication, transport and other facilities.

In relation to the 192 identified tourist centres, maximum number of tourist arrivals during 1995 was at Konark 2,127,450 followed by Nandan Kanan 1,272,202 and Puri 851,782 and the minimum number of tourist arrivals was recorded as 1809 at Vikramkhol (Jharsuguda District). Foreign tourists mostly concentrate on Puri, Bhubaneswar, Khandagiri-Udayagiri, Dhauli and Konark and very few visit other places. No tourist arrivals were recorded at many remote tourist attractions of the state because of lack of adequate transport, accommodation facilities and many of these places are unknown to the tourists. Thus, due to lack of publicity and guides, and other factors, tourism development in Orissa is limited mostly to the golden triangle of Bhubaneswar-Konark-Puri.

Total tourist arrivals during 1995 in Orissa were estimated to be 1,388,468 as against 1,350,049 in 1994 showing an increase of 2.85 per cent over the previous year. The total number of domestic tourists in 1995 was 1,360,267 as against 1,324,025 in 1994 recording a growth of 2.74 per cent. Foreign tourist arrivals were 28,201 during 1995 as against 26,024 during 1994 showing a growth of 8.4 per cent. The number of tourist arrivals in Orissa in 1985 were more than three times those of 1980 and in 1990 about twice those of 1985. But the growth rate of tourist arrivals during the period 1991-95 was minimal. The tourist arrival in Orissa since 1980 is shown in Table 13.1.

Table 13.1
Tourist Arrivals in Orissa, 1980 to 1995

Year	Domestic	% change	Foreign	% change	Total	% change
1980	190,293	35.08	23,941	16.00	214,234	32.6
1985	670,902	15.1	26,134	-7.9	697,036	14.0
1990	1,212,262	7.1	32,191	-1.9	1,244,453	6.9
1991	1,221,116	0.7	29,388	-8.7	1,250,504	0.5
1992	1,264,790	3.6	26,639	-9.4	1,291,429	3.3
1993	1,278,574	1.1	24,856	-6.7	1,303,430	0.9
1994	1,324,025	3.6	26,024	4.7	1,350,049	3.6
1995	1,360,267	2.7	28,201	8.4	1,388,468	2.8

Source: *Statistical Bulletin 1995*, Department of Tourism, Government of Orissa.

The total number of foreign tourist visiting Orissa in 1995 was 28,201 which was only 1.33 per cent of the total number of foreign tourist visiting India. Since 1991, the share of foreign tourists going to Orissa in relation to the total number of foreign tourist arrivals in India has decreased. The number of foreign tourist arriving in India is increasing but the share of India is hardly 0.5 per cent of total tourist flow in the world as a whole. The decreasing share of the foreign tourist arriving in Orissa is most probably due to lack of adequate infrastructural facilities and development of the tourist centres beyond the gold triangle of Bhubaneswar-Konark-Puri. The number of foreign tourist arrival in Orissa in comparison to India is shown in Table 13.2.

Table 13.2
Foreign Tourist Arrival in Orissa vis-a-vis India

Year	No. of foreign tourists arriving in India	No. of foreign tourist arrivals in Orissa	Share of foreign tourist arrivals in Orissa (in %)
1991	1,677,508	29,388	1.75
1992	1,867,651	26,639	1.43
1993	1,764,830	24,856	1.41
1994	1,886,433	26,024	1.38
1995	2,223,683	28,201	1.33

Source: *Statistical Bulletin 1995*, Department of Tourism, Government of India.

The total estimated earnings from tourism in Orissa during the year 1995 were Rs 1,485.79 million of which foreign tourists accounted for Rs 88.18 million. The total inflow of money to Orissa from tourist expenditure has consistently increased since 1989. The total inflow of money from tourist expenditure was Rs 708.21 million in 1989 but more than doubled to Rs 1,485.79 million in 1995. The inflow of foreign tourist expenditure increased from Rs 57.45 million in 1989 to Rs 88.18 million in 1995 showing less than a 50 per cent rise during a period of 7 years. It is thus clear that the flow of foreign tourist to Orissa is not increasing and their expenditure increases slowly. The inflow of money from tourist expenditure in Orissa is presented in Table 13.3.

Table 13.3
Tourist Expenditure in Orissa (Rs million)

Year	Domestic	Foreign	Total
1989	650.76	57.45	708.21
1990	739.59	59.77	799.37
1991	863.69	63.25	926.94
1992	998.54	64.00	1062.55
1993	1087.53	64.34	1151.87
1994	1243.86	74.40	1318.27
1995	1397.61	88.18	1485.79

Source: *Statistical Bulletin 1995*, Department of Tourism, Government of Orissa.

An important feature of tourism in Orissa is that foreign tourist arrivals in the winter season i.e. October-March are much higher than in summer season i.e. April-September. For example during 1995, out of 28,201 foreign tourists, 19,719 (69.92%) arrived during the winter season and 8,482 (30.08%) in summer season. But in case of domestic tourists (excluding Orissa), out of the total domestic tourists of 1,360,267, there were 743,688 (54.67%) arrivals in winter and 616,579 (45.33%) in summer. The maximum number of foreign tourist arrivals was in November (3,859) and minimum (887) was in June. In case of domestic tourist arrivals, maximum was 138,797 in October and minimum was 94,965 in April. It is thus clear that the tourist arrivals in general were highest during October and November.

TOURISM POLICY OF ORISSA

The Government of Orissa has formulated policies for the development of the tourism industry in the state. Its policies are in line with the national policy with some variation to allow for the regional problems. In 1979, the Orissa Tourism Development Corporation (OTDC) was set up to provide infrastructural facilities for the promotion of tourism industry. The OTDC is functioning as a departmental undertaking operating tourism facilities on commercial lines so as to supplement state resources. But the expansion of commercial activities of the OTDC have been very much limited by inadequate resources in recent years. However, the Government provided Rs 5 million during 1995-96 in the form of equity assistance to OTDC. This Corporation is operating 11 accommodation units, 4 transport units and 2 restaurants. But the commercial viability of these units is far from satisfactory due to lack of efficient managerial and the inadequate organisational framework of the corporation.

The Government has identified 192 tourist centres spread over 30 districts for all round development of tourism in the state. Out of these 192 centres only 27 tourist centres in Puri and Khurda districts are developed in terms of available transport, accommodation and service facilities. Tourists concentrate in these centres. But most of the tourist centres are languishing because both infrastructure and service facilities are not available.

There was a target to increase tourist arrivals to the state by 5% per annum during the VIII Plan. But progress in this respect is discouraging. Although there was a small increase in the domestic tourist arrivals, foreign tourist arrivals showed a decline during the first two years of the VIII Plan and slowly increased in later years. But the share of Orissa in foreign tourist at 1.33% of that of India is very low. This is mainly due to lack of vision, enterprise and aspiration on the part of hoteliers and the inadequate infrastructure facilities present in the state.

A number of projects were approved by the Government of India for the development of the tourism industry in Orissa. For example, 4 projects during the VI Plan, 12 projects were sanctioned during the VII Plan and this number increased to 26 during the period 1990-91 to 1993-94. The Government of India provided Rs 8.2 million for 7 projects and during 1994-95, 53 projects were sanctioned with a provision of Rs 31.1 million. However, this financial provision seems meagre in view of the development of a large number of projects. In Orissa, the Tourism Department regularly organises the Konark Festival and Puri Beach Festival and is strengthening the Water Sports complex at Barkul. The Government of Orissa has formed the AGolf Council of Orissa " with the Chief Secretary as the Chairman, to advise, monitor and regulate activities related to development of golf courses in the state as an ingredient of tourism development.

In order to attract more tourists, the Government of Orissa has been involved in (a) the organisation of and the participation in fair and festivals, (b) familiarisation tours for travel writers/agents, (c) sale of tourist literature and (d) advertisements in different media. However, these measures promote a few important tourist centres especially within the golden triangle of Bhubaneswar-Konark-Puri.

It is believed that the growth and diversification of tourism in the state will provide support to flourishing industrial activities and enhance the state's cultural image both inside and outside the country. It was expected that the tourism industry of the state would experience a big boost during the remaining years of the VII Plan. Apart from the on-going projects, 17 new Panthasalas are now under construction with an estimated cost of Rs 25.6 million, tourist complexes, Yatrinivas, Panthanivas, wayside amenity centres and growth of forest-based tourism are also strengthened. During 1995-96, Rs 46.8 million was provided for undertaking different activities for the development of tourism in the state.

Hotels are an essential part of the tourism industry. The growth in the number of hotels in Orissa during 1980-90 was rapid but very slow from 1991 onwards. In Orissa, there are 559 hotels of which 33 are of high standard, 93 are of medium standard and 433 are of low standard. In view of the immense tourism potential of Orissa, the Tourism Department of the Government of Orissa is planning to make joint efforts in association with the Hotel and Restaurant Association of India to expand Orissa's hotel industry. In the wake of liberalisation policy of the Government of India, private hotel enterprises have been increasingly encouraged by the Government of Orissa. The Government of Orissa has formulated an integrated tourism policy to stimulate the inflow of direct foreign investment.

PROBLEMS OF TOURISM INDUSTRY/ROLE OF THE STATE

The problems of tourism development in India and Orissa are more or less similar. However, the present study provides a comparative analysis of the problems of tourism industry in India and Orissa and the role to be played by the state in the development of tourism industry in Orissa.

Nirmal Kumar (1996) while reviewing trends in tourism development concludes that:

1. Tourism is a cause of development both material and non-material.
2. Tourism is an independent variable influencing different sectors like industry, service and transportation.

3. Tourism is an agent of social change.
4. Tourism is not a threat to environment rather it provides impetus to conservation of the environment.

In view of the above considerations, Nirmal Kumar holds the view that tourism can be seen as a promoter of economic development both in macro- and micro-spheres. Thus, logically it follows that tourism promotion can be positively influenced by state effort. The state has to play a positive role in providing the basic infrastructure and other requirements. The role of the state is emphasised because infrastructure such as roads can usually only be provided by the state. The private sector will not usually invest in such infrastructure. Therefore, the state has to take the initiative first and then the private sector.

The Government of India in its Annual Plan 1995-96 has identified four important problems in the development of Indian tourism *viz.*, (a) India's low percentage share in world tourist arrivals, (b) inadequate tourism infrastructure, (c) concentration of tourists in a few areas and (d) the short tourist season of the country. These are common and basic problems which need to be taken care of by the government. In spite of India being a vast country with rich natural flora and fauna, tourists are most attracted to the golden triangle of Delhi-Agra-Jaipur and they still do not see India as a holiday destination. The concentration of tourists occurs in this area due to transport and communication connections. In Orissa, the concentration of tourists is also in the golden triangle of Bhubaneswar-Puri-Konark for similar reasons.

As per the analysis in the previous section the tourism potential of Orissa is considerable but little developed. The tourism industry in Orissa (except pilgrimage tourism) is of recent origin and has to go a long way in future. The state has to play a crucial role in the development of the industry. The problems of tourism in Orissa like that of India are also fourfold, *viz.*, (a) poor tourism infrastructure and management, (b) declining foreign tourist arrivals, (c) concentration of tourists in the golden triangle of Bhubaneswar-Puri-Konark and (d) the short-period of stay of tourists in the state. These problems may only be solved by state effort.

Basic tourism infrastructures like roads, rail and air connections, water and sewerage systems and power supplies are very poor in Orissa and are a major impediment to the growth of its tourist industry. The development and maintenance of roads are in the public sector but technical, professional management and the required financial resources are inadequate in this sector. Similarly, preservation of historical monuments and maintenance of temples, forts are the responsibility of the public sector. But in this sector, managerial expertise is poor and the financial resources are inadequate. More should be done to overcome these problems. State effort is important because members of the private sector such as Indian hoteliers and tourist operators are not willing to invest in the development of infrastructure and maintenance of generic or common tourism products.

Economic liberalisation has had some impact on the tourism industry. Relaxation of foreign exchange rules, and reduced regulations on commission and marketing of tourism products will encourage hotel groups and tour operators to sell India abroad more effectively. Liberalisation measures initiated by the Government of India are expected to have a favourable impact on the hotel and tourism industry. At the international level, globalisation will enhance the level of Indian professionalism for developing, marketing and managing tourism projects. But at the regional level, unless basic infrastructures are provided by the state, liberalisation will have limited impact on the tourism industry in Orissa.

The Indian middle-income groups spend a very low proportion of their income on tourism and holidaying. A relatively high tax burden leaves them with hardly any income to spend on holidaying. The income tax burden on the middle income groups is regressive in comparison to the higher income groups. The higher income groups, especially company executives, spend some income on holidaying and this expenditure is often met by their companies/employers. Therefore, unless the tax structure is liberalised in favour of middle-income groups, expenditure on mass tourism will not increase rapidly and hence the level of tourism development.

The problems and prospects of the tourism industry at the national level are more or less identical with that at the regional level. The importance has always been given to the foreign tourists with the objective of earning foreign exchange for the improvement of balance of payments position. But less attention has been given to mass tourism or domestic tourism by state authorities.

CONCLUSIONS

Tourism is increasingly recognised as an industry and the state has a role to play in its development especially in the provision of basic infrastructure. The tourism potential both in Orissa and India is great but major areas of tourism interest are not developed adequately to attract tourists and consequently a low proportion of foreign tourists come to India and to Orissa. Tourism is concentrated in India in the golden triangle of Delhi-Agra-Jaipur. Coincidentally, tourists in Orissa are concentrated in the golden triangle of Bhubaneswar-Puri-Konark. In Indian tourism policy, foreign tourists are given more importance than domestic tourists. We would favour a more even handed approach.

REFERENCES

Das, S.C. (1996) "An analysis of the working of tourism industry of Orissa", *The Vision*, XV: 3-4.

Government of Orissa, *Economic Survey - 1995-96*, Department of Tourism.

Government of Orissa, *Statistical Bulletins*, Department of Tourism.

IGNOU (1996) *Tourism as an Industry* and *Tourism Phenomenon*, New Delhi.

Kumar, Nirmal (1996) *Tourism and Economic Development*, New Delhi: APH Publishing Corporation.

Lahiry, S.C. (1996) A Promoting eco-friendly tourism in Lakahadweep, *Kurukhetra*, September, 35-37.

The Hindi (1994, 1995) *Survey of Indian Industries*.

Chapter 14

Tourism in North Eastern India: Its Status, Visitors' Impressions, Problems and Prospects

K.K. Barman
Department of Economics,
Gauhati University,
Guwahati,
Assam,
India

Bhubaneswar Goswami
Barama College,
Assam,
India

Introduction

Tourism is a complex industry which deals with the physical, psychological and spiritual demands of people. The status of tourism industry depends mainly on the type of facilities and services offered to tourists and the nature of tourist item which may attract the visitors to a particular area. Visitors who are generally used to travelling to diverse economic, cultural and geographical areas have different motives, interests and preferences but mostly look into the richness of the tourist resources in an area before visiting it. The appeal of tourism resources is generally determined by factors like climate, seasons, accessibility, available accommodation, safety and security, attitudes of the local people, recreational facilities and the atmosphere of interaction among the guests and the hosts.

Natural, socio-cultural and man-made objects in an area, constitute the totality of its tourist resources.

In summary, most of the tourist attractiveness of a particular region (j) may be represented by

$$T(j) = f(Nj, Sj, Hj, Rj, Ij), \text{ where}$$

Tj = Total tourist attractiveness of a region,

Nj = Natural factors,

Sj = Social factors,

Hj = Historical factors,

Rj = Recreational factors including shopping opportunities,

Ij = Accommodation and accessibility above those of minimal touristic quality.

This contribution considers the attraction of North Eastern India for tourists taking into account factors such as those mentioned above. In doing this, it draws on the results of a survey of 100 domestic and 50 foreign tourists in North Eastern India and provides general information in the socio-economic, demographic, physical and climatic character of North Eastern India - factors which may influence its appeal to tourists. These problems of and prospects for tourism development in North Eastern India are given particular attention.

In order to obtain data, 100 domestic tourists and 50 foreign tourists were interviewed and their comments recorded. Furthermore, 50 hotel owners and eight travel agencies were interviewed. Secondary data were collected from government tourist offices, the North Eastern Council Secretariat, Shillong, and from important publications.

BRIEF INTRODUCTION TO THE NORTH EAST INDIA

North East India is comprised of seven States: Assam, Arunachal Pradesh, Meghalaya, Manipur, Mizoram, Nagaland and Tripura. See Figures 14.1 and 14.2. It lies between 21.57 N - 29.30 N. latitude and 89.46 E - 97.30 E. longitude. The region had a total area of 2,55,083 sq.kms. and a population of 31,547,314 at the 1991 census.

North East India is bounded by the international boundaries of China in the north, Bangladesh in the south west, Bhutan and Nepal in the north west, and Myanmar in the east. The region has been separated from Tibet by the McMahon Line, a boundary line drawn up by Sir Henry McMahon and agreed upon by the representatives India and China in 1914 [but the subject of dispute by China under Mao Zedong]. More than two-thirds of the total area of the region is covered by hills (Goswami, 1988). The northern part of the region is protected by the hill ranges of the great Himalayan mountains. The entire North-East is connected by a narrow corridor of West Bengal with the rest of India. This corridor has approximately a width of 33 km in the eastern side and 21 km in the western side. So the region has limited connection to the west of India and is relatively remote from it.

Figure 14.1
General Location of North East India

To a considerable extent, North Eastern India is a frontier area of India and population densities are much lower in many of its states than in India as a whole as Table 14.1 indicates. In all states, except Assam and Tripura, population densities are relatively low. They are especially low in Arunachal Pradesh and relatively low in Mizoram. Diverse tribal groups, considerable biodiversity, interesting natural features and forests are amongst the attractions for visitors to North East India.

Table 14.1 also reveals that the rate of growth of population in North East India is rapid. It is much higher than for the whole of India except in Assam. This is one of the factors placing pressure on natural resources in North East India and could undermine their value restraints in the longer run. Some sex ratios, as in most of India, are unfavourable to females. However, in some areas matriarchal societies dominate as amongst the Khasias in Meghalaya and appear to be positively associated with higher female-male sex ratios.

Figure 14.2

States of North East India and some of its Tourist Attractions

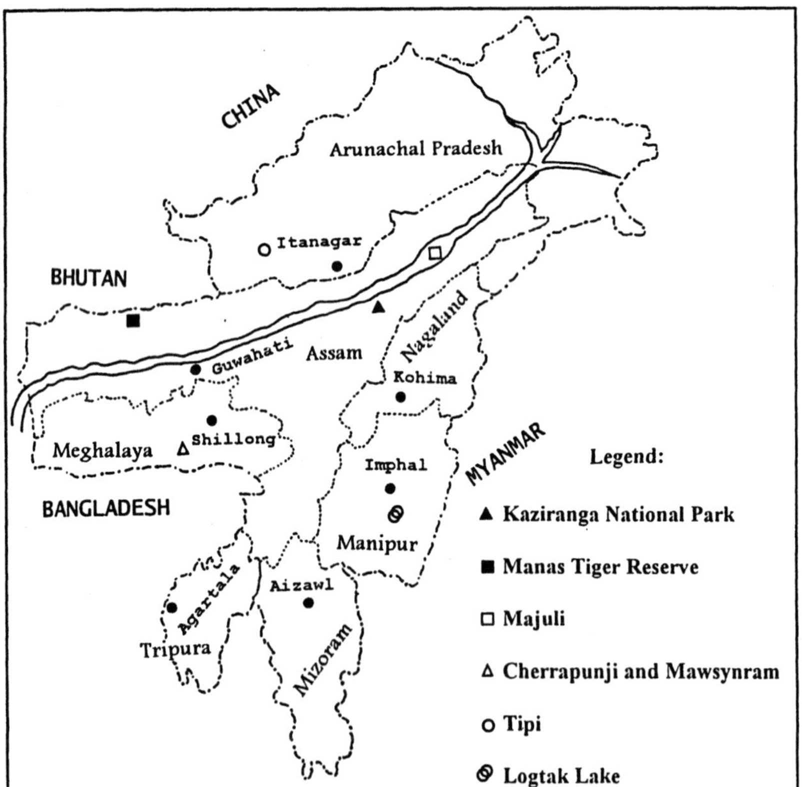

Table 14.1

Population Density, Decennial Growth and Sex Ratio of North Eastern India as at 1991

States	Area (Sq.Kms)	Population (Persons)	Density (Persons)	Decennial Growth Rate (Percentage)		Sex Ratio (Female per '000 Males)
				1971-81	1981-91	
1	2	3	4	5	6	7
Arunachal Pradesh	83,743	864,558	10	35.15	36.83	859
Assam	78,438	22,414,322	286	36.05	24.24	923
Manipur	22,327	1,837,149	82	32.46	29.29	958
Meghalaya	22,429	1774,778	79	32.04	32.86	955
Mizoram	22,081	689,756	33	48.55	39.70	021
Nagaland	16,579	1,209,546	73	50.05	56.08	886
Tripura	10,486	2,757,205	263	31.92	34.30	945
Total	255,083	31,547,314	123	35.87	--	921
All India	3,287,263	846,302,688	273	24.66	23.85	927

Source: *Census of India*, 1991, Series - 1; paper - 2 of 1992.

NATURAL GEOGRAPHICAL FEATURES OF N.E. INDIA AND TOURISM POTENTIAL, ESPECIALLY ECOTOURISM POTENTIAL

The N.E. Region of India consists of four distinct natural divisions: (1) The Brahmaputra Valley, (2) The Eastern Himalayas, (3) The Eastern Mountain Region and (4) The Meghalaya - Mikir Tableland.

(1) **The Brahmaputra Valley**: The Brahmaputra Valley, also known as the Assam Valley, is formed by the Eastern Himalayas, Patkai, Naga Hills, Garo - Khasi - Jaintia and Mikir Hills. The length and breadth of the valley are about 725 kms and 50 - 100 kms respectively. The Brahmaputra is the longest river in India and due to low gradient the river is highly braided and there exists a number of riverine islands. The biggest river island in the world, Majuli, lies here in Assam.

(2) **The Eastern Himalayas**: The region is the eastern most part of the Himalayas that extends to Arunachal Pradesh. A number of rivulets and rivers flow from this region to join the Brahmaputra river in the Assam Valley.

(3) **The Eastern Mountain Region**: Some parts of Arunachal Pradesh and the entire Nagaland, Manipur, Tripura and Mizoram are covered by this region. Innumerable rivers and springs flow through the high rocky mountains and narrow valleys of the region.

(4) **The Meghalaya-Mikir Tableland**: The region covers the area of Mikir Hills, Garo-Khasi and Jaintia Hills of Meghalaya. The Shillong plateau with an average height of 1,220 meters above sea level, is the highest in the central part;

and the eastern and western parts are about 915 meters high above sea level. The Shillong peak is the highest peak of the plateau with an altitude of 1,963 meters above sea level.

The rainy season, in N.E. India, starts during late March and early October every year. Two-thirds of the total annual rainfall occurs during the months of June to September. Of course, the amount of total annual rainfall varies in different parts of the region. In Meghalaya, the intensity of rainfall is 1080 cm in and around Cherrapunji and Mawsynram area. This area is regarded as having the highest amount of rainfall in the world. By contrast, the annual intensity of rainfall is however, low in the rain shadow area in the Nowgong district of Assam.

On the basis of the intensity and pattern of rainfall, the North Eastern region can be divided into three Zones. Zone 1 consists of the north eastern areas of the region up to the north of Dibrugarh (Assam). Zone II includes the areas on the South Dibrugarh and the area covering Kohima in Nagaland, Manipur, a part of the North Cachar Hills, Barak Valley and a part of Mizo Hills. Zone III comprises the western part of the Brahmaputra Valley, Meghalaya and south western part of Mizo Hills and Tripura. The rainfall intensities in these Zones are shown in Table 14.2. The highest level of rainfall occurs in Zone I with Zone III having the lowest level. These are generalised figures.

Although the concentration of rainfall in and around Cherrapunji and Mawsynram is very high, it is located in the low intensity zone of rainfall in Table 14.2. It is a high rain intensity spot in Zone III due to its peculiar topography. The wet season restricts tourism in N.E. India.

Its peculiar physiographic and climatic factors make North Eastern India a paradise for ecotourists. Due to her scenic beauty, the state of Meghalaya is often called the 'Switzerland of the East'. Again, the state of Nagaland is referred to as the 'Scotland of the East'. The hills and forests of the region contain a large variety of rare flora and fauna. The famous one horned Indian rhinoceros occurs in the Kaziranga National Park and the Manas Tiger Reserve of Assam, and is an attraction for the tourists. Tipi, on the bank of river Kameng, has a rich collection of rare species of orchids. The bark of **taxus baccata**, an ever-green coniferous tree, which is found at the high altitudes of Arunachal Pradesh and Meghalaya, has recently been found to be effective against some forms of cancer (Handique, 1996).

Although the forests are an important asset for the development of nature tourism or eco-tourism, recent statistics indicate a serious net loss of forest cover in the North East. The extent of this loss is apparent from Tables 14.3 and 14.4.

Table 14.2
Rainfall Intensity in the NE Region of India (in cm)

Zone	Months			
	Jan - Feb	Mar - May	June - Sept	Oct - Dec
I	10 - 20	70 - 120	240 - 320	20 - 30
II	5 - 10	40 - 70	160 - 240	20 - 30
III	2.5 - 5.0	around 40	160 - 240	20 - 30

Source: Based on Kumar (1991: 6).

Table 14.3
Change in Assessed Forest Cover between 1991 and 1993 in N.E. India (Sq. Kms.)

Name of State	1991			1993			Total Change in Total Cover (2)-(7)
	D.F.*	O.F.*	Total	D.F.*	O.F.*	Total	
1	2	3	4	5	6	7	8
Arunachal Pradesh	54,542	14,215	68,757	54,510	14,151	68,661	-96
Assam	15,842	8,908	24,751	15,998	8,510	24,508	-243
Manipur	5,309	12,376	17,685	5,307	12,314	17,621	-64
Meghalaya	3,305	12,570	15,875	3,305	12,464	15,769	-106
Mizoram	4,279	14,574	18,853	4,238	14,459	18,697	-156
Nagaland	3,351	10,790	14,321	3,487	10,861	14,348	+27
Tripura	1,825	3,710	5,535	1,819	3,719	5,538	+3
Total	88,633	77,144	1,65,777	88,664	76,478	1,65,142	-635

Note: D.F. ' Dense Forest cover O.F.' Open Forest cover.
Source: Government of India, *Forest Survey of India*, 1993.

Table 14.4
Loss/Gain in the Forest Cover in 1993 Assessment as Compared to 1991 Assessment in the N.E. States of India

State	Loss due to			Gain due to			Net (+) Gain (-) Loss
	Shifting cultivati on	Other reasons	Total loss	Regeneration of abandoned shifting cultivation areas	Other reasons	Total Gain	
1	2	3	4	5	6	7	8
Arunachal Pradesh	70	26	96	-	-	-	-96
Assam	165	190	355	104	8	112	-243
Manipur	28	36	64	-	-	-	-64
Meghalaya	110	2	112	6	-	6	-106
Mizoram	256	-	256	100	-	100	-156
Nagaland	63	-	63	90	-	90	+27
Tripura	10	27	37	15	25	40	+3
Total	702	281	983	315	33	348	-635

Source: Govt. of India, *Forest Survey of India* (Ministry of Environment and Forest) Kaulagarh Road, Dehra Dun, 1993.

Tables 14.3 and 14.4 indicate an area of 635 Sq/kms of forest land was lost in the N.E. region between 1991 and 1993. This loss has been attributed by the Ministry of Environment and Forest mainly to the traditional practice of shifting cultivation among the tribal people. The extent to which additional loss is caused by timber felling, illegal occupation of forested land and so on is unclear. Whatever may be the cause, the loss of the forest cover, is a serious threat to the stability of the ecosystems and to conservation of biodiversity of the N.E. India.

TOURIST INFLOWS TO NORTH EAST INDIA AND RESULTS FROM A FIELD SURVEY OF ITS TOURISTS

As can be seen from Table 14.5, N.E. India receives few foreign tourists. Assam is the most frequently visited state, followed by Maghalaya. There are few visitors to Arunachal Pradesh and Mizoram and relatively few to Nagaland. The statistics however are not very recent. It is a problem to get reliable up-do-date statistics for this part of India.

Table 14.5
Tourist Inflow to N.E. India (Numbers)

State	Category	1985-86	1986-87	1987-88	1988-89
1	2	3	4	5	6
Arunachal	Domestic				
Pradesh	Foreign				
	Total		13,886*		
Assam	Domestic	1,82,519	2,13,285	2,51,065	3,01,278
	Foreign	202	463	573	1,000
	Total	1,31,781	2,13,748	2,51,638	3,02,278
Manipur	Domestic	32,735	47,643	70,965	77,549
	Foreign	20	32	63	109
	Total	32,755	47,675	71,028	77,658
Meghalaya	Domestic		65,767	1,78,858	1,55,474
	Foreign		142	194	328
	Total		65,909	1,79,052	1,55,802
Mizoram	Domestic		7,896		16,465
	Foreign				17
	Total		7,896*		16,502
Nagaland	Domestic	14,550	18,870	30,660	40,800
	Foreign	25	36	60	52
	Total	14,575	18,906	30,720	40,857
Tripura		N.A.	N.A.	N.A.	N.A.

* Based on the report of the Survey of Tourism in the N.E. Region, Indian Institute of Hill Economy.
Source: NEC Secretariat.

We interviewed 150 visitors to N.E. India in 1996-1997 mostly in Assam. The origin of these visitors is shown in Table 14.6. The majority were males.

As seen in Table 14.6, the highest number of domestic as well as foreign tourists came from West Bengal (33 per cent) and from United Kingdom (28 per cent) respectively. The largest number of domestic tourists (40 per cent) travelled for business; whereas the majority of the foreign tourists (76 per cent) travelled for pleasure (Table 14.7). Table 14.8 reveals that 75 per cent of domestic tourists made their tour by train whereas 94 per cent of the international tourists came by air. However, one British national travelled by bicycle, the only visitor to do so.

Table 14.6
Origins of Tourists Interviewed in N.E. India, 1996-97

Domestic Tourists				Foreign Tourists			
States	Male	Female	Total	Country	Male	Female	Total
Arunachal Pradesh	0	2	2	Bhutan	3	0	3
Andhra Pradesh	7	2	9				
Bihar	3	1	4	Canada	1	0	1
Delhi	4	0	4				
Gujarat	1	0	1	G.D.R.	6	1	7
Haryana	1	0	1				
Himachal Pradesh	0	1	1	Holland	7	0	7
Jammu & Kashmir	4	0	4				
Karnataka	3	0	3	Israel	1	0	1
Kerrala	1	1	2				
Meghalaya	2	0	2	Italy	1	1	2
Maharastra	1	0	1				
Manipur	1	1	2	Japan	1	3	4
Orissa	5	0	5				
Punjab	3	0	3	Sweden	3	2	5
Rajasthan	10	0	10				
Tamilnadu	11	1	12	United	11	3	14
Uttar Pradesh	1	0	1	Kingdom			
West Bengal	30	3	33	U.S.A.	3	3	6
Total	88	12	100		37	13	50

Source: Authors' field study.

Table 14.7
Purpose of Journey of Tourists Interviewed (Numbers of Tourists)

Purpose	Domestic Tourists	Foreign Tourists
Business	40	2
Official	20	2
Pleasure Trip	31	38
Education	2	1
Visiting Friends	2	4
& Relatives	5	3
Pilgrims		
Total	100	50

Source: Authors' field study.

Table 14.8
Means of Transport used by the Tourists Interviewed

Means of Transport	Domestic Tourists	Foreign Tourists
Own conveyance (motor vehicle)	3	2
Chartered bus/taxi	10	0
Rail transport	75	0
Road transport	6	0
Air transport	6	47
Any other (bicycle)	0	1
Total	100	50

Source: Authors' field study.

Table 14.9 reveals that most domestic tourists to N.E. India did not stay in star-rated hotels whereas the majority of foreign tourists to N.E. India stayed in star-rated hotels or government tourist lodges. Government tourist lodges and star hotels were equally popular with foreign tourists.

Table 14.9
Accommodation of the Tourists Interviewed

Accommodation	Domestic Tourists	Foreign Tourists
4/3/2 Star Hotels	4	20
Non-Star Hotels	36	0
Govt. Tourist Lodges	15	20
Dormitory	11	0
Friends & Relatives	10	4
Govt. Rest House	1	4
Trade Fair Complex	19	0
Private Lodge	4	2
Total	100	50

Source: Authors' field study.

Tourists interviewed were asked to rate a number of the factors mentioned in the introduction to this essay, and believed to be important in assessing the degree of appeal of a tourist use. Domestic tourists rated natural beauty, pilgrimage sites and parks and sanctuaries most highly. Foreign tourists rated these factors highly also except for pilgrimage sites which on the whole would not have been of much interest to them. Relatively, foreign tourists ranked parks and sanctuaries much higher than domestic tourists. Historical monuments, local customs and traditions and mixing with local people did not on the whole rank high on the pleasure/satisfaction scale of the tourists sampled. Note that numbers for domestic tourists in Table 14.10 do not add to 100 for domestic tourists and 50 for foreign tourists because not all tourists interviewed provided a rating. 55 per cent and 25 per cent respectively of domestic tourists rated the natural beauty of the region and its parks and sanctuaries as excellent; 60 per cent and another 62 per cent of the overseas tourists rated these two respective items as excellent.

Table 14.10
'Ratings of Tourists' Interviewed of Pleasure or Satisfaction from Tourism Attractions in N.E. India (Number responding)

	Ratings(Domestic)			Ratings(Foreign)		
Pleasure/Satisfaction from	Excellent	Moderate	Poor	Excellent	Moderate	Poor
Natural Beauty	55	38	-	30	14	-
Historical Monuments	7	12	14	4	20	10
Pilgrims	40	22	-	4	22	7
Parks & Sanctuaries	25	17	4	31	5	1
Local customs & traditions	6	10	1	3	8	1
Mixing with local people	3	42	4	6	16	-

Source: Authors' field survey.

The group of tourists interviewed were asked about problems which they may have experienced. The majority seemed to experience no problems. However language constituted a problem for several (reported by 5 per cent of domestic and 10 per cent of foreign tourists) and for some safety and security was an issue as well as the climate. The results are summarised in Table 14.11. Once again not all tourists in the sample responded to those questions.

Table 14.11
Nature of Problems Reported by Tourists Sampled (Number responding)

Pleasure/Satisfaction from	Ratings(Domestic)			Ratings(Foreign)		
	Major	Minor	No Problems	Major	Minor	No Problems
Language	5	27	65	5	22	20
Cheating/theft etc.	1	8	78	-	1	44
Safety & Security	6	6	78	-	5	40
Climate/Weather	5	7	58	-	1	37
Shopping/Marketing	-	4	35	-	5	29
Transport	-	8	35	2	6	30
Medical	1	1	10	-	-	18
Conducted tour	2	14	1	-	-	14
Accommodation	3	9	68	-	7	37

Source: Authors' field survey.

Some respondents found accommodation to be a problem but not a large number. Nevertheless accommodation facilities for tourists are limited in N.E. India as can be seen from Table 14.12. The majority of hotels and tourist lodges (84 per cent) are privately owned. There is only one Indian Tourist Development Commission (ITDC) hotel in N.E. India. State governments provide some tourist and forest lodges.

Table 14.12
Category and Ownership of Hotels/Tourists Lodges in N.E. India 1997

Category of Hotels	With A/C Facility	Without A/C	Foreign currency conversion facility	Ownership ITDC	State Govt.	Private
5 Star Hotel	-	-	-	-	-	
4/3 Star Hotel	6	-	3	1	-	5
2/1 Star Hotel	1	-	-	-	-	1
Tourist Lodge	-	5	-	-	5	-
Forest Lodge	2	-	-	-	2	-
Private Lodge	1	-	-	-	-	1
Non-Star Hotel	6	29	-	-	-	35
Total	16	34	3	1	7	42

Tourists to N.E. India appear to be making increased use of local travel agencies. The number of inbound tourists using the two major travel agencies in the region are shown in

Table 14.13. Use of local travel agencies may help them to circumvent a number of the problems experienced by travellers in N.E. India.

Table 14.13
Number of Tourists who Travelled using two leading Travel Agencies in N.E. India in the period, 1990-91 to 1994-95

	Travel Agencies			
	M/S Jungle Travels		M/S Rhino Travels	
Year	Domestic Tourists	Foreign Tourists	Domestic Tourists	Foreign Tourists
1990-91	1729	60	96	-
1991-92	4981	95	101	2
1992-93	7665	150	210	-
1993-94	8590	200	176	16
1994-95	9895	215	270	29

Source: Data collection from agencies by authors.

PROBLEMS OF TOURISM INDUSTRY IN THE NORTH EAST INDIA

Despite the generally positive reaction of those tourists interviewed to the tourism features of N.E. India, several serious impediments to the development of the tourism industry in N.E. India exist. To some extent, the sample of visitors interviewed represents a particular group. They consist of those who have decided to travel to N.E. India despite the difficulties of doing so. They may be the more adventurous than most travellers and are unlikely to have expected ideal tourist conditions. Other potential tourists are likely to have been deterred by poor conditions for tourism in North East India. These include inadequate tourism infrastructure, insurgency, government permit procedures, inadequately trained tourism staff, variable weather conditions and natural disasters and loss of natural assets attractive to tourists.

Lack of a sound tourism infrastructure is one of the major problems of the tourism industry in the North East India. Transport and telecommunication systems, power and water supply, banking and insurance, hotels and other forms of accommodation are not properly and proportionately developed in the region. Absence of an international airport, unevenly distributed railway networks and poor conditions of road transport in the hills and on the plains, create barriers to tourism in the North East. After 50 years of independence in India, the states of Meghalaya and Mizoram are still without railways. Only Assam,

Arunanchal Pradesh and Tripura are provided with rail services. Nagaland has only 10.45 kms of railway and that passes through Dinapur in the Guwahati - Kibrugarh route in Assam.

Growing violence and insurgent activities have disrupted the development of tourism in the North East to a considerable extent. Ravi K. Wadhawan (1995) remarks in this context "As a matter of fact, in the entire North and North Eastern India, the syndrome of economic backwardness prevails and the stepmotherly treatment meted out to them over the decades has led to insurgency in entire hill - belt of Assam, Mizoram, Tripura, Darjeeling and Manipur".

Government procedures restrict the growth of tourism in N.E. India. Although the Central Government of India lifted the Restricted Area Permit (RAP) system for foreigners in Assam, Meghalaya and Tripura, in 1995, the other four states are still under its grip. Further the Inner Line Permit (ILP) system applies to domestic tourists wishing to visit these other North Eastern states. These restrictions are discouraging the potential tourists.

The North Eastern states are suffering a shortage of trained tourism staff. Tourism related training institutes, either along academic or in professional lines are practically non-existent. This has retarded the growth of professionalism and management skills in the tourism sector. Most of the officials and employees of state Tourism Departments and also of the hotels and tourist lodges etc. lack professional training. Trained foreign-language speaking guides are also scarce. Floods and soil erosion are two major problems for tourism in the North Eastern India. They restrict travel and dislocate ecosystems. Landslides and soil erosion are very common in the hilly areas of Assam, Nagaland, Manipur, Mizoram and Tripura. The situation of Majuli (Assam), the biggest river island in the world, is highly critical today as a large portion of island has been encroached on by the Brahmaputra river.

Encroachment and allotment of forest lands to refugees and large scale deforestation of forests for developmental activities like construction of roads, extension of railway tracks are some other factors which impede the growth of ecotourism in the North Eastern States. Deforestation of forests in the form of indiscriminate felling of trees, regular poaching and smuggling of timbers are also resulting in negative impacts on the ecotourism in the region.

Singh Tej Vir (1992) remarks "unfortunately, tourism grows faster than tourism research which creates a questionable gap for sustainable development of tourism. Meaningful impact research in various environments (ecology, economy and culture) is very much needed for community based development involving active participation of the indigenous population". Unfortunately, tourism research in the North Eastern States is not adequate and little incentive has been provided to academics to engage in this activity.

Nevertheless, the future is not completely bleak for the development of tourism in N.E. India. The Government of India has adopted a number of new schemes for building strong tourism infrastructures in the N.E. India. Gauhati (Assam) and Imphal (Manipur) airports have been proposed to be upgraded to international standards. Air services have been supplemented by introducing some private airlines to the region. The North Eastern Development Finance Corporation has been formed for providing credit and other facilities for infrastructural development. Restricted Area Permit (RAP) have been withdrawn from

Assam, Meghalaya and Tripura since 1995. Financial incentives have been provided to the hotels and tourism related travel industries. Monitoring cells have been formed for promoting adventure sports and water sports in the region. Tourist resorts and tourist complexes have been constructed in different parts of the area for the benefits of the tourists. Trade fairs and tourism festivals are being organised at national and international levels. A host of similar activities are either in operation or are proposed for the near future.

It has been learnt from the defence sources that the Army proposes to become active in the world famous Kaziranga National Park and the Manas National Park in Assam in a bid to check poaching and militancy in the Parks. The presence of Army in these parks should help combat militant activities substantially which will attract more tourists in future.

The tourism industry in N.E. India can be given a further boost by promoting adventure sports like trekking, mountaineering etc. and water sports like rafting, yachting etc. as the geographical and natural environment are suitable for such sports. Foreign tourism in the region can be increased by having at least one international airport in the North Eastern Region. This will increase the accessibility of N.E. India for foreign tourists.

Concluding Suggestions

The North Eastern region of India is an ideal place for nature tourism. There are few places in the world where tourism resources like blue hills and green valleys, exotic flora and fauna, historical monuments and archaeological ruins, multi-coloured fairs and festivals, diverse cultures and traditions occur in such profusion. The Indian Government should make arrangements for making these resources better known in the other parts of the world and encourage tourism development in N.E. India. Government, with active participation of the tourism experts, hoteliers, travel agents and tour operators, should prepare a scientific tourism policy for N.E. India to boost its tourism industry and bring economic and political stability to this part of the Indian sub-continent.

References

Batra, K.L. (1990) *Problems and Prospects of Tourism*, Jaipur (India): Printwell Publishers.

Deka, P. and Bhagabati, A. (1994) *Geography - Economic and Regional*, New Delhi: Wiley Eastern Ltd.

Goswami, P.C. (1988) *Economic Development of Assam*, New Delhi: Kalyani Publishers.

Government of India (1993) *Forest Survey of India*, Ministry of Environment and Forest, Kaulegarh Road, Dehra Dun.

Handique (1997) *Journal of the North Eastern Council.*

Hummel, John (1996) "Nature tourism in Govind Pashu Vihar (U.P.): A case for eco-tourism", in Shalini Singh (ed.) *Profiles of Indian Tourism*, New Delhi: A.P.H. Publishing.

Kumar, Yogi Anand (1991) *Development of the North East Region*, Guwahati, Delhi: Spectrum Publications.

North Eastern Council (1995) *Basic Statistics of the North Eastern Region*, Shillong: Ministry of Home Affairs, Govt. of India.

Rai, H. Laji Pathi (1993) *Development of Tourism in India*, Jaipur, India: Printwell.

Singh, Tej Vir (1992) "Development or tourism in the mountains: An overview", in Tej Vir Singh and others (eds) *Tourism Environment - Nature, Culture, Economy*, Delhi: Inter-India Publication.

Wedawan, R.K. (1995) "Kashmir - A case for economic democracy", in Sanjay Sarma and Yatish Mishra (eds) *Kashmir Tourism to Terrorism*, Delhi: Sage Publication.

Chapter 15

TOURISM DEVELOPMENT IN HILLY REGIONS OF NORTH EAST INDIA: A STUDY IN ARUNACHAL PRADESH

AMITAVA MITRA
Department of Economics,
Arunachal University
Itanagar,
India

INTRODUCTION

Tourism as a significant activity existed long before it was actually identified. Man has been fascinated by the idea of travelling since early historical times. He has had an urge to undergo new experiences, to discover new places and to seek a change of environment. At present, tourism is one of the fastest growing industries in the world. Tourist traffic has been increasing steadily and rapidly from 25 million in 1950 to 476 million in 1992 and as a result world tourism receipts increased from 2.1 billion U.S. dollars in 1950 to 278.7 billion U.S. dollars in 1992 (World Tourism Organisation, 1992). However, the share of India in the world tourism market is negligible i.e. it attracted only 0.38% of international tourists in 1992 although it is the third largest source of foreign exchange earner for the Government of India.

In India, the promotion of tourism was not emphasised in official policies at the beginning of the planning period. Government policies regarding the development of tourism were initiated with the setting up of a separate Tourism Department in 1958, the creation of a separate Ministry for Tourism and Civil Aviation in 1967 and specially with the setting up of a public sector undertaking namely, The India Tourism Development Corporation Limited (ITDC) in October, 1966 (Bhatia, 1983). The ITDC has provided a wide range of services essential for the promotion of tourism. A significant step was taken by the Government in 1986 by setting up a National Committee on Tourism which has representatives from both the public and the private sectors.

India, of course, is fortunate in having multidestination tourist attractions, of which the Himalayas are amongst the most significant. The variegated landscape, scenic beauty, healthy climate, rich flora and fauna and the magnanimous physical environment of the Himalayas are the important pull factors which attract not only domestic tourists but also foreign tourists. However, tourist inflow is limited mainly to the Western and Central Himalayas. The Eastern Himalayas, except the Darjeeling district of West Bengal, does not attract a large number of tourists. In fact, a large number of scenic beauty spots, with snow-clad mountains, picturesque and hilly terrain with colourful people, are located at various altitudes in the North Eastern Region of India. Mountain ecosystems can provide ideal conditions for the promotion of tourism which can help regional growth and rapid economic developments; but the promotion of tourism has been neglected in the development strategy of the North Eastern Region. Hence, this contribution considers the prospects and problems of tourism development in the Eastern-most Himalayan state of India, i.e. Arunachal Pradesh. For convenience, this essay is divided into three sections. The first section identifies and ranks the tourist spots of Arunachal Pradesh. However, the promotion of tourism depends, to a large extent, on adequate infrastructural facilities in the state. So, this section also highlights the relative importance of infrastructural facilities in promoting tourism in Arunachal Pradesh. The second section studies the trend of the inflow of tourists as well as the allocation of funds in the tourism sector of the state. The third section deals with the various anticipated problems associated with the promotion of tourism in the state and the conclusion follows.

BACKGROUND ON ARUNACHAL PRADESH AND THE RANKING OF ITS TOURIST ATTRACTIONS

Arunachal Pradesh, the land of the dawn-lit mountains, is the first Indian soil to greet the rising sun. Nature has endowed this difficult terrain, with unsurpassed beauty. Set in the North Eastern tip of India, Arunachal Pradesh with its snow-capped mountains, its majestic forests, the gurgling rivers and streams, is bounded by Bhutan to the West, Tibet and China to the North and East, Myanmar to the South-East and the Brahamputra valley of Assam to the South. It is a vast sprawling area occupying around 84,000 square kilometres with a population of 86 million (as per 1991 census) and has an international boundary of around 1628 kilometres. Arunachal Pradesh (earlier known as North East Frontier Agency) is the home of twenty-six major tribes[1] and one hundred and ten subtribes and it is acknowledged to be one of the most splendid, variegated and multi-lingual tribal areas of the world. At the

[1] The important tribes of Arunachal Pradesh are Adi, Aka, Apa Tani, Bangni, Khampti, Miji, Hill Miri, Mishmi, Monpa, Nishi, Nocte, Singpho, Sulung, Tangsa, Wangcho etc.

same time, Arunachal Pradesh was known as the Ahidden land" and the "forgotten frontier" before independence. However, the situation has undergone a sea change since independence with the gradual transformation of the economy from the non-monetised to a market economy and the progressive integration of the indigenous people within the national mailstream' which shows a shift from the Nehru-Elwin policy of tribal development, to a policy of progressive integration since the Indo-Chinese border conflict in 1962 (Elwin, 1957; Chowdhury, 1983; Das, 1995).

If we study the development process of Arunachal Pradesh, it is found that the state has achieved significant growth in per capita income, literacy and urbanisation[2] but the structural transformation in the economy which has taken place so far, has been lopsided - the service sector has expanded more than any other sector. Moreover, agriculture has not undergone any significant transformation and modernisation and traditional agricultural practice[3] still remains. The pace of industrialisation is very slow in the state and its industries are mainly forest-based industries and reflect the over exploitation of forest resources of the state. So, our attention is drawn to one possibility of hill area development, namely the development of tourism which has enormous potential.

In order to encourage and plan tourism development in Arunachal Pradesh, it is useful for the planners to identify the potential tourist centres and their order on the basis of an index of natural beauty and their infrastructural facilities on the basis of an index of infrastructure.

The identification of tourist spots and their order has been done on the basis of the following selected indicators:

COMPONENTS OF THE INDEX OF NATURAL BEAUTY

i. Presence of forests
ii. Presence of snow capped mountains
iii. Presence of natural lakes
iv. Presence of flowing water
v. Presence of spring
vi. Additional attracting for tourists
vii. Ideal for developing adventure and sports

---

2 In the seventies the per capita income of Arunachal Pradesh grew at the rate of 4.03% per annum and in the eighties at 4.00% which is much higher than the national average of annual rate of 1.13% in the seventies and 2.76% in the eighties respectively. However, the growth of per-capital income is largely due to the high percentage of central assistance and the smaller size of the state population. In literacy the state has made a very significant progress. With only a 7.12% literacy rate in 1961, the state covered a long route in the course of three decades in achieving a 41.22% literacy rate by 1991. The level of urbanisation increased from 3.70% in 1971 to 12.80% in 1991.

3 Most of the tribes (except Apa Tani) practise slash burn method which is popularly known as jhum cultivation.

In order to find out the order of tourist spots on the basis of selected indicators, an attempt has been made to construct an index of natural beauty. The presence or absence of any condition at any particular site was assigned the value of '1' or '0' respectively from (i) to (vi) indicators. However, in the case of indicator (vii) the scores are given on the basis of prospects of the number of games and sports facilities.

At the same time, the presence of infrastructure is the backbone of the tourism industry. Any tourist attraction is of little value if the place is inaccessible. So, an essential requirement is the availability of transportation facilities which enable tourists to reach the destination. Similarly, accommodation is another requirement for tourism. Every tourist requires facilities although the degree of comfort and the standard of amenities required by him or her varies. In order to upgrade the basic facilities in the tourist destinations, adequate infrastructure is required. So an attempt has also been made to construct an index of infrastructures for the tourist spots of Arunachal Pradesh on the basis of the following indicators.

Components of the Index of Infrastructure

i. Distance from the nearest railstation
ii. Distance from the nearest airport
iii. Road transport facilities
iv. Presence of Government accommodation
v. Presence of private hotels and shops
vi. Presence of postal services
vii. Presence of medical facilities
viii. Presence of telephone services
ix. Presence of banking services
x. Presence of power services (electricity)

As the variables in the index of infrastructure can be quantified so each variable is being weighted by its scoring and then summed up to arrive at an aggregate score. Scoring starts in the form of a scalogram giving unit score to the lowest order function with a multiplication factor to their scores as the function assumes higher order. For example, a dispensary is given a score of 1 point, the primary health centre is given 2 points and a hospital is given 3 points. Then the scores of each variable for the units are added and ranked. Finally, in order to work out the aggregate scores for each site the total scores of both the index of natural beauty and the index of infrastructure for each site are added up and sites are classified as the first order, second order and third order and so on, i.e. from most favourable to the least favourable (Gearing and Var, 1977). Thus, the hierarchy of tourist centres has been worked out which is reflected in Table 15.1.

Table 15.1
Ranking of Tourist Centres of Arunachal Pradesh on theBasis of Index of Natural Beauty and Infrastructure

Sl. No.	Tourist Spots	Index of Natural Beauty	Index of Infra-Structure	Aggregate Score	Ranking
1	2	3	4	5	6
1	Itanagar	7	21	28	1st order
2	Pasighat	4	19	23	2nd order
3	Tezu	6	16	22	-do-
4	Tawamg	6	15	21	-do-
5	Ziro	3	17	20	-do-
6	Bomdila	3	16	19	3rd order
7	Along	4	14	18	-do-
8	Daporijo	5	13	18	-do-
9	Malinithan (Likabali)	4	13	17	-do-
10	Namdapha (Miao)	4	13	17	-do-
11	Dirang	5	8	13	4th order
12	Tipi	5	7	12	-do-

Note:

Score	Ranking
25 and above	1st order
20 - 25	2nd order
15 - 20	3rd order
Below - 15	4th order

Sources: 1. Arunachal Pradesh, India, Department of Tourism, Government of Arunachal Pradesh, 1992.
2. District Census Handbooks, Census of India, Arunachal Pradesh, 1991.

Table 15.1 shows that Itanagar, the state capital, being equipped with tourist attractions and better infrastructural facilities, obtains the first rank among all the selected centres under study followed by Pasighat, Tezu, Tawang and Ziro which are of the second order (see Figure 15.1). There are five centres which fall under the third category and these are Bomdila, Along, Daporijo, Malinithan and Namdapha. Tipi and Dirang fall under the fourth order. They have good tourist attractions but lack infrastructural facilities. On the basis of geographical location, it is found that in Arunachal Pradesh most of the main tourist spots are located in the foothill region. This is because the foothills have better accessibility and better infrastructural facilities which are concentrated mainly near the foothills areas adjacent to the Assam plain. The dancing streams, lush green forests, and wild water of the rivers Kameng, Subansiri, Siang, Lohit are the main attractions for

Figure 15.1
Map of Arunachal Pradesh, India, showing the Location of Tourist Centres

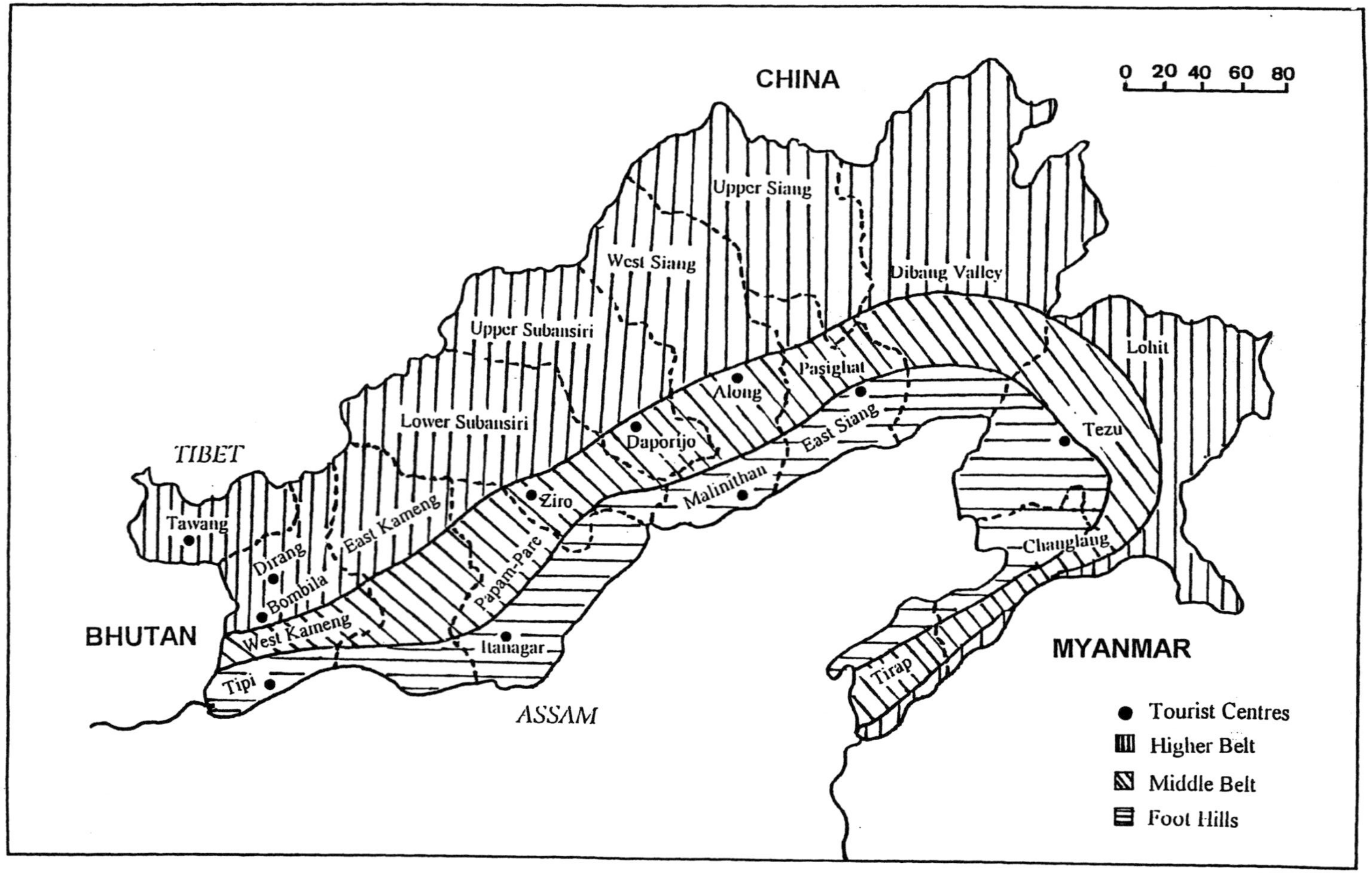

tourists in the foothill region. The historical forts and temples in some places like Itanagar and Malinithan[4] are added attractions for the tourists. There is also located in this belt one pilgrimage centre i.e. Parasuram Kund near Tezu and the only National Park of Arunachal Pradesh, which is at Namdapha. Other tourist services like trekking, river rafting, and angling can be availed of and developed in most of the tourist spots of this area. The middle belt consists of the area between the foothills and higher altitude mountain belt. The middle belt contains tourist attractions such as beautiful valleys, plateaux in the top of hills, green forests, caves etc. There are three tourist spots in our study namely Along, Daporijo and Ziro which are located in the middle belt.

The upper belt consists of land of an altitude between 2000 metres and 7000 metres adjacent to the international borders. The main tourist potentials of the upper belt are the snow clad mountains, high altitude lakes etc. This area is suitable for trekking and hiking and winter sports. There are only three tourist spots namely Tawang, Bomdila and Dirang which are located in the upper belt. They are mainly third and fourth order tourist spots, except Tawang, which has a special tourist attraction, namely a 350 year old famous Buddhist monastery, one of Asia's most ancient monasteries.

Apart from these sites, Arunachal Pradesh has a large number of beauty spots at various altitudes where nature is still magnificent, pure and unspoilt. However, the main problem lies in their remoteness and inaccessibility due to the lack of basic infrastructure. In fact, many of the tourist spots, which we have discussed, lack infrastructural facilities. For example, the nearest railway station from the tourist spots of middle and higher belt is more than two hundred kilometres. These tourist centres also lack proper private accommodation facilities, except Itanagar and Pasighat. So, it needs the serious attention of the planners to develop the basic elements of tourism which are essential for the tourists irrespective of the type of tourism. It is to be noted that a minimum amount of infrastructural facilities are absolutely necessary if tourism is to be sustained in Arunachal Pradesh.

TRENDS IN TOURIST ARRIVALS IN ARUNACHAL PRADESH AND IN STATE EXPENDITURE ON TOURISM DEVELOPMENT

The state has, no doubt enormous potential for attracting tourists from its snow-clad mountains all along the northern boundary to the river scenery of Kamang, Subansiri and Siang, the austere grandeur of the Lohit valley and the lush green forests of Tirap. However, the inflow of tourists in Arunachal Pradesh is very limited compared with the other states of India. The reasons are not only its geographical isolation and infrastructural bottlenecks but also the existence of innerline permits and restriction of movement of foreigners. For example, all domestic tourists are required to apply for an innerline permit

---

4 The Ita Fort of Itanagar was built in the 14th century A.D. Malinithan is another unique site of the 10th and 12th century A.D. It has an ancient temple housing sculptures of gods and goddesses.

for visiting Arunachal Pradesh which is valid for a maximum period of fifteen days only. All the foreign tourists intending to visit Arunachal Pradesh require restricted area permits from the Ministry of Home Affairs, Government of India. Table 15.2 shows the tourist arrivals in the state in the years from 1988-89 to 1994-95.

Table 15.2 shows an increase in the arrival of domestic tourists from 1988-89 to 1990-91 but the inflow of these tourists has fallen since then. Arrivals of foreign tourists commenced in 1992-93 and there is a slow but steady increase in the inflow of foreign tourists to Arunachal Pradesh, although the share of foreign tourists as a percentage of total tourists was only 2.21 in 1994-95.

The low inflow of tourists in Arunachal Pradesh is due to the fact that in the past there was no organised effort for the promotion of tourism in Arunachal Pradesh. Development of tourism in the state speeded up when a separate Ministry of Tourism was created in the late eighties and a separate Directorate of Tourism was set up in the early nineties. The amount of funds allotted and the expenditure incurred in the development of tourism in Arunachal Pradesh is shown in Table 15.3.

Table 15.2
Number of Tourist Arrivals in Arunachal Pradesh, 1988-89 to 1994-95

Year	Domestic Tourists	Foreign Tourists	Total	Growth Rate of Total Tourists (%)	Percentage of Foreign Tourists to Total Tourists
1	2	3	4	5	6
1988-89	2728	-	2728	-	-
1989-90	3410	-	3410	25.00	-
1990-91	3471	-	3471	1.79	-
1991-92	2978	-	2978	-14.20	-
1992-93	2853	26	2879	-3.32	0.91
1993-94	2103	33	2136	-25.80	1.54
1994-95	2209	50	2259	5.76	2.21

Source: Directorate of Tourism, Government of Arunachal Pradesh, Itanagar.

Table 15.3
Details of Revenue and Expenditure of the Tourism Department of Arunachal Pradesh, 1992-93 to 1995-96

Year	Revenue Earned in (Rs. Millions)	Annual Growth Rate of (Revenue) (%)	Expenditure (Both Plan & Non-Plan) (Rs. Millions)	Annual Growth Rate of Expenditure (%)
1	2	3	4	5
1992-93	.377	-	7.80	-
1993-94	.766	103.18	8.90	14.10
1994-95	1.20	56.66	11.74	31.92
1995-96	1.58	32.00	20.84	77.53

Source: Directorate of Tourism, Government of Arunachal Pradesh, 1996.

Table 15.3 clearly shows the allocation of funds to the Tourism Department of Arunachal Pradesh. While these funds are only 0.16% of the state budget, there was a steady annual growth of allocation of funds to the Tourism Directorate between 1992-93 to 1995-96. Nevertheless, greater allocation of funds, i.e., public investment is necessary to build up the tourist infrastructures like accommodation facilities, develop games and sports facilities, if the Government is to be effective in promoting tourism in the state. At this stage however, revenue earned falls far short of expenditure by the state on tourism. Such deficits need to be carefully monitored.

Problems Associated With the Promotion of Tourism in Arunachal Pradesh

The promotion of tourism as a strategy for the development of the hill areas has two sides, - positive and negative effects. There is a group of social scientists who are of the opinion that like other industries tourism has the capability of exerting strong backward and forward linkage effects with a number of other related areas of the economy. Backward linkages pertain to the demand exerted by tourism on input sectors namely transport, the demand for specialised equipment (for adventure tourism), services of tour agents and travel companies. Forward linkages have a more immediate and direct impact on the local economy of a tourist centre. These include the growth of local hotels, local sight-seeing services, etc. Further, local handicraft industries of the state also receive a tremendous demand stimulus for their products with the growth of tourist inflow. So, tourism development can generate much employment both direct and indirect.

Nevertheless, it appears that Arunachal Pradesh may not be able to take full benefit of tourism as an industry. This is because the strategy of development followed during the last four decades has some inherent weaknesses. For example, this state imports most of its consumption goods from outside, even the goods which could have been produced locally. So, the state has become a consumer who produces little which can be consumed by others. Hence, as a result of small economic base and weak internal links, it may have to rely heavily on imports to cater to the requirements of tourists. Thus, the outflow of money may be high and the multiplier effect of tourism in the economy of the state may be low. Secondly, tourism is, no doubt, a labour-intensive industry but at the same time it is seasonal in nature. So the indigenous people of Arunachal Pradesh may not be interested since it does not provide permanent employment opportunities and the private tourist agents have to carry non-insurable risks. In addition, in Arunachal Pradesh it is found that the local entrepreneurs do not independently and aggressively meet market competition (Das, 1995). Their preference is for collaboration with outside entrepreneurs. In such collaborations, local entrepreneurs play a passive role. In most cases, they hire out their license, buildings, machinery and so on to outside entrepreneurs and they collect mainly rent and interest. So the same thing is likely to occur with the development of the tourism industry in Arunachal Pradesh.

However, there is some hope for development of local handicrafts with the growth of the tourism industry. In Arunachal Pradesh, the Government initially tried to develop the local handicrafts through the development of craft centres and protection of the local market. The Government's achievements in this regard were not effective. In spite of the Government's efforts, the local preference shifted towards industrial goods, produced elsewhere. On the other hand, the Arunmachalee people have a tradition of artistic craftsmanship which is manifested through the products they produce (Elwin, 1957). So, with the development of tourism, it is expected that the local handicrafts of the state may receive a demand stimulus which may help in the revival of local handicrafts.

At the same time, environmentalists are worried about the ecological imbalance and environmental degradation brought about by a large number of tourists and their impact on the carrying capacity of the mountainous region. Several studies so far carried out (e.g. Singh, 1992; Paul, 1986; Chakravorty, 1995) of tourism in the Himalayan region have identified negative impacts of tourism on this environment. It is true that the excessive pressure of tourists often leads to rapid exploitation of forest resources made easier by the development of the road transport in the name of better accessibility, inappropriate construction of hotels in tourist spots, the use of firewood for cooking and heating purposes in the hotels, but how much of this is due to tourism is yet to be ascertained.

It is to be noted that the Himalayas on the whole have a fragile ecology. Certain regions within the ranges are too sensitive to absorb the adverse effects of tourism. Arunachal Pradesh is one of them. Although Government statistics show that around 61.5% of the total geographical area of Arunachal Pradesh is under forest, the state suffers from deforestation at an alarming rate, due to the practice of shifting cultivation, large scale extraction of timber and illegal felling of trees. So, it is feared that the promotion of tourism in the state may lead to more deforestation.

CONCLUSION

Arunachal Pradesh has a great potential for developing tourism provided certain infrastructural facilities are provided. There is no doubt that there are some adverse effects from tourism. However, we should take a positive view of tourism development in the hilly state like Arunachal Pradesh. The promotion of tourism is an integral part of mountain development. Moreover, tourism has another important role to play in Arunachal Pradesh. The state has little resources to support itself. Around 85% of its total budgetary expenditure comes from the centre in the form of grants-in-aid (Government of Arunachal Pradesh, 1994). The situation has worsened with the royalty of forest products declining due to the Supreme Court's interim order banning all forest-based activities. These activities had contributed more than 60% of the total revenue from local sources of the State Exchequer. So, alternative internal resources have to be generated within the state itself. In fact, the promotion of tourism appears to be the best way of generating the revenue and it is considered the least ecologically disturbing industry in hilly regions. However, certain precautions have to be taken beforehand so that the negative effects cannot neutralise the beneficial aspects of tourism.

In order to promote tourism we need to plan in an integrated manner and it has to be inter-related with the regional economic and social development. No plan for tourism and its promotion can succeed unless it is integrated with the development of the indigenous people of the state, by providing employment opportunities and means of livelihood. Secondly, rapid unplanned expansion of tourist centres should not be allowed to grow in the state. In fact, the number of tourists should be allowed to move according to the absorption capacity of the tourist centres. Hence, it is suggested that instead of tourists crowding in one or two tourist centres, there should be more tourist centres developed in different districts of Arunachal Pradesh. Thirdly, the Government should encourage tourists who select Arunachal Pradesh as their destination and are not too particular about the standard of amenities available. Such tourists aim to experience the unique culture, religion and landscape in a remote area. So, basic infrastructural facilities should be created in the state where tourists can live along with the local population. This will not only result in economic prosperity of the people but also pave the way for ecologically friendly tourism. This type of tourism does not require the construction of large and expensive facilities. However, care may be taken to control the number and type of tourists by encouraging a healthy guest-host relationship. It is to be noted that the traditional tribal society of Arunachal Pradesh is in transition. So the guest-host relationship needs to be well researched before an appropriate policy can be evolved. Unless tourism is found and practised on a healthy and friendly guest-host relationship, the very purpose of tourism will be defeated.

References

Bhatia, A.K. (1983) *Tourism Development Principles and Practices*, New Delhi: Sterling Publishers.

Chakravarti, P.K. (1995) "Mountain Tourism", in A. Pal (ed.) *The Himalaya-Environment Economy and Society*, New Delhi: Vikas Publishing House Ltd.

Chowdhury, J.N. (1983) *Arunachal Pradesh from Frontier Tact to Union Territory*, New Delhi: Cosmo.

Das, Gurudas (1995) *Tribes of Arunachal Pradesh in Transition*, New Delhi: Vikas Publishing House.

Elwin, V. (1957) *A Philosophy for NEFA*, published on behalf of Adviser to the Government of Assam, Shillong.

Gearing, C.E. and Var, T. (1977) "Site selection problem in tourist feasibility reports", *Tourist Review*, 32(2).

Government of Arunachal Pradesh (1992) *Arunachal Pradesh; India*, Itanagar: Tourism Department.

Government of Arunachal Pradesh (1994) *Economic Review of Arunachal Pradesh*, Itanagar: Directorate of Economics and Statistics.

Paul Chaya Rani (1986) "Development of tourism in Darjeeling Hill Areas (1974-84)", in R.L. Sarkar (ed.) *The Eastern Himalayas, Environment and Economy*, Delhi: Atma Ram and Sons.

Singh, A.P. (1989) *Himalayan Environment and Tourism*, Allahabad: Chough Publications.

Singh, T.V. (1992) "The malaise of mountain tourism: Searching strategies for sustainable development", in Singh T.V. *et al.*, *Tourism Environment-Nature Culture and Economy*, New Delhi: Inter-India Publications.

World Tourism Organisation (1992) *Yearbook of Tourism Statistics*, Madrid: WTO.

Chapter 16

ISSUES IN SOCIAL IMPACTS OF TOURISM RESEARCH WITH REFERENCE TO THE INDIAN STATE OF GOA

SCOTT MCCABE AND JAYNE STOCKS
Derbyshire Business School,
University of Derby,
Kedleston Road,
Derby DE22 1GB,
United Kingdom

INTRODUCTION

The impacts of tourism have been the focus of much academic debate (Mathieson and Wall, 1982). These impacts have been defined in terms of broad categories, economic, environmental social and cultural. Research into the three groups has developed unevenly, with most emphasis being placed upon the positive economic benefits of tourism initially (Burkhart and Medlik, 1981). As the late 1980s wore on, there was a shift in emphasis towards more descriptive research concerning the environmental effects, echoing a more general shift in the public opinion towards concern for the environment and a more sensitive, smaller-scale approach to tourism development. Coupled with this was an attempt to ameliorate the observed social effects after a treatise on the need for community responsive tourism development (Murphy, 1985). However, the social effects in themselves were the subject of only specialised concern by social anthropologists (e.g. Smith, 1989), since the basic theory of the social consequences of tourism was proposed by Foster in 1964.

This paper will chart the progress of social impacts research from these foundations, highlighting what is considered by the authors as a hiatus in this research, namely the neglect of the structural progression of societies as a direct result of tourism development and the inability of research to develop prescriptive techniques for the assessment of social impacts. The authors propose a conceptual framework that could be used to evaluate social changes temporally or developmentally in the same way that researchers consider developmental changes over time. In other words, as resorts develop over time, the communities of those resorts also change, not only in their attitudes (which has been the major focus of research to date), but also structurally. This conceptual model will be applied to the social effects of tourism in the Indian State of Goa and in particular to different resorts.

This paper aims to open up the debate regarding social impacts of tourism especially where previous research has neglected the changing shape and dimensions of societies, and proposes a way forward in the future research of social effects of tourism.

THE IMPACTS OF TOURISM

The impacts of tourism can be grouped broadly into three domains: economic; physical, and; social. It would be wrong to assume that these groups are distinct or that they 'stand alone', as most often, impacts interact and impinge upon one another. For example a benefit in economic terms may result in a negative environmental impact and so it would be impossible to discuss one domain of impacts of tourism without considering the others.

This paper would not, however, be an appropriate platform to review all the interacting and complex impacts that are economic and/or environmental, but a brief overview of the main aspects of these impacts is necessary.

There can be no doubt that tourism has major effects upon the economy of destinations. At a national level, tourism can contribute to an improvement in Balance of Payments. At a regional level tourism can promote economic development and growth, diversification of the economy, create employment and improve services available to the local/regional population (Bull, 1991).

The physical impacts of tourism include pressure on land resources for development which may degrade the environmental or ecological quality of the destination. Unsustainable pressure from visitors causes erosion, noise, visual, and vehicle emission pollution. Physical impacts may also be positive and sensitive to the ecological system of a destination, but environmental impacts research has tended to focus on the negative aspects of environmental impacts as these are much more evident in an aesthetic sense (Gunn, 1994).

Where environmental and economic impacts associated with tourism development occur, there is bound to be a related social impact. This is something that seems to be overlooked by researchers who consider either the economic or environmental impacts of tourism. For example, there is evidence to suggest that there are economic costs of tourism, and these are partially borne by the local population, and are manifested as a perceived and actual social cost of tourism (Mathieson and Wall, 1982). Similarly, the environmental effects of tourism are also partially borne by the communities, and perceived as social cost. However, this is not the sum total of social effects, which will be explained in detail below.

A REVIEW OF THE SOCIAL IMPACT OF TOURISM LITERATURE

It was not long before researchers and commentators noticed that the benefits brought by tourism in economic terms may not be as great as first thought, that due to the nature of ownership of tourist facilities and services these economic benefits may be repatriated to the tourist origin countries, and that the benefits are tempered by costs to the destination nation, region and resort area (Young, 1973).

These costs were identified by Young (in terms of the concept of saturation levels) as conflicts of land use. The demands of tourist developers could be opposed to the land use needs of the residents for homes, open spaces and schools. Secondly, tourism may adversely affect the employment structure of a region in that tourism industry employment can be less productive than other industries, which may depress economic growth. Thirdly, saturation levels concern pressure on transport and general infrastructure. Young argues that traffic congestion, even then, is usually the first saturation point to be reached. However it is a combination of all the above which leads to psychological saturation level in local residents, and a subsequent loss of goodwill towards tourists.

Young's keynote work highlighted the social effects of tourism as confined to the impacts of western tourists on Western, developed nations. Butler (1975) attempted to define more clearly the nature of the social effects of tourism and listed characteristics of the visitor and the destination area, and, a range of others including; distance between destination area and origin; the degree of isolation from other parts, political attitude, and degree of nationalism as factors influencing impact.

Despite it being possible to identify the range of factors, Butler acknowledged the extreme difficulty in attempting to fit all the factors into one model which would explain how a given tourist development could result in socio-cultural change and to what degree that change would be.

Based on research projects in Barbados and Niagara-on-the-lake, Doxey put forward a causation theory of visitor-resident irritants or "Irridex" (1975) which sought to explain the social impacts between visitors and residents by degrees of irritation/tolerance. The four stage Irridex was seen as a major step forward in the advancement of the research, yet it failed to recognise that resident populations are not homogenous groups. However, Doxey's work achieved more, in that it set the tone for future research which has continued right up until the present time and which can be clearly identified in much of the literature concerning the social impacts of tourism in that it focused the attention of researchers on the attitudes of the host population groups as the key indicating factor of the presence of social impacts.

As early as 1964, Foster recognised that the sociological consequences of tourism included changes in the nature and character of employment, patterns of way of life, immigration and seasonality, stratification of wealth, and heightened generational conflict, all of which lead to conflicts integral to which is the changing character of the population.

Many of these areas of change have been left unexplored by researchers, especially those who study Western, developed societies' (destination area) host populations. This is not meant as a de-valuation of the perception/attitude studies of host populations towards the impacts of tourism, indeed the perceptions of the local people may represent the ultimate end product of the above changes in circumstances and indicate how far tourism has developed beyond their control.

However, the perceptions of the host communities must be situated within the context of; stage of development; type of tourist and; type of tourism, as proposed by Williams (1979). One factor that Williams overlooked when detailing his components of domestic impact research is the cultural identity of the host population. The research he reviews consists entirely of North American studies where there may exist a culturally homogenous community, but even there, this is a dubious concept, and in the U.K. it is impossible to imagine, and this is also likely to contribute to conflict. Williams cleverly utilised Greenwood's (1972) theory of stages of tourism development. This he combined with Doxey's aforementioned Irridex and the typology of tourists proposed by Smith (1977), as well as Noroha's (1977) categorisation of tourism on a continuum of "organic" to "induced", put them all in the blender and finished up with the "Interrelation model for tourism development and impact" (p. 20).

Williams points out that;

> "...tourism development and impacts do not inevitably occur as shown. No resort community must evolve through all the stages indicated or experience equal impact."
>
> (Williams, 1979: 20)

However, Williams' model is instrumental in incorporating many of the critical factors which will affect the impacts that will be felt in communities. Factors which many subsequent studies have neglected to consider.

Rothman, in his study of two beach communities in Delaware (1978) found that visitors affected;

> "...virtually every aspect of community life." (p. 12)

Thomason, Crompton and Dan Kamp (1979) assessed the attitudes of local residents, entrepreneurs and service industry employees to long-stay visitors to their community (Corpus Christi, Texas). They concurred with Rothman in their findings that entrepreneurs perceived visitors more favourably than the local residents and service employees (who felt that visitors strained the resources of county services).

Belisle and Hoy (1980) focused on a developing area (Santa Marta, Columbia) and the local residents' attitudes to international tourists. A series of ensuing studies continued to measure attitudes and perceptions usually with some slight variation of emphasis/focus/hypothesis or theme (Murphy, 1981; Sheldon and Var, 1984; Liu and Var,

1986; Pizam, 1987; Liu, Sheldon and Var, 1987; Milman and Pizam, 1988; Allen, Long, Perdue and Kieselbach, 1988; and lately, Teo, 1994 and Ryan and Montgomery, 1994).

The contiguous link between many of these studies is that; without an acceptable tie to a theoretical base, the methodologies are fundamentally weak; an almost total lack of recognition that attitudes and perceptions can be influenced by external factors and that they (attitudes and perceptions) form only part of the fuller picture of social change as previously stated. Ap, in his review of the literature concluded;

> "Unless researchers launch out of the elementary descriptive stage of the current state of research and into an explanatory stage...they may find themselves none the wiser in ten years time."
>
> (Ap, 1990: 614 and 615, respectively)

Certainly the latest studies have not heeded the advice of Ap. Peggy Teo described the socio-cultural impacts of visitors to Singapore and attempted to evaluate the demonstration effect utilising secondary research data. Ryan and Montgomery (1994), sought to evaluate resident attitudes to tourism and planning issues in the Peak District Market town of Bakewell, Derbyshire by investigating the attitudes of residents over the season. However, they fail to reveal the essential social fabric of the community, and its particular problems as they utilised a framework not developed specifically for that destination.

The Conceptual Framework Developed Out of This Review

Researchers of the social impacts of tourism need to recognise the diversity of community types, and the essential characteristics of communities, tourism development types, and characteristics of visitor types when researching the social impact of tourism issues. What is most difficult to achieve is the development of a conceptual model that will describe the interacting elements of impacts together with the social impacts that are prescriptive for all situations. This is almost impossible to achieve without base-line data (i.e. knowledge of the essential characteristics before tourism development occurs), and social impacts researchers do not become interested with the social impacts until the development process is in the consolidation/stagnation stage as described by Butler (1974). However, by taking his model of development, with its recognition of the changes in the structure of development over time as well as the types of tourists that visit destinations, a conceptual model can be developed which may be useful in incorporating the changing social structure and the likely effects of tourism in host communities. This can be used to illustrate how far communities have changed enabling researchers to build these considerations into their social impacts research findings.

Figure 16.1
Model Describing likely Social Impact in Relation to Butler's Cycle of Development and Impinging Economic and Environmental Impact

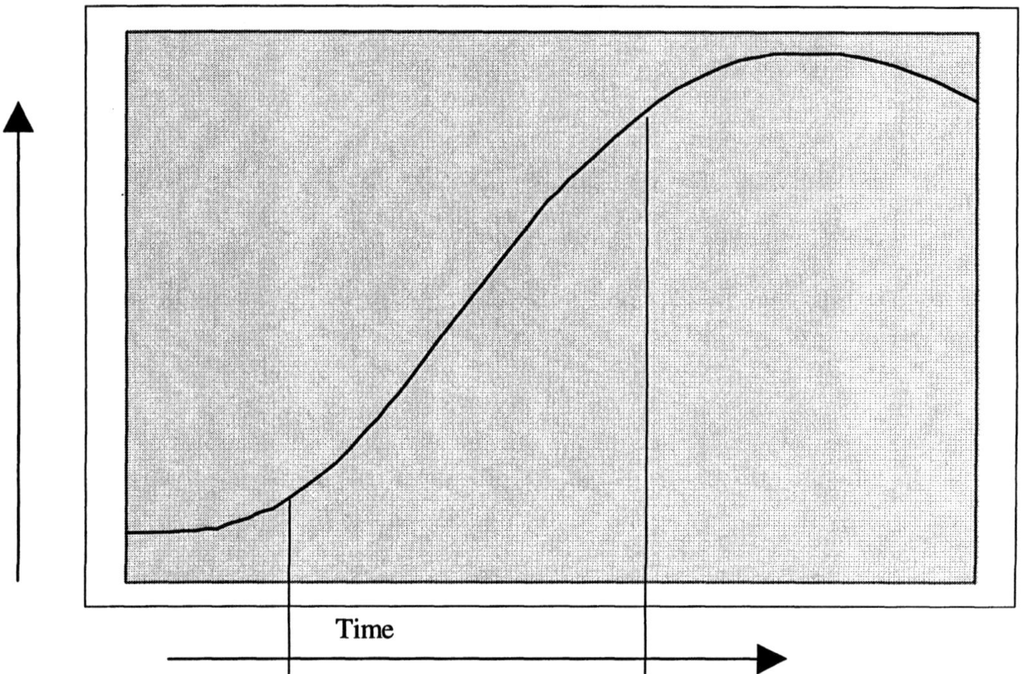

TRADITIONAL PHASE

In this segment, change is slow, and community driven. Tourists are welcome, and contribute greatly to the local economy. Likely to be positive social impacts from tourism

DISRUPTIVE PHASE

Period of rapid change. in the community. Outsiders move in and take some control of tourism. Most likely to be a stage of confusion or mixed feelings, from different segments of the population. Some member of the community will wish to encourage tourism and others will be against development. The social structures and value systems of the community will be changing constantly throughout this period. Social impacts will change and impinging impacts (negative) will become apparent, although not necessarily voiced.

RENASCENT PHASE

Societal change slows down, but is still more rapid than the traditional phase. Society is now almost unrecognisable from the traditional phase. Many original residents will have moved away, community has grown and changed beyond recognition. Economic impinging benefits will fall, whilst negative impacts will increase, environmental negative effects will continue to rise. More conflict and vocalised opposition to development, some traditional residents will oppose tourism, some will not, depending on demographic and other factors. Social impacts will be mixed among the community..

THE CASE OF GOA

Researchers of the social impacts of tourism tend only to conduct research in the 'Renascent' phase, as this paper has termed it, when the essential characteristics of the resort area are irreversibly altered, and vocal opposition to further development, or to the impinging impacts accrued from development in the earlier stages, signals that research is necessary. We accept that it would not be feasible to conduct base-line research in every case, and that community responsive tourism development should overcome some of the most acute problems. What is needed from research and planning perspectives is a clear recognition that social change accruing from tourism development is part of the **impact**, and that social impact is much more significant when this is considered. Research should always take into consideration the stage of development when conducting research and build this into their findings.

From our research visits to the Indian State of Goa, over the last three years, we have noted the changes in the scale and type of development in the different resort areas, and have attempted to evaluate the changes in social structure in various resorts at differing stages of development. We used a combination of methods, including informal interviews with residents, and observations. On the latest visit in January 1997 we also collected survey data in the form of a questionnaire targeted to business people and/or employees. With this last piece of research, we did identify a number of methodological problems with conducting this type of survey of tourism entrepreneurs in Goa. Generally, tourism businesses wanted to impress upon the researchers that their customers were all Western tourists, when this was obviously not the case. Roland Martins, of the J.G.F. and the Goa D.E.S.C., informed us that the Goan business people assumed that Western tourists would be discouraged by the presence of Indian tourists, and so gave us answers that they assumed we wanted to hear. As Westerners conducting research in the Indian context, we were often sceptical about the validity of the findings considering that the respondents did not want to express any concerns about negative aspects of tourism to Westerners. The other major problem was that we were only able to interview people with a sufficient understanding of English, and so we may not have been able to include a mostly hidden, lower-caste migrant population.

Despite these shortcomings, the use of multi-methods has resulted in a clearer understanding of the nature and extent of social impacts in different areas of Goa. We will present the observed and informal interview data, in conjunction with the findings from the survey in a descriptive format, which is more appropriate considering the interrelated nature of the social impacts in this case.

There are many different beach resorts in Goa at different stages of development, catering for different market segments. These range from domestic day visitors (e.g. Miramar), inter-state holiday makers (e.g. Colva), international charter package tourists (e.g. Calangute), Western independent travellers (e.g Anjuna), five star enclave tourists (e.g. Fort Aguada, Taj Hotels) (Evans, McCabe and Stocks, 1996). Within this classification, there are many smaller sub-categories of niche market types, however it is not necessary to detail all the types here. Some of these types of tourist development vie for the same beach space, but there is generally a dominant type of tourism development orientation within a resort area. Each of these identified tourist groups will be analysed according to the resorts they use and the services and facilities required by them, and the likely effects they have on the host communities. The resorts are at different stages of development, which will be analysed in conjunction with the other data.

Domestic day visitors comprise visitors from within the State of Goa, and from other states mainly in the form of coach tours. There is an observable difference in the activities of the two groups. The latter often tour different beaches in Goa, while the former tend to spend a longer time in one resort. We found evidence of both these types of tourists using the same resorts. Miramar is a beach on the Southern outskirts of the capital of Goa, Panaji. It is easily accessible for city dwellers, there were a lot of students on this beach (but there were three colleges in the town itself). The facilities for tourists were few, and comprised; a children's play area, some small boys selling roasted peanuts out of paper cones, four stalls selling commercialised Goa T-shirts, hats, and shell goods; one fixed shop selling cold drinks and sweets; a Goan Tourism Development Corporation complex, with accommodation, bars and restaurants selling Dhosa, Long Dog, and other Indian fast foods. There were no other hotels, although there were a couple of guest houses away from the beach area. This was a resort at the early stages of tourism development in terms of actual infrastructure, yet it has been a resort for a long period of time, as evidenced by the age of the buildings, and the road layout. Considering the length of time Miramar has been established as a resort and facilitated tourism activity, there were surprisingly few observable impacts. The community appeared to rely very little on tourism as a source of income, we noted a driving school, marketing agency and aquarium in the centre of the town. We spoke to one shopkeeper who was happy to have tourism in the town, and said that it was good for business. Yet when we asked her what type of tourists came to Miramar, she told us they were Western, as did the manager of the Goa T.D.C. complex, although we did not notice one single white face among the small number of tourists.

Dona Paulo, around 8–12 kilometres South of Miramar, is a more developed resort, catering to a mixed group of tourists. There were two observable types of group; the Indian day visitors, and the enclave starred hotels for Western package tourists. Dona Paulo is focused around a small harbour wall and jetty with an observation point and gardens. There is a market built up on this jetty with a two storey building on the landward end housing a couple of small shops selling tourist goods (films, sweets, water) and a bar/restaurant above, advertising its special Southern Indian dishes. The market stalls were mostly selling Western style clothing (Goa T-shirts), and cheap, mass-produced souvenirs. The residents of the hotels were not visible along the jetty, although we spoke to a westerner who was staying at the five star enclave resort of Cidada de Goa, across the bay. There was not a beach here of the same quality or size as the other beach resorts of Goa, the sand was dark, not golden, a result of the rocky nature of the landscape. However, there were many jet skis available for tourist use, priced at a level to attract domestic tourists (30 Rupees), something that we did not encounter at any other resort. We did not observe any other economic activity taking place, apart from tourism-related, despite there being fishing boats in the harbour. There were many tourist buses from other states including Tamil Nadu, Maharashtra, Karnataka (parking for around eight small coaches). All stall-holders asked in the survey were of Goan origin, the only migrant workers were found employed at the starred hotels. The owner of the bar/restaurant informed us that tourism led to increases in the migrant workforce, which led in turn to competition for local jobs. Other comments from the survey data indicated problems of Western tourists using only hotel facilities, as opposed to those provided by the local people.

We continued South to Colva, and the resort development there, we found, has altered dramatically over the previous ten year period. It was an established resort for 'hippy' type independent Western tourists, but these have moved away to more secluded beaches and have been replaced initially by 'neo' hippy, younger, Western travellers, and subsequently by inter-state domestic tourists. The resort is at a late stage of development, there is much infrastructure geared around tourism, yet there is also very much a diverse and vibrant economy based around fishing, and a large market in finished goods. There were many peripatetic barrow cart owners selling traditional foods and beverages (e.g. cakes and cane sugar juice), and the finished goods themselves were oriented towards the domestic market (the Goa T-shirts that we had noticed in the other domestic resorts, for example). There were ad hoc stalls on the beach itself offering games of chance (e.g. hoopla) which were very popular with domestic tourists, and the beach shacks were advertising cocktail 'happy hours', which were not evident in the Western beach resorts. The survey data show that many of the people employed in the tourism industry in Colva were local Goan people, and their main concerns were that the number of tourists was falling. The resort appears to confirm this worry, the place appears to be run-down and in decline. Yet the numbers of tourists (domestic) on the beach during the days of our visits have always been high. This could be because we visited on two separate occasions during the weekend, or that the business people interviewed were, again, lamenting the decline in Western visitors, or a combination of both these factors. The impacts on the community were difficult to assess here, the business people in many cases did not want to say anything against tourism per se, the few social impacts that were expressed were that beggars come from other parts of India, and that Southern Indian tourists come in search of women for casual relationships. Roland Martins informed us that the image of Goan women, to the men from other states, is one of easy virtue, and this was a matter of concern to the community groups.

The impacts of the enclave, five star developments have been widely documented by pressure groups within Goa (e.g. Goa Foundation), and in the Western academic scene (e.g. Tourism concern in the U.K.), and enclave development leads to particular impacts. The very fact that this type of development is 'separate' from the rest of Goan society means that the impacts are, to a certain extent, separate, and so will not be detailed here, as this is not relevant to the structure of the communities in a direct, observable sense. This is not to negate the strength of the social effect that this type of development has in a community sense, or in the context of wider Goan society, merely that this paper must focus on its explicit agenda, of documenting and describing the changes in communities as a result of different types of development within those communities. Much more detailed and long term research would be necessary to uncover the extent of the wide-ranging impacts of the five star enclave developments situated apart from actual community space.

Calangute is the prime example of a mass international charter resort development in Goa. It is becoming a sprawling, highly developed tourist resort, with little evidence of non-tourist related economic activity, or the village's original character. Over the last three years we have charted the development process of the resort, noting the continuous stretch of beach from Candolim, through Calangute, to Baga beach, no longer have distinct boundaries, but have become one continual tourism ribbon development. Also, open land within the prime areas of Calangute is now being filled in with new building works and the town is growing as peripheral developments increase. In Calangute itself there is a mix between a majority of international package tourists and a smaller proportion of domestic Indian visitors. A detailed survey of the entire resort was not possible due to the magnitude of the development and the unclear boundaries between the three villages. However, a sample of various types of businesses indicated a high level of immigration from other States compared to the other resorts previously described.

There was a clear distinction between nature of the businesses owned by Goan people and those from out of State. The migrant population tended to own craft related stalls or fixed shops, sold goods and services (jewellery and sarongs, fruit and soft drinks, massages and ear cleaning) on the beach or worked in menial positions in bars and restaurants. We found evidence of migrant workers taking up permanent residence in the village although others moved back to their state of origin in the monsoon season. Goan people owned existing hotels, bars and restaurants, and service sector retail outlets (e.g.: chemists, travel operators, opticians). It was unclear as to the ownership or nature of the new real estate developments although we were told that a proportion of them were to be time share apartments for domestic (Indian) tourists and financed from out of state developers.

The range of goods on offer was much more varied than in the previous resorts. Around the TDC complex on the beach front were grouped a small number of outlets selling similar goods to those found in Mirimar and Dona Paulo, primarily for the domestic market. The remainder of the high number of shops were almost exclusively aimed at the Western tourists, selling 'traditional' artefacts and souvenirs. These included Kashmiris selling carpets, metalwork, jewellery and carvings, Tibetans selling jewellery, clothing and bags, Rajasthanis selling embroidered textiles, crystals and carved soapstone (otherwise sold as marble!) as well as the ubiquitous sandalwood bead and drum salesmen of indeterminate origin.

Here also was a high concentration of private tourist taxi vehicles, compared to the other Southern Goan resorts outlined above. These comprised the traditional taxi vehicles, the Auto-rickshaw, the motorcycle taxis and the ubiquitous tourist mini-vans. Not only were the taxis a barometer of the extent of international tourist development at the different resorts (as the inter-state tourists tended to use organised transport, and the domestic visitors appeared to use their own transport), but also provided a valuable insight into the social issues arising from tourism development. One Taxi driver from Calangute told us about how the State government had encouraged Goans to buy their Taxis, through taking out loans (at 16-17% interest), despite the fact that the season is restricted to the winter months of the dry season, and increasingly the hotels and tour operators arrange their own tourist transport. The drivers must earn enough money in the few short months of the tourist season to pay the loan repayments, licence fees, road taxes, and insurance for the entire year. There is now the added problem of an over-supply of tourist taxis, yet the state Government continues to issue new licences far beyond the actual demand (at a lucrative benefit to itself). What would be seen as potentially a very decent business opportunity (considering the cost of journeys is high compared to other amenities such as accommodation) has become, in some cases, a millstone around the necks of local people. This particular driver was forced to supplement his income by working in the fishing industry in the off-peak season. He also informed us that his (female) cousin, as well as another member of his family no longer lived in Goa permanently, but lived and worked in the Gulf states. The reason for this was that the range and quality of employment opportunities that were available in Goa were not "suitable" for the type expected by Goan individuals. This was not an isolated case, but in the more developed resorts appeared to be a common attitude. In Calangute there were more apparent overt problems and conflicts in a social sense. These conflicts were to do with increased competition for tourist trade by service providers, the amount of migratory labour, and the apparent conflict between local business people and the inter-state tourists (see later in this paper). We noted competition and conflict between food retailers as hotels began to offer meal vouchers to guests, taking trade away from the restaurants and beach shacks. We also noted conflict between taxi operators, craft workers and Goan fishermen, who offered boat trips to see the dolphins and crocodiles in direct competition with the tour operators and hoteliers, at a much reduced rate. One boat owner had been expelled from a hotel for collecting passengers for his boat trip. The charter market that predominates the Candolim, Calangute and Baga area is the focus of this competition and conflict, and this is because of the nature of that market. Charter tourists have little time to adjust, plan their activities, book them and so on. They are transported from the airport to their hotel, given meal vouchers for that hotel, given options for trips on their welcome meeting, and all this service saves much time and effort for charter tourists, who may not feel able or secure in going out there and arranging these services themselves.

North of Calangute is the beach resort of Anjuna. This resort has developed out of being a 'hippy' attraction as long ago as thirty years, and as such it is now a curious blend of this and charter tourism. The beach is separated from the main village areas, at the beach itself is a low number of cafe/restaurants and shops, and at the other end of the beach is the renowned Shore Bar and some small independent accommodation blocks. In the main village are a greater number of shops, cafes guest houses, but there are also a couple of large modern hotels. The mix of tourists has changed at Anjuna in the last three years. We noted more inter-state Indian tourists, and charter Western tourists in 1997 than in the previous years. Our informants told us that the independent travellers had moved on to other, smaller and more peripheral beaches, such as Little Vagator where there are only three beach shacks, and a low number of (very determined) beach traders. Anjuna is still famed for its Wednesday beach market that attracts a mostly charter crowd attracted by the busy, colourful setting and the taste of hippy culture. The independent travellers still can be seen at the market, meeting friends, smoking chillums and drinking chai. Indeed they are increasingly taking over the market at Anjuna. We noticed a distinct shift in the style of the handicrafts on offer to the tourists. The bright techno colours of the clothes favoured by the younger generation 'neo-hippies', body piercing, tattooists, hairdressing, batik work, and jewellery stalls were booming. All these stalls were run by independent, long term travellers, people who stay for the season at Anjuna, then move on to Indonesia, Thailand, Nepal and other South Asian countries to buy new stock etc. The traditional Indian handicrafts section of the market with the bedspreads and cloths hanging from the palm trees by contrast appeared empty in 1997, despite the ever-popular Tibetan jewellery and Rajastani needlecraft stalls doing a good trade. This change seems to be having some social effects. The independents are moving away from Anjuna, many to be replaced by younger, less experienced independent travellers, who flock to the Shore Bar in the evenings, together with the young charter crowd, and the inter-state Indian tourists get the blame for the drop in business. We witnessed a row in a cafe near the beach, where the owner was shouting at Indian tourists for taking a photograph inside the cafe, after we had only a minute or so beforehand done the same ourselves (the reason: a storm in mid-January, a rare event indeed). We learned afterwards that the tradespeople are concerned at the drop in business and attribute this to the rise in Indian tourists coming to Anjuna to 'supposedly' photograph topless western independent women. We assume that because of the dislocation of the village away from the beach area, as well as the type of businesses that are prevalent (small, locally owned, independent) we detected few social changes and impacts, although the rise of the larger hotels in the resort.

CONCLUSION

This paper has contended that the social impacts of tourism research conducted to date has been flawed due to its lack of recognition given the changing nature of societies as a result of tourism development, and that social impacts will vary according to the scale and type of that development. We have proposed a conceptual framework, based upon an adaptation of the cycle of tourism development put forward by Butler (1974), that considers the likely changes in societies throughout the development process. We have detailed research findings gathered over a number of visits to the Indian State of Goa, that clearly identify that the social impacts of tourism vary according to the scale of development, the types of visitor, and the length of establishment of the resorts. We do not claim to have proven the conceptual model, yet we hope to open up a debate that may lead to the development of social impacts research along different lines, utilising time-series data, multi-method approaches, and comparative analyses. In many ways the research we conducted in Goa focused on two levels: at a National (Federal) and Regional (State) level (for example, the price of a loaf of bread is four times higher in Goa, than Bombay (Goa Today, 1996)); and at a local level (the different beach resorts), and this, together with operational difficulties conducting the research, and the multi-method approach, made analysis very complicated. The social impacts are varied, complex and inter-related. Future research should, therefore, concentrate on a smaller range of variables, over a longer period than was available to ourselves to build up a complex picture of the range, nature and quality of social impacts, rather than simply concentrating on limited attitudinal surveys as evidenced in the literature.

BIBLIOGRAPHY

Allen, C. *et al.* (1988) "The impact of tourism development on residents' perceptions of community life", *Journal of Travel Research*, 27(1): 16–21.

Ap, J. (1990) "Residents' perceptions research on the social impacts of tourism", *Annals of Tourism Research*, 17(4): 610–16.

Belilse, F. and Hoy, D. (1980) "The perceived impact of tourism by residents: A case study of Santa Maria, Columbia", *Annals of Tourism Research*, 7(1): 83–101.

Brougham, J. and Butler R.W. (1981) "A segmentation analysis of resident attitudes to the social impact of tourism", *Annals of Tourism Research*, 14(4): 569–89.

Burkhart, A.J. and Medlik, S. (1981) *Tourism: Past, Present and Future*, London: Heinemann.

Butler, R.W. (1974) "The social implications of tourist development", *Annals of Tourism Research*, 2(2): 107–11.

Butler, R.W. (1975) "Tourism as an agent of social change", *Occasional Papers in Geography, Number 5*, Canada: University of Western Ontario, 85–90.

Bystrzanowski, J. (1989) "Tourism as a factor of change, a socio-cultural study", Vienna Centre, European coordination for research.

Davis, D. *et al.* (1988) "Segmenting local residents by their attitudes, interests and opinions toward tourism", *Journal of Travel Research*, 27(2): 2–8.

Doxey,G.V. (1975) "A causation theory of visitor-resident irritants: Methodology and research inferences", *Conference Proceedings of the 6th Annual Conference of the Travel Research Association*, September 1975, San Diego, California, 195–98.

Foster, J. (1964) "The sociological consequences of tourism", *The International Journal of Comparative Sociology*, 5, September: 217–27.

Gunn, C.A., *Tourism Planning*, London: Longman.

Jafari, J. (1982) "Tourism and the host community", *Journal of Travel Research*, 20, Winter: 26–27.

Liu, J. and Var, T. (1986) "Resident attitudes toward tourism impacts in Hawaii", *Annals of Tourism Research*, 13(2): 193–214.

Liu, J., Sheldon, P. and Var, T. (1987) "Resident perception of the environmental impacts of tourism", *Annals of Tourism Research*, 14(1): 17–37.

Mathieson, A. and Wall, G. (1982) *Tourism: Economic, Physical and Social Impacts*, Oxford: Longman.

Milman, A. and Pizam, A. (1988) "Social impacts of tourism on central Florida", *Annals of Tourism Research*, 15(2): 191–204.

Murphy, P.E. (1981) "Community attitudes to tourism: A comparative analysis", *Tourism Management*, 2(3): 189–95.

Murphy, P. E., *Tourism, A Community Approach*, 1983, Oxford, Longman.

Pizam, A. (1987) "Tourism's impacts: The social costs to the destination community as perceived by its residents", *Journal of Travel Research*, 16(4): 8–12.

Riddick, C., De Shriver, M. and Weissinger, E. (1984) "A methodological review of research in Journal of Leisure Research from 1978 to 1982", *Journal of Leisure Research*, 16(4): 311-12.

Rothman, R.A. (1978) "Residents and transients: Community reaction to seasonal visitors", *Journal of Travel Research*, 16(1): 8–13.

Ryan, C. and Montgomery, D. (1994) "The attitudes of Bakewell residents to tourism and issues in community responsive tourism", *Tourism Management*, 15(5): 358–69.

Sheldon, P. and Var, T. (1984) "Resident attitudes to tourism in North Wales", *Tourism Management*, 5(1): 40–48.

Smith, V.L. (1989) *Hosts and Guests – The Anthropology of Tourism*, Philadelphia: University of Pennsylvania Press.

Stokes, C.S. and Miller, M.K. (1975) "A methodological review of research in rural sociology since 1965", *Rural Sociology*, 40: 411–34.

Teo, P. (1994) "Assessing socio-cultural impacts: The case of Singapore", *Tourism Management*, 15(2): 126–36.

Thomason, P., Crompton, J.L. and Dan Kamp, B. (1979) "A study of the attitudes of impacted groups within a host community toward prolonged stay tourist visitors", *Journal of Travel Research*, 17(3): 2–6.

Williams, T.A. (1979) "Impact of domestic tourism on host population: The evolution of a model", *Tourism Recreation Research*, Centre for Tourism Research, December, 15–21.

Young, G. (1973) *Tourism: Blessing or Blight?* Penguin.

ECOTOURISM AND NATIONAL PARK TOURISM

Chapter 17

ECO-FRIENDLY TOURISM AND ECONOMIC DEVELOPMENT IN THE SUNDARBAN BIOSPHERE RESERVE: A CASE STUDY

ALAK GHOSH
President,
International Institute for Development Studies and
Former Head of the Department of Economics,
Calcutta University,
India

PRABIR BISWAS
Faculty Member,
Institute of Business Management and Research,
Calcutta, India

INTRODUCTION

The 1992 "Earth Summit" in Rio De Janeiro emphasised that without better environmental achievement, the development process will be undermined and it is essential that the spotlight shifts to those areas where the poor and the down-trodden people are struggling for existence. High population growth in countries like India have created vicious cycles of soil degradation, high levels of pollution and have impaired productivity. It is alarming to note that one billion people - mostly in developing countries - do not have access to clean drinking water and 1.7 billion people do not have access to sanitation. These are certainly big challenges in countries like India which are trying to implement outward-looking and export-oriented policies for economic development. Tourism industry in India has immense possibilities as a major foreign-exchange earner and the expansion of tourism can contribute to India's economic development. But as protection of the environment is an integral part of the development process, eco-friendly tourism should be properly managed to become an engine of economic growth.

Co-Existence Between Man and Nature

The *World Development Report*, 1992 (World Bank, 1992) emphasises that the protection of the environment should get a high priority during the process of development particularly in the developing countries which exhibit a horrifying level of poverty. Alleviating poverty is both morally imperative and essential for environmental sustainability.

This *World Development Report* highlights the fact that interaction between man and nature can be mutualistic or antagonistic. For instance, exploitation of mineral resources can help the process of industrialisation, a favourable agro-climatic condition can benefit agricultural activities and scenic beauty and other attributes of nature can boost to tourism development in different areas. On the other hand, the conflict between man and nature occurs when there is indiscriminate destruction of forests and unsustainable exploitation of both flora and fauna.

Substantial synergies exist between reducing poverty and protecting the environment according to the World Bank (1992). The World Bank (1992) notes that because poor people are less able than the rich to "buy out of" environmental problems, they are likely to benefit most from environmental improvement. In the study that follows we have endeavoured to show that the Biosphere Reserve Region of the Sundarbans is distinguished by an environmental scenario which shows a dual type of interaction between man and nature - a peculiar mutualistic and antagonistic one. The Sundarbans, because of its unique scenic beauty, and natural attributes has been chosen by the Indian Government for the development of the first International Tourism Centre in India.

The Eco-System of the Sundarbans

The Sundarbans (arguably) constitutes the largest delta in the world. The total area is of 9,630 sq. km. This region forms the southern part of the Gangetic delta between the river Hooghly on the west of West Bengal and the river Meghna on the east of Bangladesh. (See Figure 17.1.) The area covered consists of fifty four low-lying swampy islands formed by the principal distributaries of the Ganges, their numerous water channels and backwater creeks from the Bay of Bengal. It is noteworthy that the rivers of the eastern portion of the forest lying in Bangladesh have connections with the Ganges and Bhramaputra and receive fresh water. Westward, in West Bengal, the rivers have been mostly transformed into mere backwaters of the sea and are consequently more saline than those in the east. The entire delta belt is covered by dense forests and vast saline mud flats. The Sundarban forests in

Figure 17.1
General Location of the Indian and Bangladesh Sundarbans

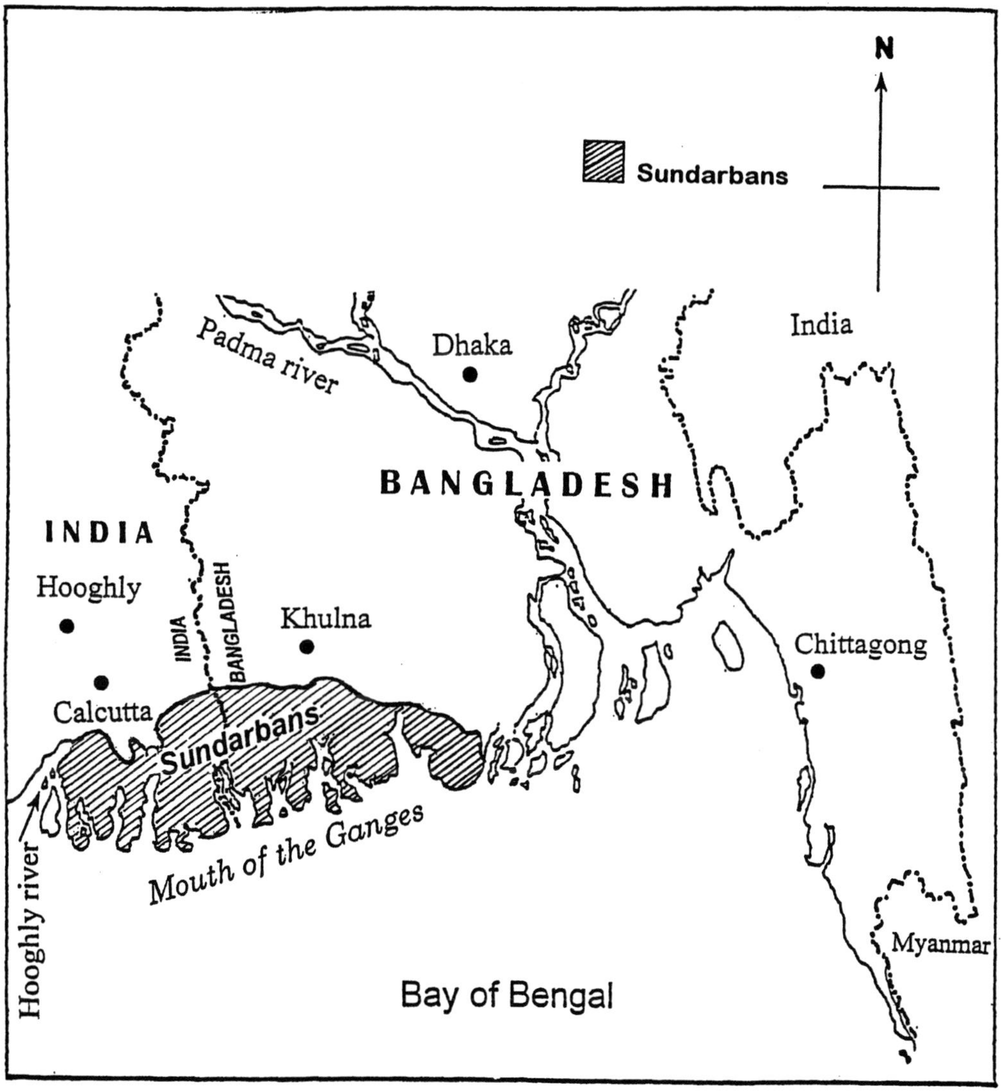

West Bengal comprise medium to low height mangrove species, with very high density of crop per unit area. The present area of mangrove forests under the control of the (Indian) Forest Directorate is 4,264 sq.km. of which 2,585 sq.km., lie between the Matla river in the west and the Harinbhanga river in the east, bordering Bangladesh, falls under Sundarbans Tiger Reserve (STR) and balance of the area, to the west of the river Matla, under 24-Parganas Forest Division. This in brief is Sundarbans, one of the world's largest estuarine forests.

It is generally known that the name Sundarbans has come from 'Sundaribans' or the forest of Sundari trees, a species which is still found in the forests of this area. But dense, often impenetrable, undergrowth of Goran trees between 1.8 m. and 3.6 m. high covers almost the entire region of Sundarbans. The rest of the flora consist of trees like Genwa, Dhundal, Passur, Garjan and Kankra. The real distinguishing feature of Sundarbans, however, is to be found in the vast stretches of mangrove forests, bayonet like roots of which stick out above the level of water during high tide to enable the trees to breathe. Within the forest areas, the kalasdwip is well known as a densely wooded island near the confluence of the river Matla and the sea. See Figure 17.2 for a detailed map of the Sundarban area.

The Sundarban forest contains many special animal species. It is the natural habitat of one of the most awe-inspiring creatures of the animal world: the Royal Bengal Tiger. Other wild animals include the jungle cat, fishing cat, cheetal or axis deer, wild boar, rhesus monkey, mongoose etc. A hatchery-cum-sanctuary which is the home of the largest estuarine crocodiles in the world is known as the Bhagabatpur Crocodile Project. This project started in 1976 for rearing crocodiles and up to April 1997, 224 crocodiles raised in the area have been released into the forests. The Sundarban forest is also remarkable for the immense variety of birds which are mainly to be found in Sajnekhali Bird Sanctuary, which is situated in the forests bordering the wide river - Matla and Gumdi, covering an area of between 11km to 12km. Herons, egrets, cormorants, fishing eagles, seagulls, white bellied sea eagles, terns as well as kingfishers are seen here. Seasonal birds like whimprel, black-tailed godwit, little stint, eastern knot, curlew, sandpipers, golden plovers, pintails, white-eyed poachards and lesser whistling teals often pay a visit here. Among reptiles one may find king cobras, pythons, chequered killbacks, lizards, monitors, the Salvator lizards and an incredible variety of marine life including the famous Olive Ridley sea turtles. The nestling place of Olive Ridley turtles and the hardshelled Batgur Terrapin is a spot of scenic beauty and has been named AKanak ". Tourists often visit this picturesque spot.

Figure 17.2
Overview of Sundarbans Biosphere Reserve Area

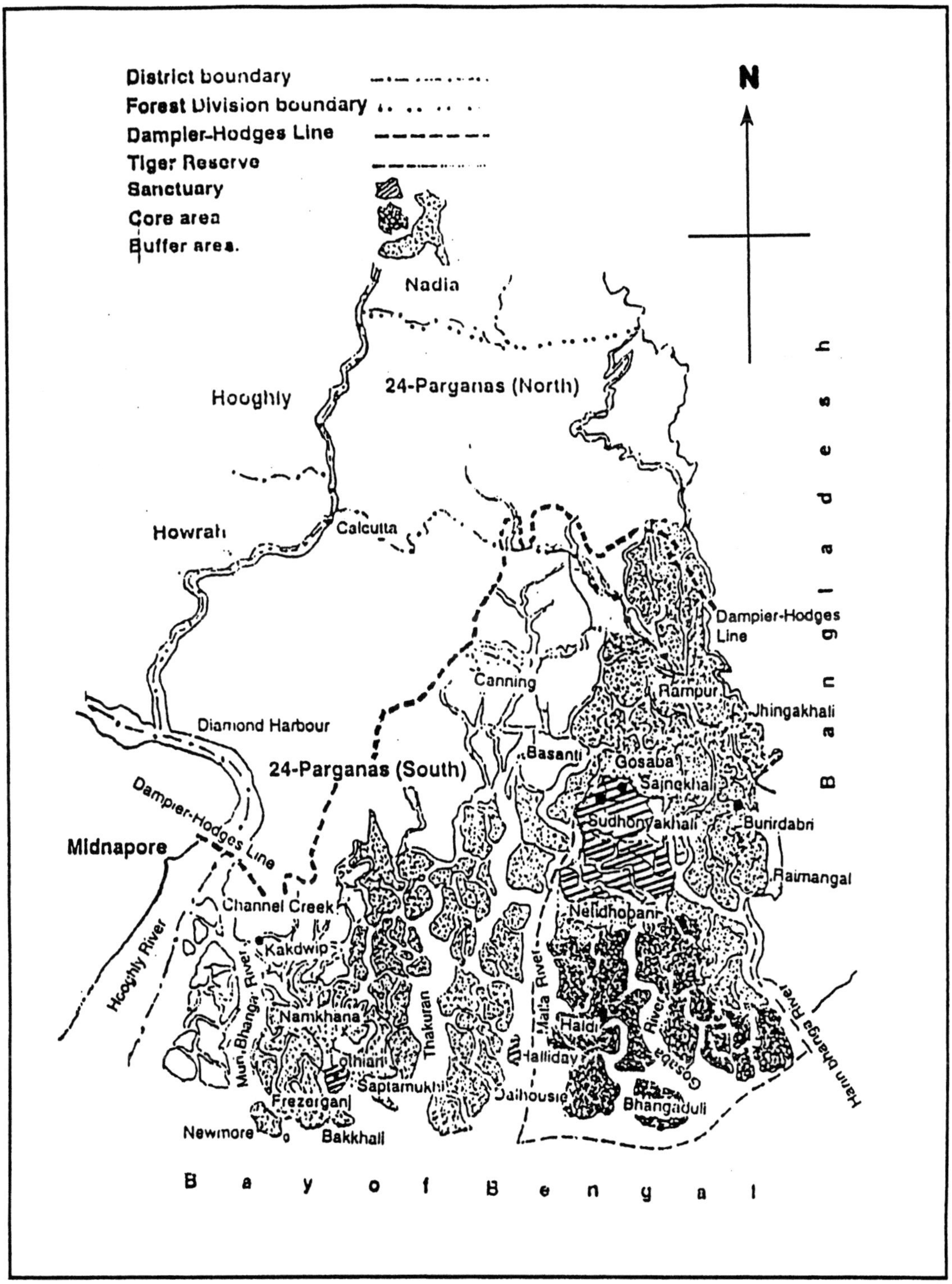

Another remarkable area of Sundarban forest is the Tiger Reserve Project which started in the year 1973. The Sundarban Tiger Reserve spans an area of 2,585 sq.km. It is by far the world's largest tiger colony with a tiger population of 287 (1984 census). There are watch-towers strategically located near watering holes at Sajnekhali, Sudhanyakhali, Netidhopani and Haldi. The core area of this Tiger Reserve, measuring 1330 sq.km., was declared a National Park in 1984. In the buffer zone of the Reserve there exists an old sanctuary named Sajnekhali Wildlife Sanctuary covering approximately 362 sq.km. The Tiger Reserve and Sajnekhali Wildlife Sanctuary attract a large number of Indian and

foreign tourists. In the eastern portion of the Sundarbans, outside the Tiger Reserve, there are two sanctuaries, viz. Lothian Island Wildlife Sanctuary measuring 38 sq.km. and Halliday Island Wildlife Sanctuary measuring approximately 6 sq.km. The Tiger Reserve National Park and all the tourist spots and sanctuaries in Sundarbans can be approached through the gateway of Sundarbans known as Piyali (which is 72 km. from Calcutta by road) where the river Piyali flows through emerald paddy fields to meet the river Matla. A beautiful tourist complex with accommodation and recreational facilities is nearing completion here. Nearby is a beautiful location known as Gosaba which is remembered as Sir David Hamilton's settlement. The main part of Sundarbans is accessible only by riverine waterways. However, embarkation points can be reached by Subarban trains to Canning. The other places near Sundarbans like Raidighi, Basanti, Namkhana, Bokkhali and Najat are also connected by regular bus services from Calcutta via Diamond Harbour.

SOCIO-ECONOMIC PROFILE OF INDIAN SUNDARBAN FOREST

We shall now provide a socio-economic profile of the Indian Sundarban forest. Inhabited villages (including Rangabelia village) are mostly located outside the northern and the western limits of this forest. The southern side adjoins the Bay of Bengal and the eastern side is adjacent to the forests of Bangladesh Sundarbans. The socio-economic condition of the people in this area is poor. Approximately, eighty-five per cent of the total population is dependent on agriculture on reclaimed land which bears mostly a single crop of paddy per year. The cultivation of mushroom is also on the rise. Mushrooms are a source of protein to poor people suffering from malnutrition. But the population living on the periphery of the forest are mainly composed of fishermen. Thus, fishing is a very important source of income.

Some people are running a profitable business by culturing fish such as tiger prawns or *bhetki*. Mainly fish captured from the Sundarbans and its periphery feed Calcutta City and the neighbouring towns of the adjoining area. A small portion of this population, however, earn its livelihood by working in forests as honey collectors, woodcutters etc. The culture of edible oysters and crabs is becoming popular. Mangrove flowers attract swarms of bees which fill the hives with honey and are a boon to honey collectors, three to four months after winter. On an average the Sundarban forests produce 500 quintals of honey which is extracted systematically every year. This honey is of good quality and is in much demand in domestic and international markets.

The Sundarban forests yield fuelwood for domestic use, some inferior timber, (for making poles for construction of village homes) and betel yards. Timber and other forest products obtained from felling trees are very much discouraged now. Timber for construction of boats and making of packing cases locally is also taken from these forests. Forest produce collected from Sundarbans not only help feed the adjoining villages but also reach Calcutta, industrial areas of Haldia and other parts of the country.

The socio-economic status of men and women in Sundarban is poor. In spite of all the efforts made by the Biosphere Reserve, fifty per cent of the agricultural labourers are still landless and extremely poor. Forty four per cent of the total population belongs to Scheduled Castes and Scheduled Tribes. Therefore, the level of literacy as well as per capita income is much lower in the Sundarbans than in other parts of West Bengal. The majority of the people live well below the poverty line. Their hopeless living conditions force them to venture into the wild to search for timber and honey. And quite often they fall prey to man-eating tigers, and other wild animals. Thus, the people living in and around these mangrove forests, infested with tigers on land and crocodiles in water, are struggling to survive.

In the core area of the Tiger Project and in Sajnakhali Sanctuary, however, no entry of local people is allowed and no commercial exploitation is permitted. Commercial activities are allowed only in a part of the buffer zone which lies on the northeastern side of the Tiger Reserve. The essence of success of conservation-oriented forest management lies in protecting the forests from the onslaught of human misuse and overuse, proper management of habitat and habitant, and developing a harmonious relationship between forest management and local people. It has to be recognized that in order to survive the local people are desperate to use forest products from the Sundarbans. To compensate for the loss of employment resulting from reduced commercial activities in these forests, a large number of special work programmes have been implemented in the periphery of the Sundarban forests and the Rangabelia Project offers an unique success story. The main aim is to see that those people, living adjacent to the forests, are not alienated by the conservation approach.

LOCATIONS, DEVELOPMENT OF INFRASTRUCTURES AND PROBLEMS OF GROWTH OF SUNDARBAN TOURIST CENTRES

Economic reforms in India have been tagged to an export-oriented strategy. Boosting of exports and earning of foreign exchange are important components of this strategy. Here tourism occupies a key position and a systematic development of tourist centres is the need of the hour. It is heartening to note that tourism is India's second largest foreign-exchange earner. (See Figure 17.3.) Nevertheless, growth in foreign tourism to India has been

Figure 17.3
Number of Foreign Tourists Arriving in India and India's Gross Foreign Exchange Earnings from such Tourism

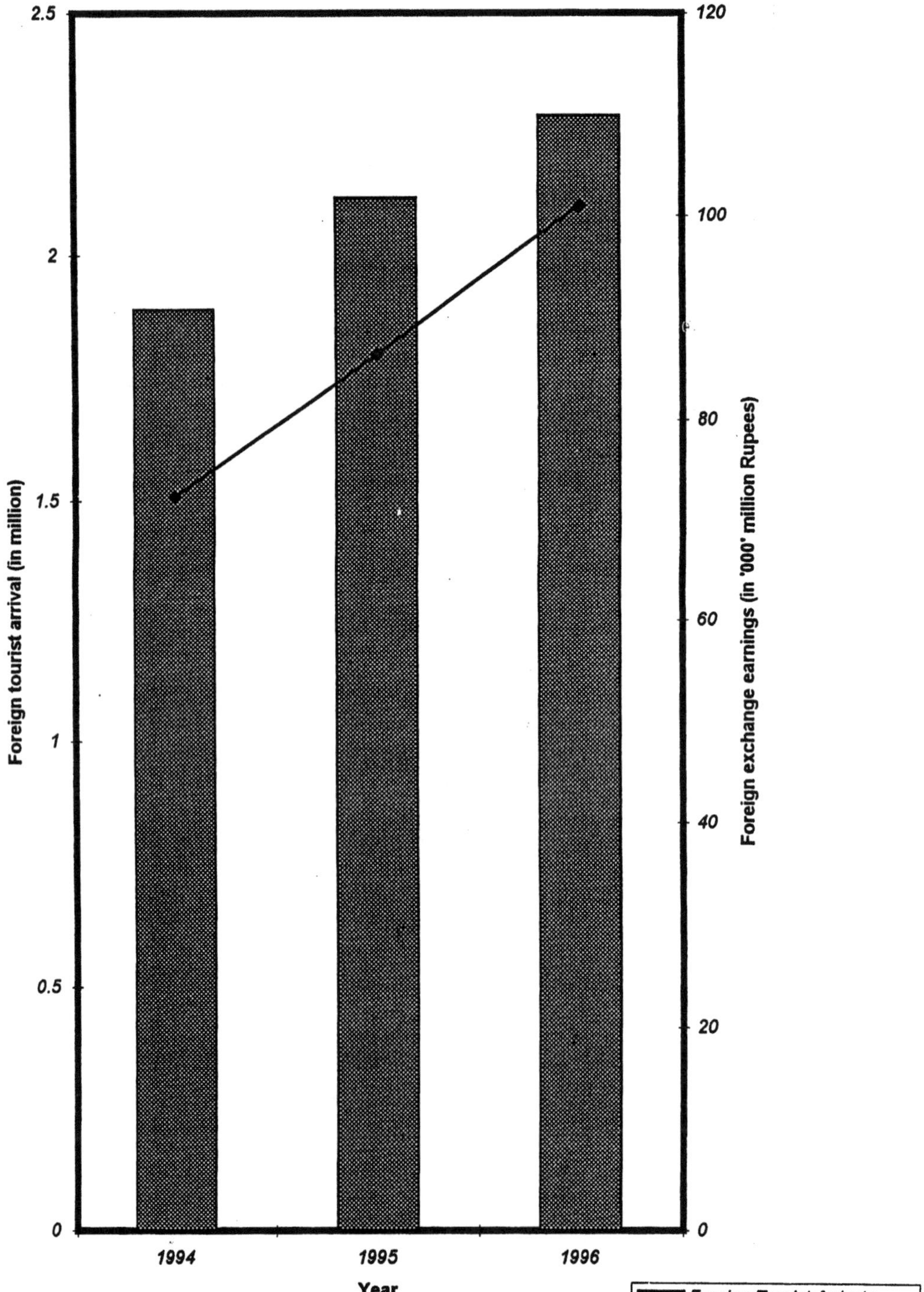

Source*: Based on statistics of Ministry of Tourism, India.*

sluggish. In the 1997-98 Budget, the Finance Minister gave important concessions for encouraging the development of tourism infrastructure. He has given a deduction of 50 per cent of the profits in respect of new hotels which are situated in places of pilgrimage or specified places of tourist interest. These hotels will also be exempted from the levy of expenditure tax. These incentives will attract private hoteliers to venture investment for new hotels in eco-friendly tourist areas like Sundarbans in West Bengal. As noted earlier, wide and wonderfully eco-friendly Sundarbans covered by mangroves has been recently selected by the West Bengal Government for development as a World Tourism Centre. Thus, the Sundarbans is destined to become India's first International Tourist Centre.

Though our aims are high and we are keen to have an international Tourist Centre in West Bengal, the State's Budget allocation for tourism is less than 1 per cent of the total. It is now expected that the considerable tourism potential in West Bengal, particularly the hilly region of Darjeeling and the dark and deep jungle areas of Sundarbans, will have to be developed by the private sector or through joint private-public collaboration.

We shall now describe the locations of the main tourist spots in the Sundarbans. (See Figure 17.4.) In the long run, however, we shall have to give top-most priority for the development of infrastructures like roads, ferry services and hotels, if tourism is to develop in the Sundarbans.

Pyali (near Gosaba), which is recognised as the gateway to the Sundarbans (where a tourist complex is nearing completion) can be reached by bus. But the roads over which buses have to ply require thorough maintenance and are narrow. If the roads are improved, it may be possible to have air conditioned buses plying between Calcutta and Gosaba (Sir David Hamilton Settlement) which is near Pyali. From Gosaba or Pyali it will be best to go to the notable tourist spots by water craft. Of course, in the years to come, when the Sundarbans becomes an International Tourist Centre, Ahover craft " service may be introduced linking the main groups of tourist centres.

The first group to be covered comprises the Sajnekhali Bird Sanctuary and Olive Ridley Turtle Hatchery and the Museum in Kanak. A kaleidoscope of colour breaks at sunrise on the horizon as the kingdom of birds at Sajnekhali enchant our eyes. Seven colourful species of kingfisher, white bellied sea eagle, plovers, lap-wings, curlews, whimbrels, sandpipers and occasional pelicans will be found here. Very near to Sajnekhali is Kanak, which attracts the tourist because of nestling place of Olive Ridley turtles. From the tourist lodge near Sajnekhali, we come to the core area (1330 sq. kms.) consisting of Sudhanyakhali, Netidhopani and Haldi. The king of the jungle (the Royal Bengal Tiger) has adapted well to this natural habitat. This core area, which has been developed as a national park, contains the Sundarban Tiger Reserve. To visit the Sundarban Tiger Reserve and Sajnekhali Sanctuary the foreigner requires special permission. If the Sundarbans is to be developed as an International Tourist Centre, the permit system has to be relaxed and permission will have to be given for starting modern hotels in the fringe areas of the core sector.

Figure 17.4
Core Areas of the Sundarbans Biosphere Reserve Area

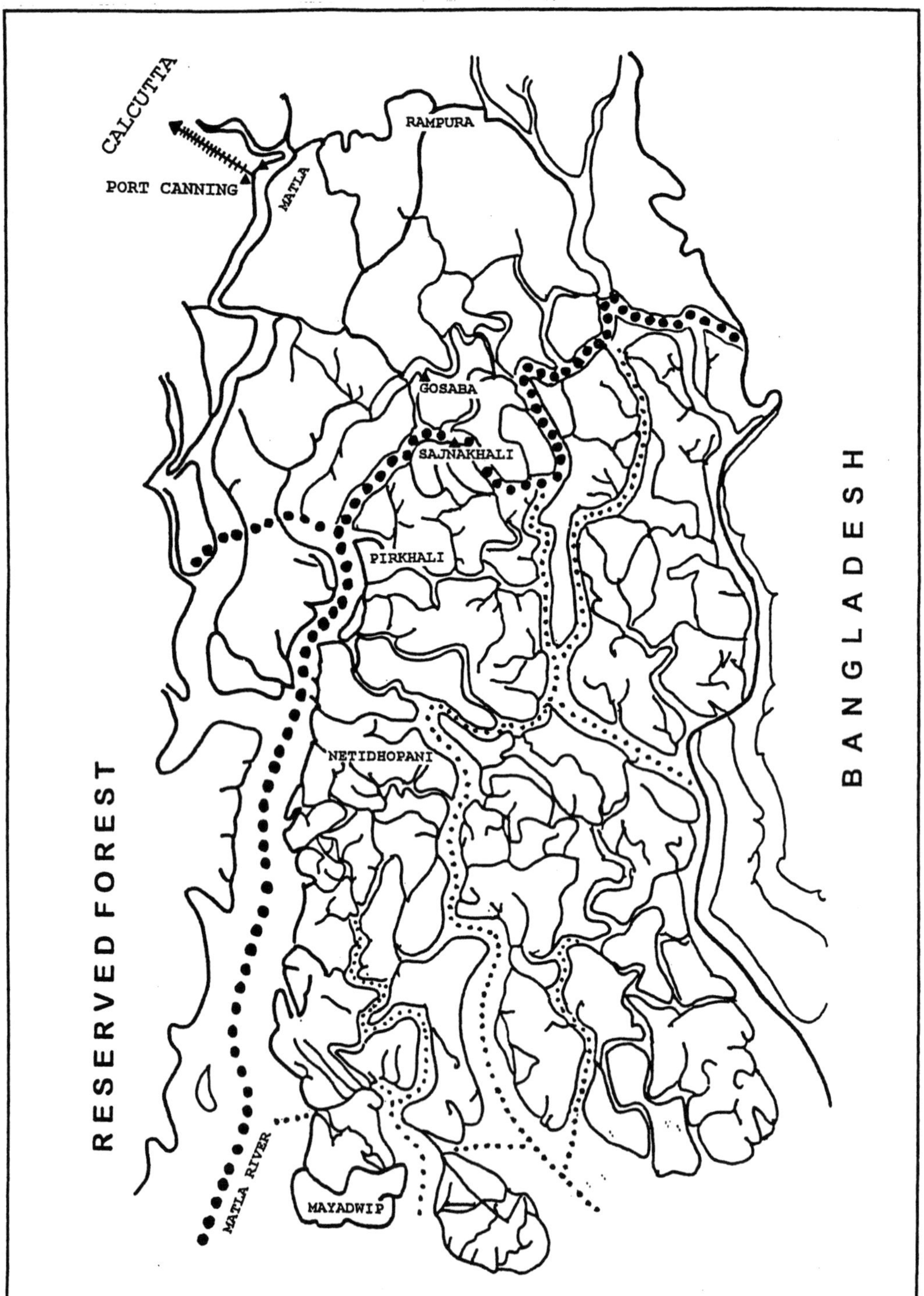

By crossing the river Matla by watercraft, we come to the next group of tourist centres highlighted by Bhagabatpur Crocodile Project and Kalas Island. Kalas Island is an eco-friendly green forest area near the confluence of the river Matla and the Sea. As noted earlier, Bhagabatpur is of special tourist interest because it is the home of the biggest estuarine crocodiles. By crossing the river Saptamukhi, we not only come to Bhagabatpur but also to another group of tourist centres which have better communication facilities and government managed tourist lodges. These are Fraserganj and Bakkhali. Nearby is the Lothian Island. Here one can see rare and wonderful specimens of wild pigs, axle deer, estuarine crocodiles, Gangetic dolphins and exquisite birds. Unfortunately, Tourist Lodge arrangements here are not up to the mark. Of these three groups of tourist spots, the first one, which is somewhat better developed, should form the central or core area for the Sundarban International Tourist Centre.

INFRASTRUCTURE CONSTRAINTS AND PROSPECTS FOR TOURISM DEVELOPMENT

The conditions of surface roads in all three groups of tourist centres in Sundarbans are extremely poor. There is a train service between Calcutta and Canning which is few kilometres from Pyali - gateway to the Sundarbans. There are, however, weekend conducted trips on board M.V. Chitrarekha, a large vessel with excellent living arrangements. Privately-managed motor launches ply from Canning and Gosaba which are near Pyali. Decent private hotels are almost conspicuous by their absence though the construction of a modern tourist complex has just started in Pyali. The Government tourist lodges, excepting those in Bakkhali, Sajnekhali and Bhagabatpur, have not been renovated for a long time and cannot attract foreign tourists.

The nearness to the Bay of Bengal causes frequent natural calamities arising out from climatic depressions on the Bay of Bengal. Cyclones, heavy rains, high tides and floods cause frequent damage to houses, crops, livestock and roads. Unless proper safeguards are taken by the government to combat natural calamities and infrastructural facilities are sufficiently strengthened, prospects of transforming Sundarbans into an international tourist centre are small. Immediate steps should be taken for the proper maintenance and widening of roads, widening and extension of railway routes, improvement of jetties, and in increase in the number of launch services.

A plan of action, with crash package programmes based on grassroots planning strategies, have to be jointly undertaken by the State and Central Governments. Collaborations with private enterprise and non-governmental organisations (NGOs) will yield fruitful results.

The first group of tourist centres comprising Sajnekhali, Kanak and the National Park with S T R has all the potentialities for becoming the core area of the proposed International Tourist Centre. Joint sector Two-Star and Three-Star hotels should be started in the periphery areas of Sajnekhali. As, in the initial stage, private sector, which aims at maximising profit in the short run, may not come forward, we propose that the government should take the help and experience of successful NGOs in the nearby areas.

The Rangabelia NGO experiment in the island villages near the core area is a success story which has attracted the attention of Indians and foreigners in recent years. In the discussion that follows, we consider the feasibility of developing an eco-friendly tourism *cum* rural development centre in and around Rangabelia. We will endeavour to show that Rangabelia project area can serve as the kingpin for the Sundarban International Tourist Centre to be developed in the near future.

The second group of tourist attractions consist of Bhagabatpur Crocodile Project and Kalas Island. As the roads are in a hopeless condition and as there is no decent and comfortable tourist lodge available, the development of this group will take time. The best thing to do will be to connect these areas with the core area and start a luxury bus *cum* ferry service from Sajnekhali to Bhagabatpur. Infrastructural constraints are heavy here and we shall have to wait until private and government funds effectively flow to this area.

The last group of tourist attractions, comprising Bokkhali and Fraserganj, is accessible by bus and ferry from Diamond Harbour which is about 80 km. from Calcutta. The tourist lodge at Bokkhali can be renovated in a modern manner to attract foreign tourists. It is to be noted here that the Sundarban tourist centres should be assured regular electricity supply. At present, frequent loadshedding and electrical cable faults make life miserable. The newly-built hotels should have their own generators. To attract foreign tourists, a helipad should in our view be constructed of Gosaba.

RANGABELIA NGO PROJECT AS THE KINGPIN OF THE SUNDARBAN INTERNATIONAL TOURIST CENTRE

The Rangabelia Comprehensive Rural Development Project, as it is known, (Rangabelia is the name of the village from where the project was launched) is sponsored by the Tagore Society for Rural Development which is an apex body of some seven rural development projects in three states of West Bengal, Bihar and Orissa. The project, initiated in 3 island villages in late 1975, now covers 256 villages in seven administrative blocks with a population of about 21,000 in 41,200 families. The project was started by and is still being guided by the dynamic and motivated leader, Mr. Tushar Kanjilal, who settled on the island in 1967 as the Headmaster of the local high school and became deeply involved in the project from 1975 onwards. A German funding organisation was involved in the initial stages. Now government and foreign NGOs provide considerable aid for the project.

The selfless work of Mr. Tushar Kanjilal can be compared with missionary zeal of Professor Muhammed Yunus the founder promoter of the Grameen Project of Bangladesh. Grameen, started as a NGO project in the Chittagong district of Bangladesh, and became an independent rural bank dedicated to poor women of Bangladesh on 2 October, 1983. Conceptually, the two NGOs are different and their areas of operations also differ. But both the experiments have turned out to be success stories. Both have achieved outstanding results during the period from 1975 to 1996. Both Rangabelia and Grameen experiments have brought about meaningful involvement of the local people at almost every stage of development. Both place emphasis on the role of women.

If we make a thorough study of the growth of Rangabelia Project we shall find three distinct phases. First, we have the ground preparation stage of three years (from mid-1975 to mid-1978). This has been characterised by a scientific understanding of the eco-friendly forest and detailed socio-economic surveys. This phase was also marked by awareness-building programmes, specially among the women.

The second phase of 10 years (from mid-1978 to mid-1988) covers the period of systematic expansion involving human engineering at the individual family and group levels.

The third, and the continuing phase since mid-1988, is marked by qualitative improvement of living conditions in the project areas. Mr. Kanjilal and his friends, with internal and external help, have succeeded in providing qualitative technical services, knowledge and inputs at different levels for economic activities. During this phase, which is still continuing, Kanjilal and his team of selfless and devoted workers are making special efforts to sustain the eco-friendly development process which have gained much momentum during the last 10 years or so.

To give concrete shape to the dream of transforming Sundarban core area into an international tourist centre, Government will have to undertake a programme for providing adequate infrastructural facilities consisting of broad and well maintained roads, modern ferry services and transform immediately existing tourist lodges into comfortable and modern airconditioned hotels. But we are afraid that private firms may not be induced to open new hotels immediately in the difficult terrain of the Sundarban area. Therefore, we suggest that a private NGO, like the one operating the Rangabelia Project, may be induced to cooperate with the government for tourism development in the Sundarbans. Lately, Kanjilal has transformed the Rangabelia experiment into a technically efficient project. Mr. Kanjilal and his team will have to be convinced that development of tourism in a successful manner int he areas surrounding the Rangabelia Project will bring about rapid economic transformation of the Sundarban region which will give an indirect boost to the Rangabelia experiment. Kanjilal should be entrusted to undertake Special Area Programmes for rapid development of tourism particularly in the border areas of Rangabelia project which are close to the first group of tourist centre attractions consisting of Sajnekhali, Netidhopani, Kanak and Haldi. The Rangabelia experiment has become internationally famous. If better communication facilities by means of luxury bus and ferry services can be provided between the Sundarban core area and the Rangabelia project area, then it may be possible to sell a package tourism programme involving Sundarbans eco-friendly sanctuaries and national park together with a visit to the successful Rangabelia Rural Development Project.

The NGO, managing the Rangabelia Project, has shown that an agro-climatic zone, such as the Sundarbans, cannot be made sustainable unless the larger issues of ecological and environmental degradation and hazards are properly taken care of. It is pertinent to note